A MEDICO'S LUCK IN THE WAR

The Stretcher-bearer at Work.
(Imperial War Museum Photograph—Copyright Reserved.)

Frontispiece.

A MEDICO'S LUCK IN THE WAR

BEING

REMINISCENCES OF R.A.M.C. WORK WITH THE 51st (HIGHLAND) DIVISION

BY

DAVID RORIE, D.S.O., T.D., M.D., D.P.H.

Colonel late R.A.M.C., T.A. (Ret.); Officer of the Order of St. John of Jerusalem; Chevalier de la Légion d'Honneur; formerly O.C. 1/2nd Highland Field Ambulance, and later A.D.M.S. 51st (Highland) Division, B.E.F.

1929

DEDICATION.

To you who deadly days have spent
While cursing in the Salient,
Or crouched in holes to dodge the bomb
And shell-burst of the strenuous Somme
Or the sharp crash upon the Square
At Arras or Armentières;
You who have seen the bullets spray
The troubled waves of Suvla Bay,
And led a life of melancholy
While fighting Turks at Gally-polly;
You, who beneath Italian skies
Ate macaroni mixed with flies;
You who in darkest Africa
Fought Bill and eke Bilharzia;
You who have tried on ocean blue
To keep what you'd put into you;
You who have learnt to love the Greek
In dear salubrious Salonique
What time the troops, in language vulgar,
Heaped wrath upon the ruddy Bulgar;
You who have found a tedious lot
Was cast for years in old Mess-pot;
You have trudged o'er leagues of sand
In what was once the Holy Land,
Or, half-baked, saw elusive winks
Flash from the eyes of noseless Sphinx;
You who, in Nissen or in shack
In dug-out, tent, or bivouac
From Wypers to Jerusalem
Just stuck it out and played the game
Of picking up and patching 'em:
M.O.s, Non-Coms and Other Ranks,
To you this book: fill in the blanks!

DEDICATION.

So it befell! Ill days? And yet
The bond's the thing we can't forget,
Nor need we argue why we should
Betray this old blood-brotherhood,
And flout the days when, one and all,
The Army held us in its thrall.
Curse it you may, as curse you did,
When some new fad put on the lid,
And, in your mess, you poked derision
At your A.D.M.S., Division,
Or else (perchance A.D.M.S.)
You damn'd the grousers of each mess,
And told some sympathetic Johnnie
"Ah! Tout comprendre c'est tout pardonner!"
While he (like eighty-five per cent)
Did not know really what was meant,
But (seeing you were a senior bloke)
Smiled blandly lest it were a joke!

I grant you there were interludes
When life had somewhat cheerier moods,
And memory calls up nights of song
And wine in merry Amiong,
Where, o'er a bottle of Pomard,
We swapped choice lies about the war;
Some night, mayhap, we'd chanced to drop
Into the famous oyster-shop,
Kept by that lass, on profits keen,
The dear tempestuous Josephine;
Or else, when on another track,
We supped with Marguerite at Acq,
Where, in old billet thirty-seven,
We gloried in a transient heaven
Of omelettes and good *pommes frites*
With drinks that warmed our hearts—and feet!
Or, harking up the trail again,
Our hostess next was Lucienne,
That maiden famed of Armenteers
Who did us all so well. (Loud cheers.)

. . . . . .

DEDICATION.

As Father Time still marches on,
Gone are those days—for ever gone!
And now in peace we sit aloof
From shells that tumble on the roof,
But link'd by bonds we can't deny—
What soulless wretch would care to try?

AUTHOR'S ACKNOWLEDGMENTS.

I HAVE to express my indebtedness to the Controller of His Majesty's Stationery Office for allowing the reproduction of such of the snapshots herein as have already appeared in "The Official History of the War (Medical Services)"; to the Imperial War Museum for the use of three photographs; to Major John Stirling, author of "The Territorial Divisions," for his kind permission to make various extracts from his work; and to Mr. A. B. McLeod, a former member of my unit, for typewriting my MS. But I have to thank more than anyone my old friend, Captain Robert Tennant Bruce, London, for the great care and trouble he has taken in drawing the maps and diagrams in this book: for freely permitting me to use his photographs (all, except the three acknowledged above and including these from "The Official History," are his); and especially for his kindness in writing Chapter VIII.

D. R.

CONTENTS.

CHAPTER		PAGE
I.	Introductory	1
II.	Estaires—Givenchy, 1915	29
III.	The Labyrinth, 1915	59
IV.	The Somme, 1916	82
V.	Beaumont Hamel, 1916	104
VI.	The Battle of Arras, 1917	117
VII.	The Battles of the Pilkem and Menin Road Ridges, 1917	135
VIII.	Battle of Cambrai, 1917	157
IX.	The German Offensive, 1918	179
X.	The Battle of the Lys, 1918	202
XI.	The Second Battle of the Marne, 1918	211
XII.	The Battle of the Scarpe, 1918	233
XIII.	The Battle of Cambrai, 1918	241

ILLUSTRATIONS.

	FACING PAGE
The Stretcher-bearer at Work	*Frontispiece*
Diagram illustrating evacuation of Sick and Wounded from Fighting Area to United Kingdom	5
On Trek—Summer	23
On Trek—Winter	26
Sketch Map of Festubert Area, 1915	47
Aux Rietz Advanced Dressing Station, 1916	78

Field Ambulance and Regimental Posts—

Somme Valley, July, 1916	89
Beaumont Hamel, November, 1916	105
1. Entrance to Farmyard, Auchonvillers	108
2. Entrance to Dressing-room in Farmyard	108
Battle of Vimy, 9th April, 1917	117

  Lille Road Collecting Post—

Arrangement of Stretchers in Trench	119
1. The Trench before we tackled it	120
2. The Finished Product—(Ecurie in distance)	120
3. The Post under Snow	122
4. Loaded Cars leave for Anzin A.D.S.	122

Battle of Arras, April—May, 1917—

Medical Posts	128

  A.D.S. at St. Nicolas—

1. Roclincourt Road	129
2. The Car Track to the Dressing Station	129
3. Entrance to Dressing-room	130
4. Entrance to one of the Tunnels	130

ILLUSTRATIONS.

FACING PAGE

Field Ambulance and Regimental Posts—
   Ypres Salient—Corps M.D.S. at Gwalia Farm—
      1. Receiving Room - - - - - - 143
      2. Feeding Tent and Nissen Hospital Hut - 143
      3. Exit from Surgical Dressing-room - - - 145
      4. M.A.C. loading Cars from Hospital Tents for journey to C.C.S. - - - - - 145

   Battle of Cambrai, November, 1917 - - - - 157

   At Trescault—Bringing wounded up from a dug-out on slides by winch, 1917 - - - - - 166

Medical Posts during the Retreat, March, 1918 - - 179

Medical Posts in the Battle of the Lys, April, 1918 - 203

Second Battle of the Marne, 1918—
   Medical Posts in the Valley of the Ardre - - 214
      " on 20th July at 10 a.m. - page 222
      " " " 5 p.m. - - " 223
      " on 28th July - - - - " 225

In the Bois de Courton—German prisoners bringing in French wounded, 1918 - - - - - - 224

Plan of Dressing Stations, Cambrai Area, 1918 - - 243

A Medico's Luck in the War.

CHAPTER I.

Introductory.

Give us again of the days gone by
A cheerier one or two,
Think of the lads with hopes so high
Whose quips and wiles we knew.
Lord! If we had not laughed with them
We had lost the half of our pay!
For the echo-less heart is a thing apart
And it goes by the Wearier Way.

To write, with even limited success, the history of any units which served in the Great War, the narrator would, I fear — and it is a large order — require to be a judicious mixture of George Borrow and Charles Lever; the Borrow part of him to deal with the marching and roadside scenes, the wind on the heath, the clouds scudding before the breeze, the sunshine and the shade and the necessary little adventures of man on the move, whether *solus* or in column; the Lever part, again, to treat of the tented field, the bivouac, the trenches, the camp-fire, the clash of arms, the cannikin's clink, the songs the soldier sang, and of whatever takes the place (in these our present degenerate days) of broiled bones and devilled kidneys. Nay, more, one might with advantage add to the *mélange* a dash of such unblushing super-egoists as Benvenuto Cellini and Herbert of Cherbury, thereby sharpening the flavour of the literary diet while possibly interfering with the truth of the story. But I have no desire to hand out laurel wreaths to individuals as the ring-master throws pointed hats at the heads of the clowns: *je prétends dire le bien et le mal sans dissimuler la vérité,* giving you neither wild deeds of derring-do nor the joyous adventures of an Aristide Pujol. And thus it falls out that, as on principle one must eschew the Rabelaisian, Benvenuto and Lord Herbert have to be somewhat regretfully abandoned and their mutely proffered aid respectfully declined.

Here, then, if you choose to read on, you will find only the plain unvarnished tale of some Territorial Field Ambulances in France and Flanders; differing in no way, doubtless, from other tales—possibly told, probably untold—of similar medical units that served there. For most of the places named in this narrative have been, time and again, the locations of other Field Ambulances. One can say, therefore, to any brother O.C. who turns over these leaves,

Mutato nomine de te fabula narratur,

whilst he, dubiously handling the book and adapting the words of the ancient and pious bishop, can reply, "And thus, but for the grace of God, goes the story I might have written." For after all, we had of necessity the same outlook, the same environment, the same experiences, the same joys and sorrows.

France and Flanders constituted our sole venue: camels, dust-storms, palm trees, pith helmets, oriental sunshine, did not come into our programme: we never

> Heard the tinkling caravan
> Descend the mountain road,

nor the East a-calling. But we certainly heard the West making a variety of curious noises, and we knew a lot about the many varieties of mud.

Two things may be said against the story—one, that

INTRODUCTORY.

small beer is unsparingly chronicled: the other, that undue stress is laid on the cheerful side of war. *Eh bien!* But therein, if you look at it in the right way, lies proof of the truth of the yarn. What else, in the rest periods, was there to chronicle? Consider, too, how consistently and invariably small the average French beer always proved to be, even when thickened—as it frequently and improperly was—with *bacillus coli*. And as for cheerfulness, what officer who was *là-bas* can ever forget the extraordinary power of the men to make the best of and magnify any little gleam of sunshine that flashed into their dull, depressing, and often sordid, routine of mud and blood; their ready response to a joke when there was, Heaven knows, little enough to jest over, and their constant good comradeship and good nature? Truly said Solomon—and has he not the more up-to-date backing of the lamented Coué?—"a merry heart doeth good like a medicine, but a broken spirit drieth the bones."

> 'Tis easy to smile when the skies are blue
> And everything goes well with you,
> But the man who could grin
> With his boots letting in,
> With a boil on his neck
> And its mate on his chin,
> With I.C.T.[1] at the back of each knee
> And P.U.O.[2] of 103,
> Was the fellow who won the War!

And of all the fellows who won the war, none was stouter-hearted than the stretcher-bearer: none carried out his job more steadily and efficiently during the campaign. He was never treated to the limelight and he never asked to be: but he is well worthy of the highest tribute that can be paid to his pluck and his endurance.

So it is mainly for him and his comrades that the yarn is spun, to ensure that in the years to come they may

[1] Inflammation of connective tissue.
[2] Pyrexia of unknown origin.

have a permanent record of their work and their journeyings abroad with that famous Scottish Division in which they took, and will always take, such a constant pride — the 51st (Highland) Division of immortal memory. Let me say here, also, that throughout the narrative I do not attempt to give any history whatsoever of military operations: I concern myself with our bit of the campaign only as it bore on medical work and R.A.M.C. matters. And the reason, by the way, that the story is written in the first person is solely because it is taken from a personal diary faithfully kept throughout: not—to use Boswell's phrase—"a log-book of felicity," but written, often enough, under curious and adverse circumstances. For many a time, with Pepys—to touch on only the minutiæ of war's varied worries—we had to say, "Up, finding our beds good, but lousy," though without his addendum, "which made us merry," seeing that the novelty of the stimulating jest soon wore off.

Technical, to a certain degree, the story must be: not too technical, I hope, for the non-R.A.M.C. reader. The names and numbers of units to whom we handed or from whom we took over may seem a monotonous and oft-repeated detail: historical accuracy demands it. Monotonous, too, may be the itinerary of the various marches, but so they were laid down in orders. If a professional historian like our old friend Xenophon, with his constantly recurring, "thence he proceeded three stadia, ten parasangs, to the river," could not get away from it, who am I that I should complain of my burden, or without protest let others criticise the way in which I have unpacked my kit of recollections?

But at this stage it may be as well to answer at once the inevitable question of the civilian reader—"What is a Field Ambulance?" If that genial — and frequently wooden-headed—individual "the man in the street" were asked, he would probably reply that it was a wagon for

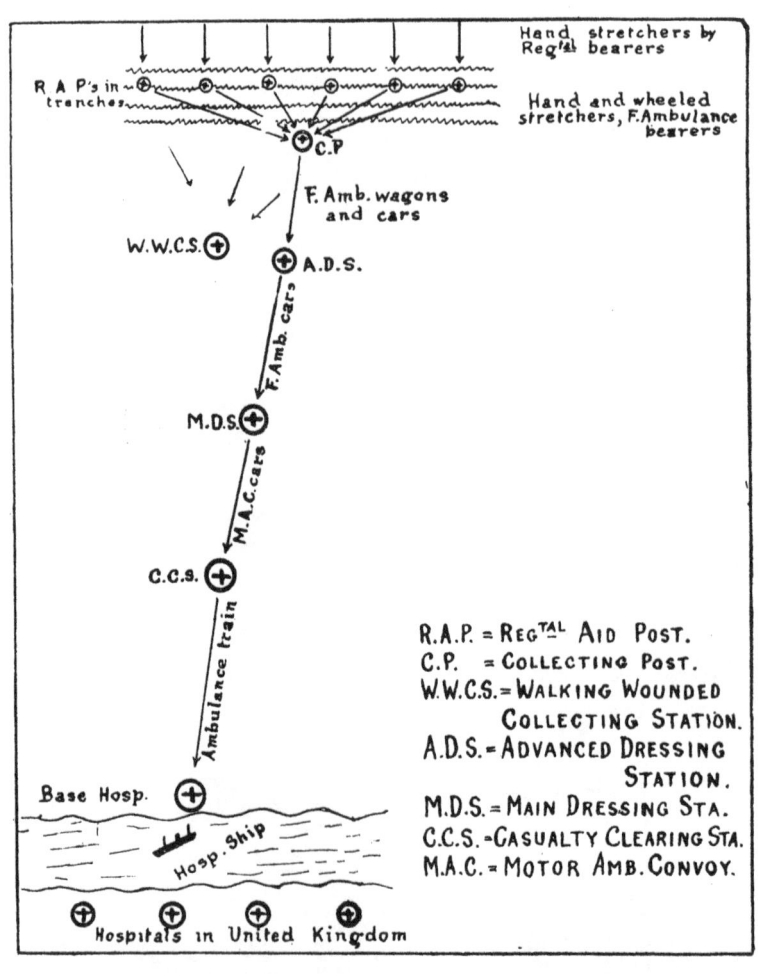

DIAGRAM ILLUSTRATING EVACUATION OF SICK AND WOUNDED FROM FIGHTING AREA TO UNITED KINGDOM

INTRODUCTORY.

carrying wounded, either drawn by horses or propelled by petrol. And even people with the high intelligence of a Brigade Staff have been known in the days gone by to betake themselves to the telephone, give a map reference, and request that a "Field Ambulance" be sent there immediately, when all they wanted was an ambulance wagon.

But a Field Ambulance is not an ambulance wagon: it is (or was) a medical unit of 241 all told, of which there were three to a Division; each in its turn made up of three sections capable of acting independently when required. For a section contained in itself medical officers, stretcher-bearers, nursing orderlies, clerks, cooks, etc., with separate equipment (tentage, surgical instruments, drugs, appliances, dressings, etc.) and horse and motor transport. The section idea was conceived with the view to mobile warfare; and, as in France this never materialised to any great extent, the Divisional Field Ambulance as a rule worked complete.

Each Ambulance generally marched with its own Brigade, whose sick, then and in the "rest" periods of the Division, it was responsible for collecting and treating; while in a push, one of the three units, plus the bearers (nominally one hundred each), ambulance cars and horse wagons of the other two, dealt with the evacuation of the wounded from the Regimental Aid Post via the Collecting Post and the Advanced Dressing Station back to the Main Dressing Station, run by another of the Ambulances. Here Divisional treatment ceased and the wounded were transferred to the Motor Ambulance Convoy, administered by Corps, and carried back to the Casualty Clearing Station; whence by Ambulance Train they went to the Base Hospital and thereafter by Hospital Ship to the U.K. The third of the Divisional Field Ambulances usually ran a Walking Wounded Collecting Station in the neighbourhood of the Main or the

Advanced Dressing Station, to which the wounded who were able to walk found their way, a route thither having previously been marked out with flags and direction posts before the push.

Now, any Field Ambulance commander that I ever met usually had two chronic outstanding grouses. One was against the medical officers of the battalions in the line, who, absolutely illegitimately and backed as a rule by their commanding officers—sometimes even by the G.O.C. himself when he had been "got at"—tried during a push to use the Ambulance stretcher-bearers in front of the Regimental Aid Posts to eke out their Regimental stretcher-bearers, with a resulting check to the rapid evacuation of casualties back to the Collecting Post and Advanced Dressing Station. The other was against the Casualty Clearing Stations. These, excellent and efficient though they were, ranked without doubt as the spoilt children of the R.A.M.C. Constant demands were made by Corps to detail officers and nursing orderlies from the Ambulances for the purpose of assisting the C.C.S.s; and it was frequently only with the greatest difficulty, and at the eleventh hour before a battle, that these parties could be recovered for their legitimate work with their units behind the front line. Further, when sent to the C.C.S., they were looked on as "nobody's bairns," and too often given all the dirty work to do: in one such case a medical officer and twenty nursing orderlies were set to dig drains! Again, it was a common experience that no proper attempt was made at the C.C.S. to return promptly the Field Ambulance's limited supply of hot-water bottles, Thomas' splints and other special appliances—things always of the utmost value to us—sent down with patients, nor to see that proper drying arrangements existed for dealing with blankets and stretchers soaked by the rain and mud of the long carry from the front line. As the war went on there was a great improve-

INTRODUCTORY.

ment effected; for each motor transport driver was ultimately given a chit at the Main Dressing Station by the despatching N.C.O., detailing what special appliances went with the patients on his car; and this chit had to be signed by the C.C.S.'s receiving N.C.O., so that a check was available. And when the Casualty Clearing Stations were at last awake to the fact that blanket-drying was not a troublesome side-show but an important factor in combating shock up the line, we had taken a step forward by which everyone benefited.

Still, great was the strife occasionally, and hotter natures made a vendetta of it; I remember one occasion when it was carried on with the aid of bombs, but in this way only. All such articles were of course removed from the person of the wounded man before he left our hands; but Tommy was a casual soul, and often carried an odd bomb or two inside the torn lining of his tunic pockets or otherwise bestowed about his person. Besides, human nature is fallible, and an overworked nursing orderly might be caught off his guard in a rush. So it happened one day that some patients found their way into a C.C.S. from the front line still bearing bombs about them. The O.C. of this C.C.S., instead of sending a friendly note of warning, chose, being a stickler for military etiquette, to complain through "the usual channels"; and in due course a strafe from higher up descended on our devoted heads. But by good luck we had a friend in charge of an ambulance train evacuating cases from this station, and he was asked to look out for bombs on cases received therefrom. Sure enough in a few days he got them, and, also employing the usual channels, discomfited our foe: on whom I called later to explain that as we were quits this kind of correspondence might, as the editors say, "now cease." It did.

Starting *la vie militaire* as an innocent-minded and peaceful civilian, one had to learn as quickly as possible the noble art of "getting one's own back" or perhaps more correctly of "not being left": outlooks had to be changed and standards of values readjusted. This was especially the case in dealing with certain brass hats. I do not wield the two-handed battle-axe of Philip Gibbs and his clan in dealing with these people: I consider the class, as a class, much maligned. But there were, *sans doute,* some extraordinary individuals amongst them, and one had, on occasion, to fight with wild beasts at Ephesus.

Now it is, naturally, medical brass hats with whom I am chiefly concerned, and on them alone I could write a book; not, mark you, to attack the Medical Service—which, taken all over in France, was as sound as a bell—but to deal with the impossible people. Some of these were only the happy-go-luckier members of the ever delightful "Fenian Brigade"; some were merely amiable cranks. But a few others, had they been horses, one would have labelled as vicious. These last were out, not—so far as one could ever ascertain—to help, but to find fault, and, when they thought fit, to try to "break" any officer to whom they had conceived a dislike. But all of this class I met were fortunately amenable to appropriate and carefully thought out treatment.

One of them, whom I remember yet with maledictions mellowed somewhat by the passage of the years, dearly loved to descend suddenly on a Main Dressing Station when a push was on, and, oblivious of the fact that the O.C. had at such times to be on duty all over the place, express great wrath if that officer was not there in person to greet him respectfully on the threshold. From my office window overlooking the entrance I saw him one day jump from his car and dive into the old barn that was our Receiving Room, and immediately hastened across to meet him, arriving some thirty seconds after his advent.

INTRODUCTORY.

"Well, you're here at last, are you?" was his genial greeting.

"Yes, sir."

"And now you *are* here perhaps you'll tell me what that —— fool there" (pointing to an N.C.O. who was standing rigidly at attention and gazing into vacancy) "can't, and that is what the devil these two barrels are used for?"

I gazed into a corner of the barn and saw there on trestles two small barrels which I had never in my life seen before. But it was no use to tell him *that*.

"We were using them for barley water, sir, but we found it didn't keep well."

"Then why the blazes couldn't that fellow there tell me that at once?" And he consumed the unfortunate N.C.O. with his eyes. I, too, gazed at the culprit reproachfully for unnecessarily withholding information so evidently essential to the well-being of an inspecting officer.

When he had left after a tour of the show (where, curiously enough, seeing the mood he was in, he found fault with nothing else), I went to the N.C.O. and asked him what on earth the barrels were for and where they came from? He was an Englishman that I had on loan, and he answered:—

"Most unfort'nit thing, sir, but these 'ere empty barrels was below a tarpaulin in the corner, and I had just 'auled the tarpaulin orf to see wot was there w'en '*e* came in."

We conjointly examined the two derelict barrels with interest, and found one was labelled "Rum" and the other "Lime Juice!" They were at once removed and broken up for firewood, the sergeant very properly remarking, "Lucky job, sir, 'e didn't pursoo the subjick!"

Yes, he was a truly great man, that same happy

warrior. Going round with him he would come, say, to the blanket store and rap out,

"How many blankets?"

It was, of course, impossible to say accurately without consulting the Q.M., as there was a constant come and go of such articles. But to reply "I'll ask the Quartermaster, sir," was fatal. His answer would have been:

"The Quartermaster be ———! You should know all the Quartermaster knows and a ——— sight more!"

So the result was that he always got an immediate answer of something like this:

"Eight hundred and seventy-two, sir, and fifteen under repair"; the sergeant-major chipping in with, "That's right, sir" (gallantly running the risk of having his nose bitten off for intervening); and the war was a step nearer being won.

On another occasion, when we were running a Corps Main Dressing Station during a push, with a very numerous personnel to look after, and the place going like a fair, a certain high-up medical mandarin sent in a demand for an immediate report as to why it was that so many safety-pins had been indented for on the Advanced Depot of Medical Stores the week before, with whatever further information on the nature, quality, merits, demerits and ultimate destination of the safety-pins supplied could be given. Safety-pins! Name of a pipe! All my work was laid aside for two hours while I concocted this report, and, with all humility, I can say truthfully that it was a work of art. The introductory paragraph, I recollect (and I managed to extend the report to two typewritten foolscap pages), ran thus:—

"When considering the subject of safety-pins, it must always be borne in mind that the best are those which most nearly follow their prototype, the Roman *fibula*."

INTRODUCTORY.   11

Then came a detail of (1) for what purposes we legitimately used safety-pins; (2) the illegitimate demands made on M.O.s of Field Ambulances and battalions for safety-pins by combatant officers and others not entitled to such luxuries; (3) the different manufacturers who supplied safety-pins; (4) the manufacturer whose products seemed specially reliable (more or less true); (5) the number of safety-pins supposed to be in each box; (6) the average number really in the boxes (probably true); (7) the average percentage of safety-pins which doubled up or became otherwise inefficient when used (possibly true); and so on to the bitter end, padded out with rolling Gladstonian periods, and really (although I say it who shouldn't) reading uncommonly well, if you took it as merely rather hurried journalism. And I remember when, somewhat wearily, I handed it over to be typewritten, I could not help thinking that the Germans had really got it in the neck this time, and that we were at last beginning to get a genuine move on in a prolonged and sanguinary war.

Later on my senior in the Corps, through whose hands it passed, and who was a thoroughly decent chap—he had Celtic blood in his veins — rang me up on the phone and said:—

"I say! I got that report on the safety-pins."

"Yes, sir?"

"Never knew so much about safety-pins before!"

"No, sir?"

"It should settle him though." (Pause.) "Oh, by the way, send me a copy of your next novel when it comes out, will you?"

Mais que voulez-vous? A la guerre comme à la guerre! To do it was, of course, painful in the extreme, but what else could you do? If you were to be left in peace and the work carried through, that kind of chap had to be spoon-fed on flapdoodle simply to get him out of the road; he asked for it all the time, and the wise man gave it to him—in judicious doses.

I remember another senior genius in the Medical Service finding quite unwarranted fault with an officer in charge of a scabies ward at a Divisional Rest Station.

"What are you in civil life?"

"An oculist, sir."

"An oculist! Great Heavens! An oculist in charge of a scabies ward?" (Then to me.) "What the devil do you mean by putting an oculist in charge of scabies?"

"Only one other officer available, sir."

"Then, hang it all, put him on!"

"Very good, sir; he's a lecturer on physiology."

I thought he was going to throw three separate kinds of fit and then burst. But he only turned an empurpled visage on me and said solemnly:—

"Now look here, this kind of thing's got to stop! D'ye hear? D'ye understand? Got to stop—got to stop at once! You'll look out an officer who's a *dermatologist*—a fellow who's made a special study of skins—chap who has done that sort of thing for years—*years*, mark you! And a junior officer with specialist qualifications too! Got that?—I'm going to collect all cases of scabies together at one centre, and *these men* are going to be in charge of them! See to it!" And in an atmosphere of "dammits" and growls he worked his sulphurous and saluted way to his limousine and departed.

Now you see "these men," as far as we were concerned, simply didn't exist: that was the worry of it: they weren't there! But Napoleon I. said that difficulties exist for the purpose of being overcome, and Klausewitz gave us the dictum, "In war do the best you can." What annoyed me mostly on this occasion was that I was only acting A.D.M.S. for the real man on leave, and he had just gone the day before: it was not my *pidgin*: however, I supposed I could make a dermatologist or two out

INTRODUCTORY.

of nothing just as well as the next fellow, if I took the matter up seriously.

It so happened that in one of our medical units was an officer—a most efficient and gallant officer—who in the piping times of peace was a dentist. I went to him and told him that I meditated turning him into a dermatologist, and that I was genuinely sorry that I had to do this: it made me feel like a magician changing a princess into a rabbit. I also reminded him that he had known me well for years, and I was sure he would bear me out in saying that, *en civile,* camouflage, bluff, casuistry, special pleading and Jesuitical reasoning were absolutely foreign to my nature. I reminded him also of the developmental connection between teeth and skin, and that really, to a man with a scientific mind and the wider outlook, the ultimate difference was so slight that, if a brass hat who knew nothing about either asked him about skins, he could quite properly reply that he had been doing "that kind of thing" all his professional life. But I told him I put no pressure on him; if he had a conscience he must not muzzle the thing to oblige me: these were matters for personal decision: I only asked him to remember that we were in the Army and that there was a war on. And next I hied me to a very smart young Canadian M.O., at that time attached to us, to whom I said:—

"Don't correct me if I am wrong! I understand you were for two years house physician at Montreal Skin Hospital. On this understanding, or misunderstanding, I have appointed you assistant dermatologist at the Combined Scabies Station. The decision is final."

Well, the dentist and the Canuck, being sportsmen, took the show over and ran it with great efficiency and success; so efficiently that they were kept at the job long after they were thoroughly fed up with it. Two days after it was opened the great man came round to inspect.

"Ugh!" he grunted, as I met him at the door of the building, "what kind of a show have you got?"

"Very good indeed, sir."

"Humph! That's for me to say, not you! Got these skin men to look after it?"

I seized the opportunity to dodge the question and to introduce the officers to him.

"Know anything about skins?" he growled at the senior.

"I ought to, sir."

"Ought to? Why the devil ought you?"

"Done this sort of thing for twenty years, sir."

"And what about this fellow"?

"Montreal Skin Hospital, sir," drawled the Canuck, diplomatically avoiding any unnecessary misstatement of facts.

"Humph!" And then he turned to me. "And you were fiddling about with oculists and lecturers on physiology while you had these other fellows up your sleeve the whole —— time! Organisation! The right man for the right job! It's what I'm teaching and preaching and you won't take it in! Just you remember this business in future as an example of what can be done when you put your mind to it."

And I said, "Very good, sir!" And I felt it too.

The officer with the chilblains is also a case of interest, although the hero of that tale was a dear, kind-hearted old chap. But I think his very arteries were made of red tape, and a Divisional or a Corps order was to him as unchangeable a decree as the laws of the Medes and the Persians. He was a good enough administrative officer, but all the medicine he had ever known had, long ago, run out of the heels of his boots. We were carrying on a Divisional Rest Station at the time, an institution where sick and slightly wounded were taken in for treatment; and if, after seven days, they were not fit to return to the line, were sent back to the C.C.S., being, *ipso facto*, struck off the strength of the Division. Well, one day a young officer came in who had nothing more or less wrong with him than very severe chilblains, and who was extremely anxious not to go further back, as he had temporary rank in his unit which he would thereby lose, while his O.C. was equally desirous of his rejoining.

But on the seventh day he was still unfit to go up the line, so we kept him on, gave his chart a touch of temperature, and trusted to luck. On the ninth day round came our old friend, buzzed cheerily through the wards, and then came to the case of chilblains, whose chart he glanced at.

"Oh, hang it all! Look here now! This is too bad! Nine days! Surely you know the order about seven days being the maximum stay here? Send him down by to-night's convoy."

"I think, sir, we should exercise great care about removing this officer: it is an acute case of *erythema pernio*." (And let it be known to the laity that this is merely the Latin name for chilblains.)

"Oh, bless my soul! I didn't know *that* though! We would need to be a bit careful here—Eh? What? But look here—he has got no temperature to speak of!"

"Some of the very worst cases haven't, sir."

"Oh, well, glad you told me about this. *What* was it you said he had? Oh! Keep a careful watch on him! Take no risks! That wouldn't do at all!" And off he went, obviously musing.

Some days later he turned up, breezy and cheery. As he went up the corridor he said:—

"And what about that acute case of ———? You know—that fellow with the ———? The case we couldn't move? How is he?"

"Much better, sir. I think he'll come round all right now."

"Dashed good job we didn't move him, eh?"

I respectfully agreed. And two days later Captain Erythema Pernio rejoined his battalion.

Of course every man has his fads, even the very best of us: I should not be at all surprised if some men who served under me thought that I had a few trifling weaknesses of that sort myself. One of my seniors was perhaps the most efficient, kindly, courteous, helpful officer whom I ever met in the Service. But he was death on thermometer-breaking, and at his conferences a most thorough explanation had to be given of all indents sent to the Advanced Depot of Medical Stores for such articles. The M.O.s of Field Ambulances, battalions, and other units, had to see to the filling in of weekly returns with the headings (1) Number of clinical thermometers broken. (2) By whom broken. (3) How broken, etc., etc. And I always remember the story told by one southron medical orderly, pouring out his soul on the form through the medium of a stubby pencil. "Under foloing circstances. Patent had thermomter in mouth when a shell burst in his visinty so he chewd on it." Which he chewed on—the shell, the thermometer, or the vicinity; likely bits of them all—is not clear, but the "patent's" conduct, "under the circstances," was excusable.

And then there was the incident of the rats: that was not a medical brass hat, though, but a "Q-monger." The iron rations of our unit had disappeared gradually, and our Quartermaster indented for 241—our total number—at one go-off, a somewhat wholesale order. And then "Q" started a correspondence which ran:—

(1)

"Reference your indent of —— for 241 iron rations. It is not understood how all your iron rations have disappeared. Please explain."

To which the Q.M. replied:—

(2)

"Reference your (1). These rations have been lost mainly through the action of rats."

What he meant was that the rats had in many cases eaten through the linen bags in which the iron rations were carried, and that the tins had fallen out through the holes so caused while the men were on the march or in billets. (It was really a bit thin.) However, in came :—

(3)

"Reference your (2). Please explain how rats can eat through tin."

Here the Q.M., with a troubled mind, brought the correspondence to me, and we tried them with:—

(4)

"Reference your (3). It is pointed out for your information that the rat prevalent in the district is not the small black rat, but the large, grey Hanoverian rat."

The correspondence ceased and we got the rations handed over—"Q" had evidently not got a good text-book on natural history at hand.

"Ay, there's queer folk in the Shaws!" And that reminds me of less important people and the tale of "Wee Ginger," which is another kind of story altogether. Divisional Headquarters were at one time in a collection of huts set on a wind-swept hill, approached from the main road by a duck-board track set in a sea of mud. From 10 a.m. to noon I had held a medical board on men claiming to be unfit for continuing in the line; and at 12.30 I was going over the papers bearing on the cases seen. Suddenly the door of my "Armstrong" was opened and a man literally "blew in"; for, as he turned the handle of the door the wind vigorously finished the operation and jerked him into the hut, all my papers whirling off the table. I asked him somewhat hastily,

B

what in the wide, wide world he thought he wanted? He was a little man with large spectacles fixed in a clock-face visage, a Scottish bonnet roguishly cocked a-jee on a mop of red hair, a kilt well below the knees of a pair of Harry Lauder legs, and a general air, probably assumed, of childlike simplicity. He saluted slowly, like a mechanical toy, and asked me with mild interest :—

"Are you the Boord?"

"Am I the *what?*"

"Are you the Boord?"

"There was a Board here at 10 o'clock. Were you summoned to it? If so, why do you turn up at 12.30?"

"Weel ye see, sir, I can explain that tae. I was tel't doon in the toon there that the Boord wis up here; but when I was hauf wev up a' thae duck-boords I says to masel' 'There canna be a Boord up *here!*' Sae I went awa' back to the toon again to speir if I wis richt, an' they said 'Ay'—an' a lot mair tae—an' syne I had a' the wey tae traivel back again, ye see, and that's the wey I'm late ye see, sir, for if I had keepit up thae duck-boords the first time . . ."

"All right, that'll do! Seeing you *are* here, what's wrong with you?"

"Weel, it's just like this, sir; *I'm ower wee for the job!* When we're marchin' I'm aye fa'in ahint. Noo ye see, on the ither side o' the watter, afore I cam' oot here, there wis a sargint—Oh, an awfy fine felly, that sargint!—and when the big chaps wis stappin' out he aye says, 'Noo haud on, boys, or we'll be lossin' Wee Ginger!' (That's what they ca' me, ye see, sir.) But the sargints here's no that kind ava, an' I dinna ken hoo often they've lost me ; they're aye daein't!"

He was about five feet two, and the tale sounded as if it might be lamentably true. Then I asked him :—

"What did you do in civil life?"

"Weel noo, there ye are! Ye see, I wis a bird-stuffer in Glescy and that wis nae trainin' ava for *this* kin' o' a' job!"

Which was incontrovertible; so he got a fresh start in military life at the A.S.C. laundry. And I do not know whether they lost "Wee Ginger" there or not, or what sad tale of a tub he told, perchance, to the next "Boord" he encountered.

At another Board a sallow individual, claiming to be the possessor of many complicated ailments, stripped for examination. A rapid glance at his salients gave the information that he was a true son of Abraham. Asked, with a stethoscope applied, to say "One, one," he responded with "Von! Von!" Now, it is always good to use the tongue of these with whom you speak, so I enquired:—

"Vat vos you ven you vos in thivil life?"

"I vos a vatchmaker in Vitechapel."

A puzzling individual was the Sassenach who gave his pre-war occupation as "'Airdresser and new-lide hegg merchant." I have often meditated over him since. How did the coalition work? Did he chop up the hair-cuttings as a stimulating diet to his hens for egg production? And did he then use the resulting eggs for the manufacture of hair-lotion? And did the vicious circle result in profit?

> How little thought each man is giving
> To how his brother makes his living!

Someone has very properly remarked that the true *liaison* between the British and the French armies was the Scottish troops. The statement is curiously true—for two reasons. One is that many of the English had never got away from the "d—— foreigner" idea of the Napoleonic wars: the other, that the sentiment of the "Auld Alliance" persisted strongly amongst the French, both military and civilian. I trust that it now exists more strongly than ever and that it will last for all time.

Less, of course, the Gunners, R.E., M.G.C., A.S.C. and R.A.M.C., the 51st Division was a kilted division. I think it was Max O'Rell who gave as a reason for the Scots wearing kilts that their feet were too big to get into trousers. And we all know Joffre's classic criticism of the garb of old Gaul, so I need not—fortunately—quote it. But I once overheard in Picardy a somewhat Joffrian explanation given by an R.A.M.C. private to a French lady, of why his unit, then billeted in a village amongst kilted troops, did not also wear the *courte jupe*. The lady's knowledge of English was on a par with his knowledge of French, so the conversation started by her pointing to his slacks and ejaculating "Anglais?"

"Na, na!" said he, "Ecossy!"

Whereupon she indicated a passing Jock and stated her case briefly:—"Ecossais—Voila! Vous—Anglais!"

"Ach! The kilt!" he replied: "Na, na: owre muckle bendin' aboot oor job, wifie! Compree?"

I do not think she did, and perhaps as well. But the honest woman, as she set off up the road, must have gathered from the laughter of his comrades that there was some "dooble ong-tong" in the answer.

It often took the expatriated Scot some time before he understood enough of the language to feel quite at home in this new country. "Napoo" was perhaps the first expression he fully grasped when disappointed in his visit to shop or *estaminet*, always in search of something to fortify the inner man.

> "C'wa man, Jock! See, here's an estaminit
> Lat's gang inside an' try, man!
> We'll maybe get twa oofs an' some ham in it,
> An' a bottle o' beer forbye, man!"
>
> But, alas for the pair! I can hear them swear
> As they leave the place, a-damnin' it!
> "Och ay! *Oui, oui! Napoo! Fee-nee!*
> To the crows with her giddy estaminit!"

Yes, the last line is bowdlerised: I frankly grant the

INTRODUCTORY. 21

necessity of so doing. On occasion the genial Jock had some excuse for his verbal carelessness, and he sometimes could put forward the excuse pretty well, as I shall try to show.

Many will remember Martinsart and the conditions prevailing there in 1915. Four g.s. wagons from each Divisional Field Ambulance were detailed to assist the pioneer battalion in the construction of a road over the hill just beyond the village. The weather at the time was atrocious, and the place where the horse-lines and bivouacs were pitched was a veritable sea of mud. So bad was it that it reached to the horses' bellies when they left the road, and they had practically to swim across the field to their stance about four hundred yards away near a battery of 4.7's. The bivouacs were in constant danger of being submerged, and the effort necessary to reach a little shed where the men's cookhouse was situated was no small one. One day, while watering horses at a big tank in the village, a shell burst near at hand and a horse swung round with a jerk and toppled into the tank. A staff officer passing at the time "nearly chewed the head off" the driver (the words are the man's own) for "contaminating the water!" But the poor old horse had the best of it, for he got a much needed bath.

Rats, too, were there in battalions. So numerous were they that the men used to go out after dark with sticks and lay about them indiscriminately, and in the morning usually found a dozen or so lying dead. No place was safe to keep the rations from them: even when a wire was run from one end of the bivouac to the other, and they were hung thereon in a bag, these little indefatigable tight-rope walkers got at them. One humorist declared they ate up his hairy jacket and all his tobacco, and that he heard them playing at night on a derelict and damaged set of bagpipes that were lying in the "bivvy." Which is as may be.

And he it was (and this is what I am working up to) who, when reproved by a passing chaplain moved to dire wrath by the lurid language emanating from a shelter, ventured a quaint excuse. "It's no muckle godliness ye'll find here, sir, but the Lord'll maybe forgie me, for I practise the next best thing at hame." "Oh!" said the angry padre, "what's that?" "Cleanliness, sir! I'm a scaffey wi' the Aiberdeen Corporation!"

As a linguist—using the term comprehensively—Jock seldom stuck. From my bedroom off a farm kitchen in the Somme I once overheard two diplomats interviewing the lady of the house, who, incidentally, did not understand a word of English, much less Scots.

"Bong swarr, wifie!"

"Bonsoir, messieurs!"

"Hae ye ony pum-de-tairs, mistress?"

"Pommes de terre? Non, non! *Napoo!*"[1]

"Och, awa' wi' your *napoo!* I ken ye've some spuds: I saw ye peelin' them yestreen!"

"Vraiment. *Napoo!*"

"*You* hae a try at her, Tam!" said number one—and Tam had a try. He decided for the pathetic touch, and started off in a wheedling tone,

"Noo look here, wifie, it's no for oorsels we're seekin' tatties, na, na; it's for a *camarade* o' oors, sick in billets, puir sowl, an' a tatty's the ae thing he's fairly greetin' for!"

But even this sad—and, I fear, imaginary—story did not, curiously enough, get through the old lady's defence, and only drew forth another negative.

"Och, come on, Pete! The auld besom winna gie's ony: lat's try some ither gait! Bong swarr, wifie!"

And off went the two disappointed potato-hunters. Coming into the kitchen, I asked her:—

---

[1] The inhabitants very early adopted this Anglo-French expression when addressing the troops.

On Trek—Summer.

INTRODUCTORY.

"The men billeted here do not trouble you?"

"Au contraire, monsieur: toujours très convenables!" And then she told me how number one regularly drew water for her from the well, while number two had that morning washed down her door-step for her. "Always kind and polite, monsieur! And had I *pommes de terre* they certainly would get them!"

And who, when memory is releasing its roll of films, does not remember the innumerable treks, each unit, with its inevitable attendant train of mongrel dogs (our own total once rose to fifteen, embracing every variety from a mighty mastiff to the little prolific black and tan terrier bitch beloved of the M.T.), passing through the winding streets of village after village, dotted with *estaminets* ("A l'Aube," "Point du Jour," "Aux Pêcheurs," etc.) and *débits de tabac*, with gables and windows embellished either with notices calling up new "classes" of the French Army, or with other war time posters? Prominent everywhere was "Taisez vous! Méfiez vous! Les oreilles ennemies vous ecoutent!" (*Cave quid dicis, quando, et cui!*) And this, the home newspapers told us, was best translated:—

> There was an old owl sat on an oak,
> The more he heard the less he spoke,
> The less he spoke the more he heard,
> Why not imitate this old bird?

(All very well for the ancient bird of wisdom! But was the rash speaker's information always valuable to the foe? Did not the Chinese philosopher, Lao Tsu, long, long ago, lay down the golden truth—"He who speaks does not know: he who knows does not speak?") Other posters there were—the artistic "On les aura!" chief of the series advertising French War Loan; or those of *tombolas* for the *Croix Rouge,* in one of which a man of ours actually won a hundred francs, and liquidated it, to his own downfall.

Each village much like another; differing somewhat, perhaps, in the amount it had been knocked about, or in the age and picturesqueness of its church. One might contain the Headquarters of the Division whose area we were crossing; or be less important in possessing only those of a brigade or a battalion. And yet very few were without interest if one set oneself deliberately to dig it out. It was enough, often, when all were settled in at the end of a day, to stroll in the dusk through some—to the casual and fed-up observer—dead-and-alive hamlet, and think how generation after generation of toil-worn folk like those one saw had lived and moved and had their being here, had made this their local habitation and here gained their name. For it was often in the smallest *hameaux* that one found the true Jacques Bonhomme. Loves, jealousies, hates, ambitions all were here: the churchyard—or the *curé*—told of sorrows and tragedies. Folk-beliefs were always ascertainable: quaint rustic tales could be told to sympathetic ears. Here was a British name, twisted to suit French lingual powers; for had not the great-great-grandfather of the present possessor of it been a sergeant in Wellington's army who had stayed behind at the behest of Cupid? Or again, one discovered a purely Protestant village—*rara avis in terris*—where a common anti-papal ancestor's will had for monetary reasons involved the inter-marriage of his descendants, to their great mental and physical hurt.

Sad, more or less, the villages always were: black was the common wear of the women-folk; while the men were either bent with age, or, if youthful, weak in body or mind, left behind solely because they were unfit material for the strong hell-broth of war.

And the burial places. Everywhere in the war area the communal cemetery had been crowded out, and new ground broken; full, row upon row, of neatly regimented mounds with the little white-painted wooden crosses at their heads. On these hung the metal tricolour of the Republic, while on the upright was painted the inevitable black tear of sorrow. On a summer's night, when a sighing wind gently and with mournful persistence moved these little tricolours to a faint metallic rustling up and down the rows, one could stand alone there amongst the crosses and imagine the spirit of *la Patrie* was whispering a message through the earth to tell those lying below that they had not died in vain; to have patience yet awhile and their country's freedom would come. "Fear not the tyrants will rule for ever, nor the priests of the evil faith": it could not be that a great land and a greater people were doomed to lie forever under such an accursed yoke.

On the graves were the wreaths or the souvenirs of those who mourned their dead, shewing the same desire as at home for *in memoriam* rhymes; following, however, more fixed types, and free from the terrible originality we too often see in our cemeteries and daily papers. The more usual—printed on square or oval china plaques—were:—

>Tout ce que l'amitié
>Peut offrir,
>Une fleur, une larme,
>Un souvenir.

Or again:—

>Souvenir !
>Nous ne t'oublierons jamais !

One verse often seen :—

>Si mort inattendue
>A déchiré nos cœurs,
>Ni le temps ni l'oubli
>Ne tariront nos pleurs.

Another:—

>Autrefois des fleurs,
>Maintenant des pleurs.

The most common inscriptions were simple:—

> Tué à l'ennemi pour la défense de la France.
> Froide terre! Tu caches à jamais notre trésor!
> Mort au champ d'honneur.
> Mort pour la patrie.
> Mort pour la France.

Of great beauty, too, were many of the village names. Owen Wister says rightly:—"All France is musical with names; names sonorous that chant like legends, or gay, that trip like the dances of old *jongleurs:* names full of overtones, where the vowels and syllables fall into cadences so melodious, that to read them aloud is like a song." Bellinglise was his favourite: mine, I think, of them all, was Fleury-la-Rivière.

And then, after a night in some such place, spent more or less comfortably as Fate might decree, bundle and go again at an unearthly hour in the morning on the old tinker's trail. As the sun got higher and higher and our spirits rose with it, songs and choruses to the accompaniment of penny whistle or mouth organ burst out at intervals from the marching men: while, if we had pipers to lead us, who does not recall the response of the French cow to the shrilling of Caledonian music? When Corydon fluted to his Phyllis, Allan Ramsay tells us:—

> E'en the dull cattle stood amazed
> Pleased with the melody.

But these were phlegmatic Scottish kine! The cow of *la belle France,* with all the Gallic vivacity of her owners, went one better; and shewed her pleasure, not by stationary amazement, but by prancing, tail-up and with evident appreciation, to the "Pibroch of Donuil Dhu," or to what she considered the even more appropriate air of "The Muckin' o' Geordie's Byre."

By night again we might be once more in the devastated area: hawks and magpies the only birds and rat-ridden ruins again our environment. Even there in

On Trek—Winter.

Facing page 26.

INTRODUCTORY. 27

remnants of garden or orchard were the poppies, the marguerites or the blue cornflowers, unexpected little oases of beauty in the desert of destruction. And your evening stroll was devoted to poking about here and there amongst desolate hearths with a stick and murmuring :—

> This was the house that Jacques built.
> This was the roof that covered the house
> That Jacques built. . . .

and cursing the war and all its many hellish ways.

One could talk, too, of cellars further forward still, amongst even greater devastation, where, as Walpole said of Rome, "the very ruins were ruined." Therein one sought shelter for advanced posts of all descriptions— creepy-crawly, verminous and damp; but safe enough when the roofs were propped a bit, and always getting safer the more the shattered house above was knocked down, and the head-cover thereby grew. It is a wonder we did not see ghosts in these places, in the older buildings at least, for they must have been there to see. And many a restored villa or château will run the risk, in its after history, of khaki-clad and mud-covered spectres intruding upon its below-stairs life.

> As you went up by Windmill Farm
>   An' down by the *shemmin croo*
> You came to the edge o' Dead Man's Wood
>   An' there was the old *shattoo*,
> A heap o' bricks an' a cellar stair
>   With the rest o' the show *napoo;*
> Yet it was a Relay Bearers' Post
>   An' sheltered a tidy few.
>
> A cracked old bell still hung on the wall
>   An' often some silly cuckoo
> Would tip it a-jangle by way of a joke
>   When he found nothing better to do,
> While the rest o' the blighters would chortle out
>   "*Toot sweet!* We're a-comin', *Mossoo!*"
> A-shammin' as they was the *domey-steeks*
>   O' the Count o' the old *shattoo.*

> For a ruddy aristocrat owned it once
>   Till, all in horizon blue,
> He left his bones away in the South
>   Done in by a Jerry *oboo.*
> Ay, he left his bones, but he left no wife,
>   No kids, an' o' francs *tray poo,*
> For he'd gone the pace when he was alive
>   As a lot o' them Frenchies do.
>
> You mark my words when I prophesy,
>   The things as I say bein' true,
> If it's ever rebuilt in the years to come
>   (I speak o' the old *shattoo*),
> The *domey-steeks* a-sittin' downstairs
>   Will huddle and squeal "*Mongjoo!*"
> When a ghostly chorus answers the bell,
>   "*Toot sweet!* We're a-comin', *Mossoo!*"

So now, an it please you, gentle **reader,** let us have done with character sketches, generalities and the methods of Silas Wegg, and, in more chronological detail, to our muttons.

CHAPTER II.

Estaires—Givenchy, 1915.

Then, in a train, they hauled us up to Flanders,
Near where a big canal so sluggishly meanders,
There with high explosive the beggars tried to floor us,
And we got to understand the value of the chorus:

    Strafe the Kaiser! Strafe the Huns!
    Strafe the devil that invented guns!
    Strafe their Army! Strafe their War!
    Oh, what a giddy lot of fools they are!

        (2nd Highland Field Ambulance's *Hymn of Hate*.)

"The Division left Britain at the end of April and beginning of May, 1915, and, on arrival in France, was immediately sent to the neighbourhood of the firing line. . . . On 17th May, Sir John French gave orders for the 51st Division to move into the neighbourhood of Estaires to be ready to support the operations of the First Army, and on the 19th the 2nd Division was relieved by the 51st. . . . On 15th June the 51st, along with the Canadians and 7th Division, took part in an attack near Givenchy, which met with little success."—(*The Territorial Divisions*.)

WE landed at Le Havre on 1st May, 1915,[1] a beautiful, clear, sunny morning, every man heartily glad to be at last on French soil. For even the many allurements of Bedford—kindly, hospitable Bedford, our war station since August 1914, whose name still recalls benefits bestowed, Bunyan, and the blistered feet of the military pilgrim's progress—had not reconciled us to home

[1] G.O.C. Division, Major-General R. Bannatine Allason, C.B.; A.D.M.S., Colonel C. C. Fleming, D.S.O.; D.A.D.M.S., Lt.-Colonel T. F. Dewar; O.C. 1/2nd Highland Field Ambulance, Lt.-Colonel F. Kelly; O.C. 1/3rd, Lt.-Colonel W. E. Foggie; O.C. 2/1st, Lt.-Colonel J. Robertson.

service. Hard work we had done there, and in lecture room, field and hospital had learned many things—much of which we had to unlearn later in the bitter school of experience—but our stay in England had been far longer than we had expected, and hope frequently deferred had made us yearn all the more for what we held to be our legitimate work across the Channel.

In bulk, mark you, we were an untravelled folk; to most of the unit France was as yet a *terra incognita*. And as my party, with other divisional troops on that ancient Thames service paddle-boat, the "Golden Eagle," glided between the piers of Havre harbour, everything that savoured of the foreign — especially if it were feminine—was eagerly scanned and cheerily and audibly commented on. In response to a hail from a fellow countryman on the pier, our burly French pilot gave a shout from the bridge of "Oui! Oui!—Oui! Oui! Oui!," and seemed both astonished and annoyed when some five hundred voices took up the refrain and "Oui-Ouied" in chorus like a cargo of stout-lunged mice whose tails had been individually trodden on.

As the men fell in, a guide was waiting who led us round the quays of the historic old seaport to where the rest of the unit, with the transport, disembarked shortly afterwards from a Canadian cattle-boat, the "Mount Temple." Ambulance and g.s. wagons, with limbers and water-carts, were rapidly swung out-board by crane; donkey engines puffed and rattled; officers— military and mercantile marine, British and French— exhorted, objurgated and gesticulated; horses snorted, clattered and stumbled down the long gangways and were hooked in; and the unit at long last marched off to the Rest Camp on the outskirts of the town. There, in all the discomfort characteristic of such places, we stayed till 11 p.m., when we set off for the goods station; and, profiting by much home practice in that line, entrained with wonderful rapidity, men and horses being stowed away in trucks blazoned with the then novel but soon too familiar legend, "Chevaux 8, Hommes 40."

At the station we were joined by our first interpreter[1] who, during his stay with us, was in every sense the comrade, guide, philosopher and friend of all ranks—absolutely just as intermediary between our allies and ourselves when questions of difficulty arose, and from the beginning entering sympathetically and heartily into our daily life. Lucky was the unit to whose members were interpreted not only the language but the soul of France! And our "interrupter" proved himself eminently capable of doing both.

Travelling all night—and for May a singularly cold night it was—we stopped soon after daybreak at a roadside station to water the horses and get breakfast. Hot coffee laced with brandy—*betterave* brand, certainly not *fine champagne,* but palatable enough: it heated you and that was much—washed down sandwiches and biscuits or bread and cheese; and I remember being destitute of tobacco there and getting a packet of Maryland cigarettes from a hospitable French officer—cigarettes whose novelty made the briefest of appeals to the British smoker's palate. When the penny trumpet *toot-toot* of the guard's horn at last warned all aboard and the cheery, noisy crowd had tumbled into the wagons, in bright sunshine and warm weather we spent a long, enjoyable summer day journeying slowly north with many stops via Abbeville and Boulogne.

The country was looking its best, with the fresh greenery of spring and the *fleurice* (*Scotice* "flourish") of the fruit trees. At every village level crossing were children with their shrill cries of "Cigarette! Souvenir! Biskeet!," while if we stopped, women did a brisk trade

---

[1] M. Alfred Lelièvre of Havre.

in chocolate and fruit. Then gradually night fell, cold as before; the laughter and talk ceased as, wagon by wagon, the men closed the sliding doors of the trucks; a certain amount of broken sleep was got, what time we were not by the dim station lights trying to find out our whereabouts as we dragged wearily through; and at 3 a.m., with the muffled drumming of distant gun-fire booming in our ears, we reached, in the chilly dawn, our detraining station, Merville.

Merville—later to meet a sad fate at the desecrating hand of the enemy in April, 1918 — was then an undamaged, modern, small industrial town of 7,000 inhabitants, well laid out and flourishing, with an artistic little monument in its square, *aux morts de 1870*. Trekking briskly off at 4.30 a.m., we passed some time afterwards through the straggling village of Calonne-sur-la-Lys, and, after a march of about ten kilometres, reached our destination—Robecq, a little country town with a population of some 1,500.

To most of us, I think, the sensations and impressions of that first march on foreign soil will always be vivid; for at last we were in France and on active service —at last we were on the way to do what we had hitherto merely practised so long. Everything that for years was to be part of our daily life was then still novel—the long poplar trees lining the dusty highways; the large crucifixes at communal boundaries; the wayside shrines; the type of houses in the villages and the monuments in their cemeteries, where especially did we look with surprise on the large, black, band-box arrangements containing wreaths and portraits, so beloved of the French peasant.

At Robecq we took over the major part of the village school as hospital accommodation for Brigade sick and as billets for the men. Near by was the old church, dedicated to Saint Maurice and dating back to the days of the Spaniards; while in the space adjacent to it the transport was parked and the horse lines established. Then, when everything was fixed up "ship-shape and Bristol fashion," those off duty started exploring their environment.

With its narrow, winding streets and old-fashioned houses, the little town was as picturesque as it was insanitary—rural France knows so well how to be both!—and the curious groups of strolling Scots found, Quentin Durward-like, much to interest them and to criticise, while holding, like him, to the subconscious national motto of *nil admirari*. Firstly, the beer was too thin and the "vang blang" too sour; until both, *faute de mieux*, became a somewhat expensively acquired taste for the rank and file. But the bread of the village baker, new and hot from his oven, found such favour in their sight and their bellies, that the civil population ran a risk of a shortage; and, on urgent representation from the Mairie, next day's Divisional Orders forbade its further purchase by the troops. Well, well! "All is not good for the ghost that the gut asketh," as "Long Will" Langland said; and Army bread was no doubt better in the long run both for gut and for ghost.

New sights there were on every hand: the town crier going round with his drum making unfollowable announcements to languid audiences of three or four: the people kneeling to *M. le Curé* as he passed in procession with the Host to a death-bed: and, after the death, the cross of corn sheaves laid on the ground outside the door to notify the occurrence to the passer-by. On top of the centre of the cross was a little pyramid of clay, with a sprig of boxwood stuck in its apex. (I remember some time later seeing an unsentimental Tommy sitting on one of these crosses outside the estaminet at Le Hamel and tossing off his beer; thus proving at one and the same time his thirst, his contempt for folk-lore, his lack of imagination and his Protestant ancestry.)

c

In the yard of the baker aforesaid was a wheel fixed against the wall, like a mill wheel without the floats, and some seven feet in diameter, into which a large dog of mongrel mastiff breed, when he was free from pulling about the town his little cart laden with loaves, entered and stolidly set in motion a dough mixer inside the *boulangerie*. At a farm down a side street was a much larger wheel, where a horse placidly did his darg and supplied the motive power for a threshing mill.

Through the open half-door of a small barn could be seen an old peasant with a short and very dumpy flail methodically thrashing out his haricot beans, a feat that looked very easy to the onlooker until it was tried. For while *grand-père*, without any difficulty, brought the flail down with a heavy thump, missing his ear by an inch, the Scots novice—and I saw him do it—included the ear in the hearty blow meant for *les haricots*.

In the fields on the outskirts of the town you could see the full-uddered family cow harnessed to the plough, while gangs of boys were cutting the shoots off the pollarded willows lining the deep ditches, and tying them in bunches to be taken to buttress up the trenches. One evening I had a long talk with an elderly peasant on agricultural methods; he, anxious to know the nature of our Scots soil and what crops we grew there, and I, with my slow-going French, more anxious than able to tell him. If he adopted Scots methods of agriculture on my instruction, I grieve for him, and perhaps more especially for his dependants. Still, we both enjoyed the conversation, and, after mutual felicitations and a *petit verre* at the cross-roads café, parted duly edified.

Roadside shrines there were in plenty, one dating back to the eighteenth century, and offering a hundred days indulgence from the Bishop of Arras to anyone saying the required number of Paters and Aves. It sticks specially in my memory, for opposite it in April, three years later, I was to dress the head of a wounded Australian, while our Divisional Headquarters, under the exigencies of shell fire and the Boche advance, were hurriedly leaving Robecq for Busnes.

My own billet, shared with four other officers, was in the house of the local tailor, a large, stout, kindly man, who told me there had been one of his craft in each generation of his ancestry for the past 345 years—since 1570—and this he had documents to prove. I never doubted it, so I never saw the documents. The front door opened from the street on his little shop, where was our orderly room; the shop opened on the kitchen; and the kitchen opened on a lean-to greenhouse facing his garden. Here, under glass, he sat cross-legged in the sun and plied his needle, always ready for a chat on things in general. A bachelor, his household consisted of a spinster sister with chronic rheumatic arthritis, and an unafflicted niece of eighteen. In hen-coops in the back garden he kept a choice selection of game-cocks, which he fought, on occasion, with needle spurs mounted in leather. "Was cock-fighting, then, legal in France?" "Ah non, Monsieur! Contre le loi, mais c'est toléré!" The law was evidently pleasantly elastic, and, equally evidently, he, as a sartorial sportsman, appreciated the privilege of being a citizen of such a model state.

To get to your bedroom you opened a door in the kitchen and at once commenced to climb a dark, winding wooden stair. I say "at once" advisedly; for strangers such as we were, not expecting the first step to be where it was, usually and unintentionally commenced the voyage *en haut* on hands and knees. Batmen carrying jugs of water lay down incontinently on the first three steps and sent Niagaras coursing out on to old Mademoiselle's kitchen floor, where she sat in her arm-chair beside the large stove like King Canute defying the tide: or later, descending with slops, did a water-chute from halfway up and burst harlequin-like through the door into the kitchen. But anything the old lady said—and she said a good deal—they did not understand. So there was no unnecessary unpleasantness.

It was in this town that, next morning, I made a *faux pas*. Having been appointed to look after the sanitation of the place—in so far, at least, as our troops billeted there were concerned — I called, along with a battalion medical officer, to ask *M. le Maire* for a map reference as to where, if anywhere, some sanitation could be found. On entering the Mairie there were various inhabitants to be seen sitting, dressed in sober black, on forms against the wall. One came forward at our entry and we exchanged the usual preliminary courtesies. "Could I see M. le Maire?" "C'est impossible, Monsieur." "Impossible? Nothing is impossible to a brave man. Napoleon showed us that!" (I thought this was a happy and appropriate local hit: I remembered it in my Marryat from boyhood's days. Had not O'Brien said it to a French soldier—and gained what he asked for—when he and Peter Simple were escaping from a French prison?) And again came the suave, "C'est impossible, Monsieur!" "Impossible? Mais pourquoi?" "Parcequ'il est mort, Monsieur!"

Hence the black clothes! Hence the people collected for the funeral! Hence, now I came to think of it, the slow clanging of the church bell! Naturally, I said that under the circumstances I would not insist on seeing the Maire; and then, outside in the street my colleague and I exchanged acrimonious remarks about the lack of intelligence of people, who, with a church bell tolling and inhabitants in funeral black sitting about, wished to interview obviously defunct civic dignitaries. He had a very caustic, bitter tongue, that M.O.

But, not to be beaten, I took my little sixpenny "Soldier's French Conversation Book"—what a library of these things every fellow had then!—to our "interrupter" and asked him to write down, on the blank page at the end, the French for scavenger, broom, filth, gutter and barrow. And thus armed I started in search of the *balayeur,* so that with his *balais* he might brush up the *immondice* from the *égouts* and remove it in his *brouette.* When found, barrow, brush and all, however, little could be made of him. Was not he the only one? Were not his colleagues at the war? And his constant placid smile and his "Que voulez-vous, Monsieur? C'est la guerre!" helped him satisfactorily to account for all acts of sanitary omission.

Ultimately, after several ineffectual interviews, he developed the power of seeing me round a corner at five hundred yards; whereupon he dived with his eternally empty barrow down a side road—I should imagine into the next commune. There he stayed until darkness set in and allowed him to return uninterrupted to sleep at Robecq. Peace to his ashes if he be dead! If living, to his ash-heaps, to his middens and to his dirty gutters! For, if not a sanitarian, he was at least a laughing philosopher, which, perhaps, is the next best thing to success in any sphere of life; and, if he had never heard of Mark Tapley, he had, independently, developed his tenets.

We stayed in Robecq—where we were in the Indian Corps of the First Army—for eleven days, collecting Brigade sick, as aforesaid, and new experiences. During that time three of our officers, one from each of the Divisional Field Ambulances, were sent up to the 130th Indian Field Ambulance, then opened out at Zelobes, to see work under active service conditions. Their collecting post was a series of dug-outs in an orchard at Croix Barbèe, whence to the R.A.P.s ran little trolley trains propelled by man power on wooden rails, each trolley holding two patients.

In the vicinity our field guns were banging away merrily, while a horse ambulance wagon stood among the trees waiting for its load. New as such an environment was, we were much struck by the *sang froid* of the horses, which, regardless of the guns, were browsing on the grass, swishing their loins with their tails, and occasionally jerking their heads round to bite at their sides when the flies annoyed them; and all in the most natural, placid manner as if they had been brought up at the gun mouth. On the road to and from Zelobes were various shell-damaged villages, with churches, châteaux, estaminets and farmhouses all knocked about by enemy fire — our first close view of scenes the next four years rendered too familiar.

Night in the town of Robecq—for those, at least, billeted on the main street—was always broken during our stay by the passage of troops. Over the rough cobbles went, with little break, horse, foot and artillery—Scots, English, Indian. To lean out of window on the *premier étage* at 3 a.m. and see dimly in the street below a halted, heated battalion, or hear the "W-o-oh!" of the drivers as the rattling of a battery's wheels ceased, to give place for the moment to the occasional stamp of a hoof or the jingle of a chain, was to recall Erckmann-Chatrian and the descriptions of Private Joseph Bertha of Phalsbourg. If anyone who has served in France has not yet re-read his "Conscript" and "Waterloo" he will still find it worth his while; for a new sympathy and a subtler *camaraderie* will develop with the home-loving and wordy little Alsatian watchmaker in his many trials and adventures.

When we bade farewell to the hospitable little town— to the English-speaking lady teacher at the school, who had held French classes for the men; to the doctor's widow with her lively record of a good man's thirty years of hard and ill-requited work in country practice; to *M.*

le Curé; to the hereditary tailor; to my ally and, 1 trust (in spite of all that passed between us), my friend, the scavenger; to many more; we trekked northward at 10 a.m. in rear of our Brigade, via Merville, Neuf Berquin, Vieux Berquin and Merris to Strazeele, a village on the crest of a hill not far from Hazebrouck, and looking towards Bethune over a very pleasant prospect not unlike the Howe o' the Mearns as seen from Cairn o' Mounth.

We reached our destination by afternoon and again took over the village school as billeting and hospital accommodation, while the field in front of it accommodated the transport, the personnel of which bivouacked in the open, as in the main they did whenever opportunity offered—and very clever at the job they became—to the end of their service. With several other officers I was billeted in a newly built house belonging to the village priest. Him we did not see—the Huns had seen to that—but his ancient and voluble housekeeper pointed out the many things we were not to do, and gave us a list of domestic "don'ts" to which it was difficult to adhere.

Here we were in country which, at the outbreak of war and their first flush of "frightfulness," had been overrun by the enemy; and a Boche grave in the marketplace was used as a dump for the village filth, to emphasise duly the angry feeling of the community towards *les barbares.* In the neighbouring village of Fletre the *curé* had, on his refusal to detail mistresses for Hun officers, been shot by Von Kluck. So went the local story, anyhow, and few of the inhabitants of the district could speak of the enemy without spitting. A small wayside shrine on the outskirts of Strazeele had been deliberately desecrated, and the walls were covered with the obscene *graffiti* of foul-minded scribblers. To us all this was then new; but until the end of the war religious emblems and buildings seemed specially to call out the spite of "the blond beast," and to excite a degenerate ingenuity in destruction and insult.

From Strazeele it was a short ride to Mont des Cats, a hill some four miles distant, crowned by a recent Cistercian Monastery built in 1892, a large part of whose outbuildings had been accidentally burned down some weeks before our arrival. From the hill one gained a commanding view of the surrounding country; Hazebrouck, Poperinghe, and, above all, poor tortured Ypres. Three high buildings were then still visible above its smoking ruins, amidst which shells were continually bursting; and various interested groups of French soldiers and civilians were beside us on the hill to watch the scene. One of the latter, a stout lady with very badly inflamed eyes, traded on my courtesy and the *entente cordiale* to the extent of borrowing my binoculars, and left me in the unfortunate position of not being able to use them again that day until I had returned home and washed the eye-pieces with an antiseptic.

On the 15th May our motor transport joined us with seven ambulance cars, and next evening amid drizzling rain the Division started south via Neuf Berquin and La Gorgue to Vieille Chapelle, which we reached at 5 a.m. It was a tiring march in the dark, with many prolonged halts and no falling out for rest. Further, the orders were silence and no smoking, to avoid noise and lights which might attract air-craft. Guns were booming steadily in the distance, and the horizon was lit up by a steady series of gun flashes.

The checking of the forbidden cigarette during halts led to occasional misunderstandings, as many of the men had, even then, luminous wrist-watches, and "Put out that cigarette!" often got the reply in injured tones, "It's not a cigarette, sir; I'm only looking the time!" When halted and on a hill the column ahead was dotted irregularly with glow-worm-looking specks of light, due to the desire of all ranks to see at what rate Father Time was stepping out. Surreptitious smoking, of course, there was; but to detect tobacco one had to trust to the nose rather than the eyes.

Much has been written on the question of the "Angels of Mons" and the hallucinations produced by exhaustion. During that night march, towards daybreak, several of us had like experiences—lakes spreading away from the roadsides; battlemented castles with gigantic warders standing to arms; ghostly bodies of troops silently marching parallel to us.

All the time we were looking forward to our billets with rest and food; and when at last we separated from the main body, met our billeting party who had gone on ahead, and made for our destination, it was no agreeable surprise, an hour after dawn, to find that "our lodging was the cold, cold ground" of a muddy field, with some ruins and roofless farm buildings at the entrance to it. The in-going track was so cut up with previous traffic that we had to man-handle the transport and ambulance wagons along it, through mud at some parts well up to the axles; and, this done, we looked dismally enough at the landscape and each other, finding little comfort in either view.

The field, however, was fringed with pollarded willows, and the "hooks, reaping" and axes being got out of the wagons, we—most illegitimately—set about cutting the shoots off the trees and laying them on the ground; while the men benefited by previous training, and showed adaptability and ingenuity in knocking up bivouacs with their ground-sheets and tarpaulins. These, floored with the willow shoots, were soon full of blanketed, tired and wet occupants, snatching an uneasy slumber on an empty stomach, what time the cooks took possession of the ruined buildings and set about preparing a meal.

It was one of the lesser iniquities of the campaign that field-cookers were not issued to Field Ambulances, in spite of continual representation to the authorities on the subject; for while the infantry and other branches of the Service, during and at the end of a march, were readily supplied with hot food, the Field Ambulance men had to wait until the cooks, struggling against manifold difficulties and working with the primitive regulation dixie outfit, could get a meal ready. This, however, merely *en passant:* a grouse of the Red Cross against Red Tape which was always with us, cribbing, cabining, confining, and curse-causing, to the end of the war.

When the men were fed and once again safely under cover for more sleep, several of us, tired and hungry, set out for what remained of Vieille Chapelle, and found a fairly intact estaminet, where we got some hot coffee and bread. The place, close and stuffy to a degree, with its smell of vegetable soup, stale *caporal* and coffee, was at least warm; and while waiting for our food we got an uncomfortable quarter of an hour's nap on hard wooden chairs tilted against the wall. (There is a trick in this that you won't know unless you have country-doctored for years. Take two chairs and place them face to face: tilt one back against a wall in a corner: get on to it and tilt the seat of the other up to meet it. Then put your legs on number two and stick your feet against the back of it. In this way can some sleep be got.)

Later, we strolled down the road to a partially ruined school, which was the Dressing Station of an Indian Field Ambulance, and tried to slumber on some straw on the stone floor of one of the unoccupied rooms; but it was too cold and soon had to be given up as a bad job. So we returned to camp, knocked up a bell tent, and consoled ourselves with tobacco and some *vin blanc* from the estaminet, until our tired batmen had had their sleep out and could give us a meal of sorts. For in these early days our officers' mess arrangements were primitive in the extreme, and slowly evolving from chaos as we gradually realised that the campaign demanded considerably more than the outfit for a somewhat prolonged picnic.

It dried up a little by afternoon, and two things happened—we had our introduction to shell fire and sent our first parties off to do Advanced Dressing Station work, as the Highland Division was taking over the sector held by the 7th Division. While squatting in our allotment of Flanders mud the preliminary "whizz" was followed by the inevitable succeeding "bang," and a shell burst in a field across the road in front of us. We were gazing in dull surprise at the smoke clearing away, when another shell burst in the field behind us; and a pessimistic authority amongst our officers rapidly informed us that this was what was technically known as "bracketing," and that the third and succeeding shells would land in our midst. This cheerful news naturally aroused a keener interest; but *grâce à Dieu,* like most prophets, he was absolutely wrong; and shells three, four and five burst on a road leading to a canal bridge which seemed to be the Hun gunner's objective.

A little later orders came in to despatch a party of bearers to an A.D.S. at Richebourg St. Vaast, and two officers went off with a couple of bearer sub-divisions. Gun-fire up the line was continuous and heavy and lasted all night, our immediate neighbourhood getting intermittent attention. The A.D.S. was situated in a three parts ruined farm building, the less damaged rooms of which were cleared as dressing and store rooms. A battery of R.F.A. was immediately behind and hard at work, while the Boches were hammering the houses in the Rue du Bois across the fields on the other side. Altogether, even the most bigoted optimist could not deny that Bellona was getting busy over her job of work.

Six days later the Ambulance moved to new quarters, trekking through the ruins of Vieille Chapelle to a hamlet on the other side of La Couture. Shells were whining overhead as, in the gloaming, we reached our destination — an orchard where we started erecting bivouacs in the rapidly gathering darkness. After a bit the shelling got hotter, and as some landed in the next field, causing casualties to the troops there, orders were given us to fall in again; and, folding our tents like the Arab, we silently stole away for another venue, Le Vert Lannet. This we found a kilometre or so further on, up a side road leading to a canal; and off this road, in the kindly semi-darkness of a summer's night, we once more turned into an orchard, sweet-smelling and ghostly white with apple blossom, knocked up our tents and bivouacs afresh, and slept through what remained of the night as best we could for the incessant gun-fire.

In the morning it shewed up as a pretty little spot, with a small one-storied farmhouse facing the orchard, while behind was a field where a deep and wide ditch gave facilities for bathing and washing clothes, both by now pretty necessary operations.

All day it was close, warm and sultry; so in the afternoon, with two tubs borrowed from the farmer's wife, the Quartermaster and I went down to the waterside for our ablutions. As we filled our tubs from canvas buckets, a bull-frog, hidden in a bunch of the plentiful yellow iris lining the banks of the ditch, was raucously applauding the ineffective efforts of a cuckoo to outrival a big gun in the wood beyond—an attempt futile but none the less gallant—while up above, high in the blue, an observation balloon of the earlier pattern hung like an old-fashioned horse pistol with a shortened barrel. It was pleasant to sit drowsily in the tepid water, with only your head and shoulders visible above the tub's rim to the outside world (like the children reassembled successfully by

St. Nicholas after they had been cut to bits, whose effigies are found at the saint's feet in so many rural French churches), and think, like the Glasgow man, "how guid a thing it was to be alive and weel."

Alas, for our *dolce far niente!* Appears suddenly from nowhere a stout middle-aged female! And leading, by a rope, a cow whose appointed grazing ground was evidently a few yards from my bathing stance! There, anyhow, the lady unconcernedly drove in the usual big iron staple to which she tethered her cow, and, seating herself on the grass, began leisurely to knit a long grey stocking. I turned "eyes left" to see how the Q.M. was taking it; but he must have observed her approach from afar, for his tub was already vacant, and his half-dressed form was dimly discernible in a thick clump of bullrushes. I pondered bitterly—for had he not treacherously failed to share his observation with me?—whether he was liker the great god Pan "down in the reeds by the river" or an enlarged edition of the infant Moses.

A timid fluttering of "eyes right" again still showed the solid, stolid female. Abandoning my first inspiration of rapidly turning everything upside down and crawling off snail-like with the tub on my back, as savouring of cowardice in the face of the enemy, I tried, being in the Army, to recollect precedents for necessary action, and Mr. Pickwick's little difficulty with the spinster lady at Ipswich flashed across my brain. In somewhat similar circumstances had he not, to announce his presence, coughed? I coughed, therefore—a little nervous cough—but as the song goes:—

> Aye I saw her sittin' and knittin',
> And aye my heart went tittin' and flittin'.

A louder bark on my part, and later a storm suggestive of *coque-luche* (*Scotice* "kink-hoast") had no further effect: gentlemen coughing in tubs were evidently not any novelty to her, *c'etait l'habitude du pays, peut-être*—for how much did *l'habitude du pays* always account in the course of our wanderings!

But the kindly cow, working round in her grazing orbit, gave momentary cover from the lady; and, grabbing wildly at my garments, I dashed from my tub and told the Q.M. my private opinion of him in the decent obscurity of the bull-rushes. Later, clothed and independent, we passed her as we made for the orchard, but our "bonsoir" remained unreturned. She was either a deaf mute or a practical joker: possibly both. France was so often a country full of surprises.

On the night of 22nd May, when the Division joined with the Indian Corps in a movement on the south of La Quinque Rue, the constant gun-fire up the line and the more occasional loud bursts of shells near us were blended into one terrific chorus by a mighty thunderstorm, the rain playing havoc with the apple blossom, and showing too well the weak spots in tent and bivouac; but as the morning broke bright and sunny everything dried quickly, while the only record of successful Hun gunnery, so far as we were concerned, was the smack of a shell splinter on the boot sole of one of the motor transport drivers.

Next afternoon over twenty-five shells landed in our vicinity, and, as we had no cover except canvas, the experience was not pleasing; while a day later the inhabitants of the estaminet at the foot of our road were shelled out and came up to our farmhouse for shelter. One was an old man of seventy-six, a sufferer from weak heart and asthma, who arrived in a pitiable state of breathlessness and exhaustion: another was a terrified girl of twelve, in spite of her terror sticking pluckily to two smaller children whom she dragged with her up the road. And all this seemed the more out of place that it was a lovely, warm, sunny day, with Nature at her best.

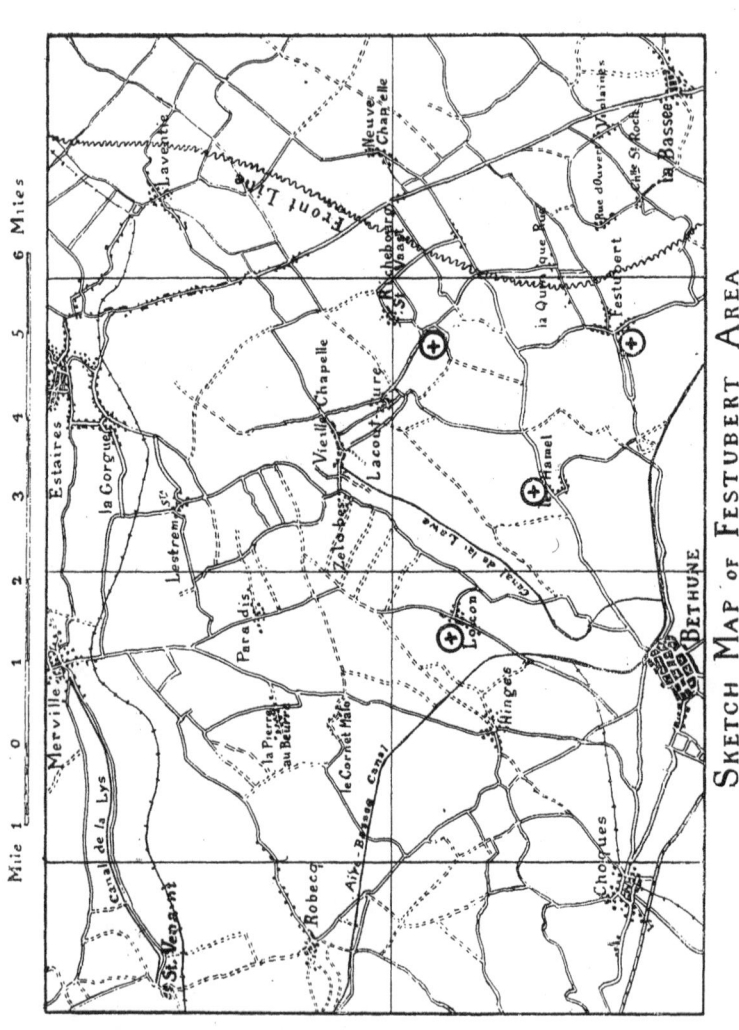

Sketch Map of Festubert Area

Supplying relays of bearers to the Advanced Dressing Station at Richebourg St. Vaast, visiting it and the neighbouring town of Bethune, and drawing medical material from the Advanced Depot of Medical Stores at Lillers were the chief excitements of our stay, over and above the intermittent shelling of our locality. Lillers, at that time intact, a town of about 8,000 inhabitants and *chef lieu de canton,* was busy and thriving, with good shops; and, especially on market days when all the country folk were in with their goods, an interesting enough place in which to wander about. The old church dated back to the XIIth century, and owed its origin and importance to the possession of the bodies of two Irish saints, Lugle and Luglien, who had been assassinated in a neighbouring forest about the end of the VIIth century. Above the chief altar was a large figure of Christ carved in oak, called the *Christ du Saint-Sang,* the name being due to a characteristic legend that, when the Low Countries revolted against Philippe II, a Huguenot fired his arquebus at the figure and blood thereupon ran from the wound.

Bethune, although even then considerably damaged by shell fire, was a historic and still pleasant old town. With over 15,000 inhabitants, when we knew it, and surrounded by well laid out boulevards and highly cultivated marshy fields (known locally as *houches*), it was in existence as far back as 984 A.D. It, too, had its miracle; for in 1184, when a plague was devastating the countryside, St. Eloi appeared to two blacksmiths and enjoined them to form a charitable association and provide, free of all charge, decent burial for the dead. Was it not so? Who knows! But at any rate *La Confrèrie des Charitables* with its many curious traditions was still in existence in 1915.

I doubt me much, however, whether many of our khaki Gallios cared for any of these things. To most

Bethune meant that one could sit in that excellent (and ultimately wrecked) café, *Le Globe*, drink *bière de la Meuse* and watch with interest the gay, gallant and nattily dressed officers of our ancient allies, as they met, saluted, laughed and exchanged news and cigarettes in *La Place*.

And if gay, gallant and well-bedecked, so much the more appropriate; for was not this once the adventure country of "The Three Musketeers?" Not far from here had Madame's head fallen to the axe of the red headsman of Armentières. Had D'Artagnan swaggered in amongst us, flung his rapier on the table and called for and quaffed at one draught a litre of Spanish from a silver flagon, I, for one, would have been little surprised. Spanish wine in a silver flagon—Yes! But I often wondered later how the gay Gascon would have liked rum in a tin mug, or what he would have said and how he would have faced up to four years of trench warfare? *Quien sabe?*

In a few days we trekked to Les Choquaux, a hamlet some kilometres behind Locon, billets being in a large farmhouse there, with bivouacs and horse lines in a field adjoining. These were pre-salvage days, and in this field were hundreds of well-finished ammunition boxes, with copper fittings, left by the previous occupants. Many of these cases had been smashed up for firewood; but out of what were still intact several of our men built comfortable shacks, a job as easy as playing with a child's box of bricks. With a tarpaulin as roof they made excellent dry-weather shelters, and the usual fancy titles of "Ritz," "Hotel Cecil," etc., were soon in evidence over the doorways. Here again our occupation was collecting Brigade sick and taking them to the Casualty Clearing Station near Bethune, overhauling equipment, doing sanitary work, and supplying reliefs to our Advanced Dressing Station. Bathing parties went daily to the neighbouring canal, and life was pleasant and uneventful.

One night a Hun spy, dressed as a Canadian, was

caught near this canal by a Gordon; and some Canucks, still seeing red over the crucifixion outrage, came up and asked, "Can we have him?" "O, fairly!" said the obliging Jock, "fat eese[1] hae I for him?" If he had not the Canadians certainly had; and Mr. Boche went promptly west. So the yarn—*ben trovato*, anyhow—ran, to the obvious satisfaction of all who heard it and passed it on. For if "what the soldier said" was not evidence according to Mr. Justice Stareleigh, it was always—out of court and in the field—good "gup" over a pipe and a drink; and, throughout the campaign, we "never spile't a story by considerin' gin 'twas true."

On the evening of the last day of the month we moved to Pierre au Beure, a little hamlet some two or three kilometres from Calonne-sur-la-Lys; a short march in dusk, and ultimately darkness, as we did not get in till 10 p.m. Here we found our new A.D.S. was fixed at an estaminet in the hamlet of Le Hamel, with a Bearer Relay Post ahead of it in the cellar of a demolished house at the entrance to the ruined village of Festubert; a fairly lively spot. We were now in the Fourth Corps of the First Army, with our Division in the line in front of the village. The weather kept good, and our men, bivouacked in the orchards, were fit, well and in good fettle.

And it was here, if my memory does not play me false, that a jar of rum got served out amongst the horse transport, surreptitiously, without authority, and by night, resulting in a *fracas* next day with injury to the feelings and forefinger of a stout lady of the district. She came in tears to me with her bleeding digit and my heart bled in sympathy. But yes! The malefactors were *Ecossais!* And of our unit? *Mais oui! Sans doute!* Two had entered her cottage asking for water wherewith to dilute

[1] What use.

something in a bottle! And she with a kind heart sympathetic to the allies—and could not all the neighbours testify to her well-known kindness of heart?—had given it. Not content with water, one of the malefactors had further asked for bread, and when she said no—for was the bread not needed for her offspring?—had seized her loaf and started cutting it with his knife. And not only the loaf—Ah! no!—but her now bleeding finger which called to Heaven, as she did to *M. le Commandant,* for justice! And much more to the same effect.

But O, the eternal feminine! When two men were identified and run in, down she came to plead for their release! It had been an accident, and she herself much at fault. For had she not snatched at the loaf while he was cutting it nothing would have gone wrong! And was not her own husband also a soldier? Were not *les règles militaires très strictes?* Who knew what consideration her husband might, even at the moment of speaking, himself require? Wingéd words flew like a chattering cloud of starlings, and it was more difficult to get rid of her on her new errand of mercy, than on her original one of vengeance. But the rigour of next morning's orderly room was, I trust, duly modified by the memory of her copious tears.

I remember, too, that I was billeted in a little farmhouse with an ultra-religious family, although in spite of that the house was well-kept and clean. But any time you passed through the kitchen to get to your room, you found the family engaged in voluble prayers; and one dear little chubby soul of six used to disengage her face from her hands, open one eye and—praying audibly all the time—watch your progress as you stepped respectfully and quietly through the kitchen. It was extremely disconcerting, and tended to make you stumble against the noisier portions of the furniture in your painful efforts to be unobtrusive.

ESTAIRES—GIVENCHY, 1915.

And it was at Pierre au Beure also, down at the canal, that I saw The Man who Searched for Something. Coming along the tow-path one fine morning, I noted from afar a mother-naked man who dived into the water, remained under as long as he could, and then reappeared gasping and puffing. By the time I got up to his stance he had done this three times, and with raised hands was again making ready to go in. When—as he fixed me sideways with a moist and glittering eye—I asked him why he thus behaved and what he sought to do, he explained, edentulously and in the dulcet tones of Glasgow, that he had lost his teeth there "las' nicht when dookin'," and, having marked the spot, he had now returned by daylight for salvage operations. I watched an ineffectual fourth effort and left him under water for the fifth time; but my pious hope was that St. Mungo, who had to thank the fish for returning Queen Langueth's ring from the water, would in due time pay sympathetic attention to his distressed fellow-townsman's submerged denture.

Here, too, it was that a complaint came in from a supersensitive lady, living in a house at the canal side, to the effect that she could not look out of her back windows without having her finer feelings shocked by the sight of our uncostumed men bathing. We sent her a polite message that the difficulty could be met on all such occasions by her seizing the opportunity to enjoy the purely pastoral landscape visible from the front of her establishment.

The route to our A.D.S. at Le Hamel from Pierre au Beure ran through a series of narrow winding roads to Locon, and then across the La Bassee Canal in the direction of Festubert. In the beautiful summer evenings it was a fine run to go up with the rations and medical stores. The A.D.S. itself, in a dirty little estaminet where the owners still hung on and conducted a desultory business, had little of the romantic; but the return trip in the dark was a series of rapid impressions of camp fires lighting up the swarthy faces of turbaned Indians squatting in the orchards; of our headlights flashing on the bayonets and glittering teeth of Sikh and Ghurka sentries; of the little roadside shrines at the corners bright with votive lights; of cottage windows, open for air and *buckshee* mosquitoes, shewing officers in their shirt sleeves poring over maps or writing their home letters close to a solitary, guttering candle.

And then on 11th June we moved to the village of Locon, to act as a Main Dressing Station. A Divisional push was imminent; and, in an orchard opening off the main street, we laid out our lines and ran up the canvas necessary for our work, with a large dwelling-house as accommodation for wounded officers, and the village school for sick cases; while the 3rd Highland Field Ambulance was also busy rigging up an old brewery further up the street for the reception of casualties.

In the evening, four days later, our attack came off; an attack dismissed curtly in official history with the words, "on the night of the 15th June, east of Festubert, we took a mile of trenches but failed to hold them." But that brief statement meant heavy casualties to the Highland Division; meant that for us and for the 3rd H.F.A. we had by 18th June conjointly handled over 1,200 wounded, and that a set of Territorial orderlies, most of whom had previously never seen any wound worse than a cut finger, had, with only odd snatches of sleep, faced up unflinchingly for three days and nights to some of the worst sights that mortal man could see. And the knowledge that they were efficiently dealing with their cases was enough reward to them for the many years of pre-war Territorial training and hard work.

It was, of course, an experience to be repeated time and again in the future; but the first "opening out for wounded" and the first appreciations of our work will always linger specially in the memory of those who took part in it. For we received later the appreciation of the D.M.S. Army "of the smooth working of the medical units during the recent operations," and of the D.D.M.S. Corps of "the excellent work done by all ranks of the Medical Service of the Division. The Field Ambulances had to work under very trying conditions, but all difficulties were admirably overcome, and the manner in which the work was done is worthy of the highest commendation." And all ranks duly "sat up and took notice," knowing that they were now a practical bit of "It."

We stayed in Locon until 26th June, busy with Brigade sick and the treating of scabies cases—one of the minor curses of war—which latter were isolated near the schoolhouse in the loft of a barn, the only approach to it being up a very long and shaky ladder placed against the outside of the building. The main difficulty was the supplying of sufficient hot water for baths; and half a dozen *lessiveuses*—the big, metal, covered tubs used locally to heat water for washing clothes—were procured from Lillers and built into improvised brick ovens; the "bathroom" being a windowless and shell-damaged house. To get all the patients bathed and inuncted was a day-long job; but this improvised *lessiveuse* method held sway until Divisional Rest Stations later got on to a firmer footing, with properly built spray-baths attached for the benefit of all such cases.

Here, too, we first tackled the problem of attendance on the civilian sick, work which was kept up wherever we went in France and Belgium until—and for months after —the Armistice. My first patient was a young woman suffering from a wound in the ankle accidentally caused by an English soldier monkeying with a revolver. Her husband was in the south, a *brancardier de La Croix*

Rouge, one of our own craft. She was a grateful and emotional little soul; and my orderly and I were, after each dressing, entertained to a glass of wine and a tearful *résumé* of her previous history.

Old Madame D., my landlady, who had a truly Rabelaisian wit, kept me *au fait* as regards the village life and the few merits and many demerits of her neighbours. Hers was a clean house and a comfortable billet; but she —good housewife as she was—cordially disliked our national habit of sleeping with open windows as tending, by the resulting *courant d'air,* to damage her white curtains. After she thought I was asleep she would steal into the garden, and from the outside silently insert a ghostly hand to pull the two halves of the window together. Later, with equal silence, I rose and reopened them, and then in the morning had to be "bright and early" so as to close them once more before she quietly came round amongst her cabbages to reconnoitre. Kindly and humorous old dame! I wonder how it fared with you and your little dwelling in the Rue de Bethune when Locon was again over-run and totally destroyed by the Hun in 1918?

On the 26th June we trekked to Estaires and took over the *Institut Libre du Sacré Cœur* in the *Rue du Collège,* with the horse lines in a field across the street. The Division was then in the line in front of Laventie, and we were dealing with wounded and sick officers and infectious cases. The Institute was a large Catholic seminary, three stories high, with good accommodation for patients and orderlies, the officers' mess being in the theatre on the top flat—a large room which we also used in the evenings to hold occasional and very successful concerts for the men. The rector was a youngish priest, expecting soon to be called up for combatant service. But, unfortunately for us and himself in addition, he was an "early bedder" and much disturbed physically and mentally by the noise the Army Pattern British boot made on the feet of our personnel as they nightly retired to their dormitory over his head. "Ah! Quel tapotage!" And pathetic indeed was the wording of his numerous written complaints!

Another interesting co-adjutor was the janitor, an old man with a lame leg got from a Prussian bullet in 1870; a curio picked up—as he loved to tell at length—while saving the life of an officer.

Much work we did there in the sanitary line: field work of our own (chiefly—to keep down flies—evolving methods of burning horse manure, of which, like the construction of tribal lays, there are a hundred different ways); combined with—*salus populi suprema lex*—lifting and mending the long and badly choked drains of the establishment.

Here, too, one of our officers, with the requisite staff, was detailed to institute and look after Divisional Baths, as trench life with its mud and the impossibility of changing shirts, underclothing, etc., resulted in the troops being attacked by "undesirables"; while billet life rarely furnished an adequate supply of water for complete private bathing. Every one who was *là-bas* will remember the familiar scene in the rest areas,

> . . . A simmer's day, the auld barn wi'
>   The orchard at the back.
> The sunlicht tricklin' throw the leaves
>   Fell flickerin' on the wa'
> An' the flourish o' the apple trees
>   Was floatin' doon like snaw,
> While ilka man o' oor platoon
>   Sat strippit to the waist,
> An' seekin' owre his flypit sark
>   To see wha'd catch the maist.

Later on this baths-and-laundry job fell into the hands of the Army Service Corps, but at the beginning of the war it was R.A.M.C. work. One big bathing establishment was, therefore, quickly set a-going at La Gorgue, where an old factory of two stories was secured for the purpose.

The various units were notified of the days and hours when they could use the baths, and the commanding officers had to intimate a day in advance to the officer in charge of the baths how many men would be sent. It was essential, also, that strict punctuality should be observed in the matter of attendance at the hour specified; for the baths officer had to work out how long it would take to bathe the numbers of men coming forward and what supplies of fresh shirts and underclothing would likely be required, as these had previously to be indented for by him.

The bathing party of a unit was marched in, and the men went to a room where they stripped. Each man's dirty shirt and underclothing—almost always lousy—were made into one bundle, which was taken to a disinfecting chamber. (Luckily, at the old factory there was a room capable of being heated to a temperature of $240°F.$, which served the purpose without a new installation.) The bundles were then sent off to be washed and mended by a staff of French women for reissue, when ready, to other troops. Uniforms (tunics, trousers, kilts, etc.) were made into a second bundle and carried off to be turned inside out and carefully ironed along seams or pleats so as to be louse-free for the wearers after bathing was finished.

The men having bathed (which was done in the large ground floor room running the whole length of the building, by using ordinary wash-tubs set in rows and filled with hot water by a hosepipe from two big tanks heated by steam), went upstairs to another room where the clean rig-out of shirts and underclothing was now ready. Thence they passed to a third room where their uniforms, thoroughly ironed (and mended where required by a staff of nimble-fingered needlewomen), were handed out to them. They then dressed and went outside to a large shed for a cup of coffee with bread and butter; and, at last, cleaned, clothed, fed and in a better mind, were marched off to rejoin their units. In a working day of ten hours a thousand men could be thus dealt with.

It was a great sight to see the sheer physical enjoyment a man got from making himself clean again:—

> They gave me a bath and I wallered
> For Gawd! I needed it so.

And it was curious, too, to note the innate conservatism of the individual in the matter of his own belongings, and his active objection to being dealt with on communal principles. One man, perhaps, had discarded a fancy shirt sent out from home by wife or sweetheart, and loudly expostulated against a system which involved his loss of it in favour of some unknown soldier later on; while another, in similar case, would swear in revenge his new issue was lousy. Hence the tale of the worthy who said of his shirt, "I'd rather hae the auld ane; I kent *them* better!" Making new acquaintances was tiresome: he preferred his old familiar "friends!"

But to be "officer in charge of baths," steam heated, worried, groused at throughout a long working day, and always liable himself to be attacked by the minute enemy he fought, was no sinecure.

I do not think that Estaires was popular with the men, for the orders were that troops had to be confined to their billeting areas, and one soon exhausted the limited resources and estaminets of the *Rue du Collège*. The town itself, a place of some 7,000 inhabitants, was not of marked interest, unless, as at Merville, when filled with the peasantry of the district on market day; but the *Hôtel de Ville* had a square belfry of the XVIth century and the church was also old, dating back to the XVth century, with some good stained glass. La Gorgue and Lestrem were practically parts of Estaires, and the chief industry was linen manufacture.

One memory that I have of the place was the taking, in an ambulance wagon, of a piano, hired from the beadle of the kirk, to an open-air concert of the 5th Gordons at their camp on the La Bassée road, some seven kilometres outside the town. This was held in a field on a fine summer evening, and as darkness fell the audience could be seen only as a semi-circle, several rows deep, of glowing cigarette ends. In the morning the site had been shelled, and between songs the guns boomed a perpetual chorus in the distance. On the road home, at a late hour, we were held up by a sentry at the bridge crossing the Lys canal, and in response to his challenge the car drew up and the reply, "Ambulance wagon!" was shouted. Inside the car our capable corporal cook (and pianist) seized the opportunity of the halt to burst into a joyous rag-time; and the sentry's face was a study as, open-mouthed, he let us pass—the uncanniest ambulance wagon up to date in his experience of such vehicles.

CHAPTER III.

The Labyrinth, 1915.

How to live in holes like a set o' furry foxes,
How to make the things you need out o' biscuit boxes,
All these we have learnt now, and generals adore us,
And often after dinner you can hear them sing the chorus :—

Strafe the Kaiser! Strafe the Huns!, etc.

"In July, 1915, the Division was ordered to join the X Corps, Third Army, and on the last days of the month took over from a French Division a section about Hamel, near the Ancre. About this time the Division seems to have gained the confidence of G.H.Q., as in August and later various New Army Divisions were attached to it for instruction, including the 18th, 22nd, 32nd, etc."—(*The Territorial Divisions.*)

ON the 26th of July we handed over at Estaires to an Indian Field Ambulance and trekked to Ferme Roussel, three miles north of Merville, all three Divisional Field Ambulances going as one column, and next day went through the wood by St. Venant to Berguette, arriving at midnight with "Macfarlane's lantern" full overhead. Here the unit entrained and travelled by Calais, Abbeville, Amiens and Corbie to Mericourt-Ribemont, where we encamped in a field near the communal boundary.

The Highland Division (the first Scottish troops the district had seen) was now in Picardy, right among the French, taking over the Labyrinth from them; a sector where that lying jade Rumour had it that cows, pigs and poultry were kept in the trenches, and that these trenches (laid out as market gardens) were twenty-five feet deep—

a sufficiently interesting yarn manufactured by the humorous *poilu* for the credulous stranger to put in his pipe and smoke!

Mericourt was rather a pretty village—we were to know it better next year in July—but, owing to heat, wood and water, flies and mosquitoes abounded, interfering unduly with feeding and sleeping.

My own billet was in the house of the village "bobby," the local *garde-champêtre,* a very worthy old man with a very deaf wife; and, in addition, with one of the best wells of the village in his little brick-paved front yard. Thus it comes to me again that one day from my bedroom window on the second floor I saw a party of French Territorials straggling past, dusty and footsore, too tired even to chant "La Madelon," or the famous:—

"Soleil! Soleil!
Tu n'as pas ton pareil."

One thirsty soul, suddenly espying my landlord's pump, promptly broke the ranks and made for it with his empty water-bottle, an example which those behind him immediately followed, resulting in a general break-up of the column, and very nearly of the pump as well. Seeing what had happened, the officer commanding shrugged his shoulders with great nonchalance, sat down under a convenient tree and lit a cigarette; being joined there at intervals by such of his men as had slaked their thirst. After half an hour he gave a perfunctory order to fall in, and started off with those of his command who saw fit to follow him; but fully one-third of them, having taken off their boots and incontinently fallen asleep by the roadside, stayed behind, setting out later as the spirit moved them by twos and threes. It was an easy-going performance, and fitted in well with the sleepy, sultry, summer afternoon.

A week later we trekked some seven kilometres north to Warloy-Baillon, and took over the *Hôpital-Hospice* from the 16/16 French Field Ambulance, who had been there for nine months; a genial, kindly lot of officers and men, between whom and our fellows there was the most hearty fraternisation. Their O.C.[1] was a true son of the *Midi*, a big, burly, black-bearded, merry-hearted man, with a fine bass voice which he used in song to great effect after our conjoint dinner in the hospital that evening. "It's a long way to Tipperary" was then still bulking as the characteristic British war-song in the minds of our allies, and the great ambition of our French *confrères* was to get air and words thoroughly and correctly off by heart; so we had to sing and re-sing the wretched effusion and coach their pronunciation of the chorus till a late hour. When their unit left next morning, after exchanging a tricolour for a Union Jack, every mother's son of them was shouting it; and they marched tunefully enough down the village street, with the British flag waving at their head, and all of us giving them a hearty send off.

That evening, too, by invitation, we attended a concert given by the local French troops in the *Cercle des Sous-officiers* at the hall adjoining the *Hôtel des Voyageurs* in the main street, a hall where we were to have many cheery functions of our own in the next five months. The performance included violin solos, songs serious and comic, conjuring entertainments and ventriloquism; while a very good orchestra, conducted by a Parisian professional, rose to its greatest heights in the concluding rendering of "The Marseillaise" and "God Save the King."

A luncheon next afternoon with the Commandant of the neighbouring village of Vadencourt and a dozen or so of his officers, under a rose-trellised shelter in the garden of the château there, finished off the international

[1] Lt.-Colonel A. Batailler.

courtesies, and the rest of the French troops in the district departed the following day, leaving us to settle down in Warloy to our work as a Divisional Rest Station; the 3rd H.F.A. functioning as Main Dressing Station at the neighbouring village of Millencourt, while the 2/1st H.F.A., at Esbart, some kilometres nearer Amiens, supplied personnel to the Advanced Dressing Station at Authuille, outside Albert. This A.D.S. was in the cowshed of a much battered farm, on the slope of a hill down towards the Ancre; but, pit-propped and with the roof and walls well sand-bagged, it was ultimately made fairly safe. In the vicinity of Authuille, at Aveluy, were many good French shelters cut deep into the solid chalk; and some erotically artistic souls amongst the *poilus* had left typically Gallic evidence of their powers of carving on this appropriately soft medium.

Going to and from Authuille the wayfarer had to pass through Albert, desolate and destroyed, with its war-famous statue of the Virgin hanging head downwards at an acute angle from the top of the church tower. Viewed from a distance, it looked like the head and neck of some huge long-billed bird—a much magnified heron or stork. The church itself—*Notre Dame de Brebières*—was renowned in pre-war times for its miraculous statue of Our Lady, which had now been removed elsewhere for safety. This statue, according to *une tradition immémoriale,* had been discovered in the second half of the XIIIth century by a shepherd pasturing his sheep near the Ville d'Ancre, as Albert then was known. He noticed that one of his sheep kept continually nibbling at a certain tuft of grass without searching elsewhere for pasture, and although he called it and sent his dogs to bring it back, it was in vain. Becoming impatient the shepherd hit the tuft of grass with his crook, when, to his great surprise, he heard a voice saying, "Hold, shepherd! Thou woundest me!" Drawing back his crook he found it stained with blood, and, his anger leaving him, he stood stupefied while the stick slipped from his hand. Coming to himself again he knelt and dug gently into the earth at the spot whence the voice had come, and discovered a statue of the Virgin Mother with the Child in her arms and bearing on her forehead a wound caused by his stroke. This is the legend of the discovery of the miraculous statue.

On the tale getting abroad, several of the larger and more powerful towns tried in turn to have it removed from its site near the Ville d'Ancre. But the horses attached to the various *chariots*, on which it was placed, refused, in every instance, and in spite of shouts and blows, to move a step, and a temporary shrine was erected to house it. Later, one horse was yoked to a cart wherein once more the statue was laid, and, headed for Albert, without any driver, drew it thither with ease. The desire of Providence being thus definitely ascertained, in Albert the statue had remained for nearly six hundred years until the German advance sent it to seek another sanctuary.

Although we did not know it when we arrived there, we were to be in Warloy for five months; and as this was by far our longest stay in one place during the whole of our wanderings in France, it is of Warloy and its kindly inhabitants that most of us found time to acquire a wealth of pleasant memories. Life here was typical of that spent in many French villages; so it may be excusable to give it in some detail, for it was the average life of any British Field Ambulance in such surroundings.

"War-loy" we cheerfully called it, taking it as spelt, and with no attempt to accommodate ourselves to French ideas thereanent. Hence the senile jest of an aged inhabitant of over four-score years that he had been born and had lived all his life in the place yet had never known how to pronounce its name properly until *les Ecossais* had arrived! But Warloy-Baillon, to give it its full title (as like many other French villages it was a combination of two communes), had a pre-war population of about eight hundred souls, mostly *cultivateurs,* although there were also several *brasseries* and a small weaving factory. It consisted of two parallel streets, the Senlis-Amiens road running through the main street of Warloy, and the Rue de Baillon lying down in a dip of the ground towards the neighbouring village of Baizieux on the hill beyond; while between the two larger streets ran a number of intersecting smaller ones.

The *Hôpital-Hospice,* a gift to the village from one of its sons who had acquired wealth, was a large, modern two-storey building, used before the war both as a cottage hospital and as a hospice for the aged poor of the district. The French civilian nursing staff consisted of three *religieuses,* the Mother Superior and two nuns, Sœur Andrée and Sœur Marie, who were put on our ration strength and stayed on in residence, readily giving us their skilled and kindly help in our work. In the orchard behind, we ran up some canvas where the ground sloped down to the old church and to the village school; and the schoolrooms there and a small farm building beside the hospital were also used for divisional sick and the inevitable scabies ward. The men were billeted in the old school in the Rue D'Harponville; while further up the same street the officers' mess was established in a disused and somewhat dilapidated villa, the summer residence in happier times of an Amiens citizen; the transport lines being at the Senlis end of the village.

Near the *mare contaminée*—for so the village pond was very justly placarded—on the Amiens road, stood a little building where the venerable village fire-engine— with its courtesy title of *la pompe d'incendie* on a board above the entrance—was stored; and by a trap-door therefrom one descended a series of steps leading into the large caves that ran under the village. It was said that, in days of yore, a passage ran straight to Harponville, some four kilometres distant, where also were similar caves; but this passage—if it ever existed—was now blocked. A visit below with electric torches showed a series of chambers cut in the chalk and opening off the main tunnel; some for human inhabitants, and some for cattle or horses, as was evidenced by the hewed out mangers and feeding troughs to be seen. A deep well—now fallen in—had been dug, and there were good ventilating shafts.

The local story was that these *sous-terrains* had been used as refuges for man and beast when the Spaniards, centuries back—one informant said in 1200, and he was obviously wrong, but we had neither knowledge nor reference books wherewith to confute him—had over-run the country. On one visit we found some parts of a human skeleton in one of the chambers at a depth of about a foot below the accumulated debris of the floor; a discovery that aroused the keen interest of *Monsieur le Maire*, as possibly throwing some light on a bygone and unsolved local tragedy.

Life in Warloy was uneventful, and, many of us thought, even monotonous and dull; although in later years and more stirring times we often enough looked back with a mighty longing to the quiet days spent there. The surrounding country was prettily wooded in parts, and gently undulating. The greatest excitement was a trip with patients for the special hospitals (eye, ear, throat, etc.) to Amiens, then fairly normal, busy, and cheerful, with its glorious old cathedral, and quaint, picturesque, narrow side streets. But shopping could be done there, books could be bought, and a good dinner was always obtainable at the *Hôtel du Rhin* or the *Ecu D'Or*—best of all, perhaps, at the establishment of

Josephine, *alias* "Hurricane Jane," the tempestuous, whirlwind lady of the oyster shop in the *Rue des Corps nuds sans teste:* "the street of the headless naked bodies" as most of the inhabitants interpret it. What the legend was from which this somewhat dirty little side lane took its name I never, in war time, could find out. Even the learned *archéviste* of the *Hotel de Ville* of Amiens cannot throw much light on the matter. In a letter to a friend of mine who, later on, kindly made enquiry on the subject, he wrote:—"It is not surprising that you have not found any book reference concerning *la rue des Corps nuds sans teste,* as no such reference exists. One is reduced to conjecture, and first one thinks that the true spelling is *rue des Cornus sans teste.* Personally, I have found two documents containing the name; one, *rue des Cornus sans teste,* in 1809, and the other, *rue du Cornu sans tête,* in 1848. The spelling, *corps nuds sans teste* (the present sign), would thus seem to be a modern invention which nothing justifies; for if there had been, even in the last century, any sign or sculpture of any kind representing naked bodies without heads in this street, we should have known of it. It is, then, probable that there formerly existed in this street, which is adjacent to the ancient rampart, some *cabaret* of evil notoriety, having for its sign the horns of a stag (the emblem of deceived husbands) as exists in other towns, whence the name of *cornus sans teste.* Unfortunately, no trace of such a sign exists in the old records. Recently, another reading has been proposed, viz., *la rue cornu sans tette.* In old French, as in the *patois* of Picardy, this word *tette* signifies a breast, a nipple, a teat of an animal. In this case, the sign would have represented a cow without teats, that is to say, an ox. This would have been a rebus, and one knows that such things are very frequent in Picardy: witness that of *l'homme aux trois visages* of the *Passage Gossant,* which has not yet been completely explained." So there (even after the persistent efforts of a skilled local antiquary) the matter rests—in obscurity; and we can quite appropriately quote the old Scots rhyming conundrum:—

> As I lookit owre my father's castle wa'
> I saw a body stan'in',
> I took aff his heid and I drank his bleed,
> An' I left his body stan'in'.

For the answer to that was—"A bottle!" Suitable—is it not?—to the "cabaret of evil notoriety," unless, alas! at this unsavoury "howff" it was a case of butt, leather jack and flagon.

But, be all that as it may, if you booked a seat in Josephine's little restaurant, with its pile of oyster shells outside the door, and were willing to face up to a fairly long wait when you turned up to claim it, you were certain of a well-cooked meal; enlivened by the furious bustling about of the hostess bringing in the various dishes, collecting multitudinous orders and shouting them volubly down the steep little twisting stair to the cook below— exhortations, recriminations and explanations being delivered, exchanged and received in rapid and vigorous French. Worthy woman! It is said she came from the south as a maidservant, took over the business, ran it successfully, made a small fortune, and out of it installed her aged parents in a comfortable house in Amiens. And yet her charges were by no means immoderate, and her fare always good.

In our village itself we mixed freely in the daily life of the inhabitants. The local doctor was on military service, and the care of the civilian sick fell into the willing hands of the ambulance: we were *locum tenentes* for an unknown brother of the craft. Every morning there was a dispensary for those who could attend as outpatients for tooth extractions, minor surgery and medical advice; while the afternoons, when the convoy for the

Casualty Clearing Station had gone and hospital work was slack till the evening "rush" again, were devoted by many of the officers to visiting the sick in their homes. All such work was, of course, gratuitous: but they were an independent folk and *très reconnaissants;* so many a payment in kind was given in the shape of poultry, eggs, fruit and butter, to refuse which would have put us for ever beyond the pale of their esteem.

And the types of invalid were much the same as with us. There was, *par exemple,* the old lady who was *très nerveuse avec beaucoup de gaz*—"nervish wind" we call it in Scotland. She remained *très gazeuse* and in varying states of inflation — dear old Zeppelin! — till we trekked elsewhere, and left her to the carminatives of our successors.

Our only Irish officer, who talked French fluently with a slight Tipperary accent, dealt chiefly with the out-patient department; and by his unfailing *joie de vivre* inspired a confidence that to us, his somewhat jealous friends, was phenomenal. For the first month his directions to all patients commenced with a stereotyped and stentorian "Il est necessaire pour vous"; and a coldness ensued for some days between him and our interpreter, who, wishing to be kind and yet evidently suffering, had pointed out that this expression was neither idiomatic nor used by even the older writers. Our colleague then grudgingly adopted—after getting a second opinion from a brother officer learned in the language—*il vous faut,* followed by the infinitive. Still, when a trembling female with a finger on a decayed molar asked him mumblingly "arracher la dent," he was ready of tongue, strong of wrist, and gallant of mien. Moreover, did he not, with an attachment to principle that was entirely admirable, invariably address in the most soothing accents every female from fifteen to seventy as "ma pauvre petite?"

Then there was the aged agriculturist with a Potts' fracture. He was not my patient, but I saw him occasionally in friendly consultation, what time our surgeon was otherwise occupied. However, as the weather was warm and a glass of good wine always forthcoming at these visits, the surgeon consulted with fair regularity, and my opportunities were few. Poor old *cultivateur!* Overcome with much unaccustomed professional attention, he used to kiss our hands at the end of each seance! But he ended with a useful leg.

I do not think that any Picard can justly laugh at our island climate, as we so often find done in French literature. In "Twenty Years After," the musketeers when in London said, "Let us take a turn about town! Let us imbibe a little fog!" And Porthos, gigantic and gallant gourmand, added, "Yes, that will be a change for us from beer." But in Picardy, to speak truth fearlessly as it should be spoken, we found the climate as thick as across the water and the beer much thinner. Even "Le Petit Parisien," an unbiased witness which circulated freely amongst us, described the district in a *feuilleton* as "un pays très agricole òu il pleut beaucoup," and we found the weather part of the statement most damnably true!

Now, if anyone a year before had told me that one mirk midnight, twelve months later, I should have been trudging through the mud down a back street in a picturesque and insanitary French village, my light, a three parts worn out 1 fr. 50 electric lamp, my companion an excited peasant (whose one plaintive and constant remark was "Mais depêchez-vous, Monsieur!"), and my errand under the auspices of Lucina—then to that man I should have said "C'est un cauchemar!" But I depechied, all the same, and it was a fine baby, *la petite Suzanne.* (I trust she is now as well and thriving as she was when, two months subsequently, I, at the request of *maman,* kissed the infant goodbye. It was a tearful parting, and in the confusion *maman* kissed me. *Que voulez vous? C'est l'habitude du pays!* And, *grâce à Dieu,* I dodged kissing the father, who wished to share in the compliments!)

When we passed from labour to refreshment, we broached (*sans cérémonies,* as my still excited host put it) an excellent bottle of St. Julien; and over it *la belle-mère* waxed confidential, giving the births, deaths and other medical memorabilia of her married career. She roused in time the spirit of competition in her *commère* (*kimmer* of our Franco-Scottish past) who beat her at the post, after a ding-dong race of tongues, by two infants and three dangerous illnesses. *Monsieur,* overcome with paternity—it was his first experience—nearly brought bad luck on the house by thoughtlessly lighting a third candle; and I assisted the old ladies to rub in the wickedness—especially on an occasion like this when it behoved us all to keep the auspices favourable—of trifling in this way with the popular beliefs of Picardy. He described himself, with an abandon of gesture, as being *désolé;* and I think he felt it, for he was of the large-bodied and simple-minded type. Then, after much interchange of felicitations, into the darkness and the mud again, with the big guns booming in the distance, and the occasional gleam of the star shells as "merry dancers."

The Lucina department grew and multiplied. Rumour had it that *chariots,* filled with matrons in the straw thereof, were arriving from neighbouring villages under cover of night; and this rumour we, the regular practitioners, ultimately traced to the Transport Officer, who held himself horsily aloof from general practice. But, in any case, it so happened one night that we needed an important piece of the obstetrician's armamentarium, which, *nom d'un petit bonhomme!* is not in the Mobilisation Table, nor yet in the Field Medical Panniers!

The Quartermaster, interrupted in his evening bridge, wearily suggested trying Ordnance, but curtly refused the ambassadorship. And yet it was necessary to act! Therefore in a motor ambulance wagon to the neighbouring medical unit at Esbart. Did they keep a "Simpson's, long, pair, one?" *Hélas, non!* But (happy thought!) they had heard of a retired French medical practitioner who, fallen heir to a paternal *brasserie,* had shown his commonsense by abandoning medicine and brewing beer —"and very doubtful stuff at that"—in the vicinity. To him, then, post-haste at midnight to rouse him from his slumbers and recall his pre-beer days!

A long parley through shuttered windows with his good lady, ultimately ended in our admittance; although, misunderstanding our design, she insisted that under no circumstances could *monsieur* go out as he was a sufferer from *la bronchite.* Bearded, stout, asthmatic yet amiable, he at last descended, with all his kindly soul in his "Qu'y-a-t-il pour vôtre service?" The case is explained. A Simpson's, long, pair, one? "Mais non, monsieur! Mieux que ça! Tarnier! Did we in our country know of this immortal?" Duly assuring him that all true Scots obstetricians grovelled at this shrine, we left with a highly rusted museumesque antique—a candidate for the steriliser.

Cœlum non animum mutant! Il n'y-a rien de nouveau sous le soleil!

> Through broken nights and weary days
> Lucina! Still we hymn thy praise!

It was 2 a.m. before we—three of us, for it was teamwork—sat down to the first bottle of sweet champagne, in the company of the father of *la petite Jacqueline,* the two grandfathers, the two grandmothers, some cousins and other *parents,* and the *sage-femme.* It was somewhat later still when we got to the château where we were billeted and wakened our totally unsympathetic brother officers to tell them the glad news about France's new inhabitant. There are some souls in whom the spirit of romance is as dead as Queen Anne.

But we did not specialise. There were many other cases, e.g., the stout female agriculturist with "trench feet" contracted amongst wet turnips: it was she who gave me, as a souvenir of her recovery, the large celluloid pin-cushion which now adorns my dressing-table. And I remember vividly, too, the child with *la gorme*, which I fear is *patois*, and anyhow is a scabby business at best, most properly treated by a large boracic-starch poultice all over the head. The nature of the case was obscured for some days by the mother misinterpreting my minute instructions in French as to the making of such things. I rather think, looking back on it all, that she must have put some glue in it.

There were two outstanding personalities in the village whom we shall always remember—*M. le Maire* and *M. l' Instituteur*.[1] The former was a thin, active old gentleman with white Dundreary whiskers, a retired business man from the neighbouring town of Albert, who was indefatigable in his efforts to serve his commune and our troops. Nothing was a trouble to him; in all business relations he showed an unfailing courtesy and kindness, and in a social capacity much hospitality, ably seconded therein by his capable wife. The schoolmaster, whose house faced the little village school which we had converted into accommodation for the sick, was also the friend of all ranks; and he, his wife and daughter will always be gratefully thought of as genuine friends—patient, tactful, helpful and kindly.

And there were two special occasions when we saw the mayor and the schoolmaster at their best. One was on the 5th of September, when the first anniversary of the

---

[1] M. Gaffet and M. Preuvot. Both these amiable functionaries—along with the gentle Mother Superior—have since died.

battle of the Marne was celebrated in Warloy by a procession, taken part in by French and British troops, and by school children bearing a large wreath, to the little village cemetery at the east end of the village. Here all the graves of fallen soldiers—each with its little white cross bearing the man's name, rank and regiment, the black tear of sorrow painted on the upright, and the metal tricolour badge attached—were decorated with small French flags; and in the midst of these graves *M. le Maire* and other notables made eloquent speeches on what the battle had meant for France.

The other occasion—one entirely free from sadness—was when they attended our St. Andrew's night supper. We gave them broth, "saut herrin'," "biled hens" and a haggis—made by the skilled hand of our sergeant-major—with "Auld Kirk" to wash the solids down; and for their edification our junior officers danced perfervidly (and more or less correctly) our national dances, what time the seniors and our guests discoursed of Marie Stuart and tied tighter old international ties. *Monsieur le Maire* said, with some emotion, at the close of the function—and I think he spoke truthfully—that he had never spent such an evening before. And he called before breakfast next morning to ask for us; thus at once demonstrating both his extraordinary vitality and his kindness of heart.

And when we are dealing in happy memories, the hall of the *Hôtel des Voyageurs* will always bulk largely in our minds. When handed over by the French troops, who had used it as the *Cercle des Sous-officiers*—"the Non-com.'s Club"—a good stage and some rough and ready scenery had been left us; and here we held regular concerts, largely attended by the troops of the district and by the French civilians. We had an energetic committee who saw to the drawing up of good programmes; and if anything went wrong, and a concert party failed us, a "free-and-easy" could always be got up by having a singing competition—"1st prize, 10 fr.; 2nd prize, 7 fr.; 3rd prize, 3 fr."—with a bench of referees (against whose decision there was no appeal) sitting critically on the stage, awarding or withholding marks for each solo, and stimulating the unfortunate performers by free, caustic and personal comments when required.

To view a full house from the wings was a great sight. In the somewhat meagrely lamp-lit hall the floor space was packed with a cheery khaki crowd, drawn from all the units in the vicinity; while above, in the rickety gallery—and it was always a mystery why it never came down—were about twice the number of men Board of Trade regulations at home would have allowed, countable, if you had cared for the exercise, by a multitude of cigarette ends glowing through an atmosphere of tobacco smoke so thick you might have cut it with a cheese knife. At the top of some steps from the floor, a side door communicated with the *hôtel*—a somewhat grandiose name for the old *estaminet*—and at the foot of the steps old madame and her handsome daughter presided over a large beer barrel set up on trestles in the hall; drinks between items on the programme being available to those of the audience who happened to be in funds. The civilian element, mainly composed of youngsters, was usually at the back of the hall, and chiefly appreciative of the knock-about comic turns—the only part of the performance it could really follow with complete understanding.

On one famous occasion a burly French *poilu* in his horizon-blue, back to his native village *en permission*, asked if he and a friend would be allowed to contribute to the pleasure of the evening by a duet on the *cor de chasse*, the circular go-round-the-body hunting-horn of France. Their offer was, naturally, accepted with gratitude as a highly novel item; and when, bowing gracefully, they appeared on the stage they received an ovation. They then walked to a wing and commenced, facing it like pipers, to tune up, with all the apoplectic facial contortions peculiar to those who play wind instruments. This, received as a comic effort, drew forth laughter and applause, which the performers, owing to their own noise, fortunately did not hear. I happened to be chairman that night; and, when they were ready to begin, asked the audience, whatever the result might be, good, bad, or indifferent, to cement the *entente cordiale* by giving the duet a rousing reception. It certainly got it, and got it on form, for the players were old hands at the game; and when, again bowing profoundly amidst yells of "encore," they were told that this with us meant "bis," their faces shone with satisfaction. What would their allies *les Ecossais* desire? And the question being put by me to the assembled troops, they, with an exquisite tact which was purely unintentional—for it was the only French air of which they at that time knew the name—demanded with one voice the *Marseillaise!* Visibly touched by the sentiment of the occasion, the Frenchmen gave us a fine rendering of the air of Rouget de l'Isle's immortal masterpiece, and left the platform amidst prolonged and tumultuous applause.

Do you remember that night, you fellows who were there and may perchance read this? Or have you forgotten it? It sticks in my memory anyhow; for it fell to my official lot to entertain the hunting-horn heroes to several bottles of more than ordinarily *vin ordinaire* in the hotel, to smoke black *caporal* cigarettes with them in the damp little stuffy sideroom, clinking our glasses as we had to *trinquer* times innumerable over toasts that included the destruction of *les sales Boches*, the success of the armies, and *bonne chance* to our noble selves! I learnt their names and those of their respective wives, the story of their simple lives, and the number and sex of their families; and I communicated, by special request, much of my own domestic history in return. But we parted the best of friends, although next day I suffered from acute dyspepsia. Still it was worth it all; they were *braves gars, ces bons Picards,* and I enjoyed every minute of their honest, cheery company.

For, take him the right way—and that was nearly always the way he wanted to take you—the French peasant, in or out of uniform, was a thoroughly good fellow; and many a happy hour I have spent in conversation with him at his fireside or on the road. Emotional if you like—had he not much to stir his deepest emotions? But open-hearted, witty, laughter-loving and optimistic, a long-suffering *jusqu'au-boutiste* who, even in his darkest hour as a refugee or in retreat, believed rightly in the final victory of his cause and his country. One often heard the careless statement that he was always "on the make." Suppose, for the sake of argument, that the truth of that were granted. Had the man whose all was lost, whose home was in ruins, whose wife and children, mayhap, were in enemy hands, whose land was desolate, not every incentive to be so? Reverse the relative positions and what would our people have done? It is so easy to criticise, and yet so difficult to imagine oneself in the position criticised. *Tout comprendre, c'est tout pardonner.* Personally, I have nothing but the kindest recollections of him; and I owe him—and his wife— much gratitude for many acts of single-minded hospitality. *Vive la France!* May Fortune ever smile on her! And, whatever alliances go, may the spirit of the old Franco-Scottish alliance remain true and steadfast.

On 29th December, after making innumerable farewell visits and receiving a courteous testimonial on *papier timbré* from M. le Maire concerning our medical attendance on his people, we left our village and trekked some ten kilometres to Mirvaux, a rather dirty and poverty-stricken place of about 170 inhabitants. Our chief work there—and there was ample scope for it: it was virgin soil—was sanitation. We, according to orders received, renamed the streets; and, as befitted our Aberdeen origin, did so after the "braif toun of Bon-Accord." Soon newly painted signboards pointed out "Market Street," "Union Street" and "Marischal Street." Even "Shuttle Lane" was not forgotten, a narrow street where an old hand-loom weaver and his wife carried on business. It was a curious partnership; for he made veiling for the headgear of *les religieuses,* and she (true daughter of Eve) material for the powder-puffs of frailer females. Here, then, you had Holy Church in one corner of the room; the World, the Flesh and the Devil in the other; yet able to converse in *patois* on matters of common interest to both sides, when the clacking of the loom permitted it. And I remember that "Constitution Street," on the ancient principle of *lucus a non lucendo,* was so named by us because no one's constitution could have long withstood the infernal smell of it.

And yet Mirvaux was the only place, I think, in our musical history where we got two lady performers to appear on our concert platform—blonde Suzanne, the baker's daughter, and a girl friend, favouring us one eventful evening with *Sous les plits du drapeau* as a duet. It was to this air that the famous and illiterate doggerel:

> "Après la guerre finee,
> Et les Anglais partee,
> Toutes les demoiselles vont pleurer"—

was always sung by the troops; and in sublime and cheerful ignorance we rendered this as a chorus to each verse. The item was a *succès fou,* and one back benchful of enthusiasts fell through the tarpaulin curtain which walled in the open side of the cartshed concert hall, landing incontinently in the near and moist neighbourhood of the midden, to the uproariously unconcealed joy of those not taking immediate part in the impromptu "extra."

And then for three months followed a series of treks, and much routine work, while the Division had a spell of training in the back areas—to the ancient town of Corbie via Querrieux, on to Pierregot, to Gezainecourt near Doullens, to Ivergny, followed by an eighteen mile march through snow to Aubigny. Here, on 10th March, we took over from the French four huts near the railway station and the *hospice* in the village, opening as a temporary Casualty Clearing Station under the XVII Corps. A few days later the C.C.S. itself took over, with one section of ours to help; while the rest of the unit moved to Haute Avesnes, doubling up there with a French Field Ambulance, but moving next day down the Arras-St. Pol road to Berles. Here a section took over the Advanced Dressing Station at Aux Rietz, near Neuville St. Vaast, on the south end of the Vimy Ridge, to evacuate wounded from the famous Labyrinth. This post we largely extended and improved, and the sketch plan shews a characteristic type of dug-out suited to R.A.M.C. requirements. It was a freely shelled locality, and the old Territorial Trench leading to it from Brunehaut Farm, near Marœuil, was regularly attended to by enemy gunners. Ambulance cars only came up the Marœuil-Neuville St. Vaast road after night fell, as it was under observation; and cases reaching the A.D.S. by daylight had to be kept there till dark, the cars being parked by day in a sandpit at the roadside on the other side of Marœuil.

Berles was a little place, *assez pittoresque,* with a fine old château in whose pleasant grounds the nightingale sang with silvery tone in the still summer night. It was our first acquaintance in France with *le rossignol,* whose reputation, according to Shakespeare, largely depends on

Aux Rietz Advanced Dressing Station.
Neuville St. Vaast road and entrance to trenches leading to underground chambers.

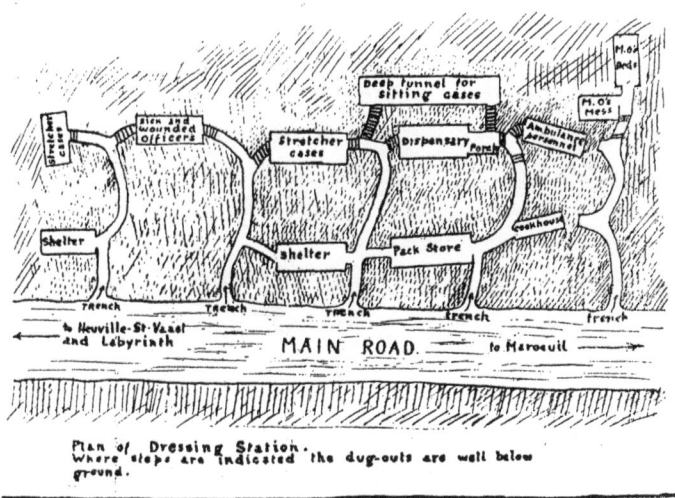

Plan of Dressing Station.
Where steps are indicated the dug-outs are well below ground.

Facing page 78.

his careful avoidance of competition; for, as every one knows,

> The nightingale, if he should sing by day
> When every goose is cackling, would be thought
> No better a musician than the wren.

I never saw him at Berles, but later, in a wood at Marœuil, I caught a glimpse of him in the semi-darkness, and was surprised at his small size. In any case, no connoisseur would give a "blackie" for a dozen of him; and here again I am on solid ground, with Henley beside me:—

> The nightingale has a lyre of gold,
> The lark's is a clarion call,
> And the blackbird plays but a boxwood flute
> But I love him best of all.

The owner of the château, a tall, stately, old Bourbon aristocrat, condemning all things Napoleonic, was, nevertheless, by force of ironic circumstances, the Maire under a Republican Government. But he dwelt in the past, he and an old retainer of the Caleb Balderstone type, who by day wore a blue baize apron, and in the evening an early nineteenth century claw-hammer. It was a pleasant, rambling old home, a suitable environment for both the old worthies; and two russet-chinned swallows flew in and out of my bedroom window there as soon as dawn broke, twittering and fluttering as they, without let or hindrance, plastered mud on a half made nest under one end of the curtain pole. For who would break his luck by interfering with a swallow?

We left Berles to take over the Main Dressing Station at Ecoivres, a *pavé* streeted village within a few hundred yards of the base of Mont St. Eloi, on whose summit stood the village of that name crowned by the twin towers of the old abbey—that well-known landmark of the campaign, standing out prominently for miles around, and in pre-war days a great picnic centre for the inhabitants of Arras. some eight kilometres distant. On one of the towers was a crow's nest observation post for the gunners; and an illicit visit by night to the hill showed a magnificent view of the line marked out by starshells and gun-fire. Not a soul was to be seen in the higher part of the village: the cobbled streets were overgrown with grass, and the solid old stone houses all badly battered and scarred by shells. The remains of the ancient abbey were surrounded by the ruins of large farm houses, farm buildings and dwellings; but the only tenants were night birds and rats. It reminded one of the lament for the past glories of Walsingham:—

> Owles do skrike where the sweetest hymnes
> Lately were songe,
> Toads and vipers holde their nests
> Where the palmers did thronge.

On the further side of the wood, east of Mont St. Eloi, lay a large military cemetery, *la cimetière de la Motte*, containing many hundreds of French and British graves. Some were surrounded with railings of wood or iron; many had wreaths—one very pretty one was of artificial violets. In several cases the only clue to the man resting there was his name on a slip of paper inside a bottle laid on the grave; but most were marked by large or small wooden crosses. Frequently one saw a shattered rifle with its muzzle stuck in the mound of earth; and on the butt a soldier's bullet-holed *képi* or a metal helmet dinted or perforated in a manner tell-tale of how the owner had died. But the cemetery was even then overgrown with weeds and thistles, some of the latter nearly six feet high. I visited it late one evening, and in the gloaming the eerie sadness of it gripped hard. It was a relief to come back again in the darkness through the woods, where the 6th Gordons were bivouacked in tents, shelters, dug-outs and old gun emplacements. Lights were twinkling everywhere, and the place hummed cheerily with the honest old north country accent.

THE LABYRINTH, 1915.

Taking over from the 75th Field Ambulance, we had —as so often happened—the village school for our hospital accommodation; and the rest of our work was largely the sanitation of the village. We made a "midden map" of Ecoivres—a large scale map of the place with the middens marked by dots of red ink—and that map when finished had a marked attack of roseola. For it must always be remembered that most of the French villages we knew were aggregations of small farmyards, and that the social importance and success of the *cultivateur* was largely measured by the amount of manure he managed to accumulate. Hence the existence of his natural objection to have it meddled with. And hence his constant joy in that malodorous environment which has been so aptly described as a "quadrilateral smell!"

At this date the square incinerator, made of four sheets of corrugated iron, had deservedly come into sanitary fashion; and several of them, carried about from place to place where the need was greatest, did yeoman work in disposing of much accumulated rubbish and filth. In Ecoivres, however, there was one of the finest and most plentiful springs of water that we ever struck in France— clear, hard, cool water, which, under the auspices of the R.E., was piped and pumped for years over a large surrounding area.

During the latter part of our stay at Ecoivres we had several parties of a London Field Ambulance up at Aux Rietz A.D.S. for instruction, and on the 13th July we handed it and our headquarters at Ecoivres over to them and moved back to the neighbouring village of Acq, preparatory to trekking south for the Somme.

CHAPTER IV.

The Somme, 1916.

*O, it's fall in and for'ard
On the Route Nationale,
South'ard, mayhap, or nor'ard,
On the Route Nationale;
Whither we go we know not.
Better times? We trow not;
Nevertheless we slow not
On the Route Nationale.*

"On the 22nd-23rd July the Division attacked but failed to gain much ground. On the 24th the enemy launched two powerful counter attacks, the one directed against our new position in and around High Wood (51st Division, Major-General G. M. Harper) and the other delivered from the north-west of Delville Wood. Early in August the 51st . . . was in other operations involving much fierce and obstinate fighting. . . . About the 7th the Division was relieved and taken to Armentières."—(*The Territorial Divisions.*)

WE lay for some days in huts outside Acq, a village of no great interest, although in its vicinity were two large stones—*les pierres d'Acq*—said to have been raised by Beaudouin Bras de Fer in 862 in honour of his victory over Charles the Bald, but in reality old prehistoric monoliths. A visit to the village cemetery shewed the more common names of the local families to be Delcour, Allart, Richebé, Genel, Bacqueville, Cuisinier, Gauchy, Delassus, Masclef, Dubois (of course), Cuvellier, Goudemont, Compagnon, Leroux, Lantoine, Delettre, Bayart and Bulteel. And if one had, like Hervey, to spend one's spare time in meditation among the tombs, it can be guessed that there was not much else to do. For, knowing we were soon to be on the old tinker's trail again, we wasted no time on landscape gardening round about our hutments to catch the eye of itinerant medical brass hats, but stuck in to that never-failing operation, the overhauling of equipment.

So, having got orders late on the previous night, we left Acq on the morning of the 15th, and spent a very hot and dusty summer day in trekking via Haute Avesnes, Habarcq, Avesnes le Comte and Grand Rullecourt to Ivergny, a picturesque little place of some 400 inhabitants. It was a longish march of fifteen miles through pretty, undulating country, with good crops well forward everywhere; and we got down comfortably enough, as the motor ambulance cars made repeated (and illegitimate) trips, picking up our men in relays, and allowing them to settle down early, and not too tired, in bivouacs and the village school. My own billet had the unlooked for disadvantage that my hostess retired to rest through my bedroom; but as her catching me *en chemise* obviously did not disturb her beyond eliciting the customary "Pardon, Monsieur," I, with equal courtesy, did not allow it unduly to disturb me.

Next day we left Ivergny and trekked fourteen miles in rear of brigade transport via Lucheux, Gorges and Doullens to Candas. The pace set was rapid, and (until we broke off from the column at Doullens) very trying alike to men and horses, owing to dust and heat. To Lucheux the route was a very pretty one and lay through extensive woods (the scene, in bygone days, of the murder of the famous St. Leger), with a steep descent into the village; while at Gorges the Divisional band was discoursing cheerful music by the roadside to enliven the dusty column as it passed through.

Doullens, a fine little country town of 6,000 inhabitants, was looking quite gay with its *pavé* streets and its cafés thronged by citizens in their Sunday best; and, on leaving it, the *citadelle*—later to be the scene of a most diabolically deliberate outrage on the Red Cross—stood out on its rock as a war-worn relic of days gone by, with a history going back to the middle ages.

Out of Doullens our route lay up a steep hill, to negotiate which the bearers had to buckle to and assist the transport horses; so everyone was glad to get at last to Candas, where the men were bivouacked in a good field. An Empress Club bath unit—a water-heater and a nest of tin baths, some of which lasted out the campaign—had turned up as a kindly and welcome gift before we left Acq; and this, set going in the lee of a hedge, afforded a much appreciated chance of a dip for the footsore and weary.

At night I found a reversal of my previous night's billeting arrangement; as, in the small earthen-floored cottage where I slept, I had to pass through my hostess's room, in which she and her family were abed, to reach my own chamber further "ben." But here again the arrangement seemed a customary one, and only elicited a sleepy "Bonne nuit! Monsieur," from the lady of the house.

At Candas we stayed three days. It had the widest streets of any village that we ever saw in France, and was even then a great Air Force centre. In one little *épicerie*, where we went in search of picture post cards, the owner was well read in Franco-Scottish history, especially in the career of the unfortunate Marie Stuart; while the *cordonnier* (the village "souter")—a sturdy old septuagenarian with large spectacles—sought out by us for bootlaces, also supplied us with a vigorous denunciation of the enemy to the accompaniment of equally vigorous hammering on the sole of the boot he was repairing.

"Ah! monsieur!" (tap!) "Les Boches!" (tap, tap!) "Les barbares!" (tap, tap, tap!) "Les féroces!" (tap, tap!) "C'est une race à détruire!" (tap!) "A détruire!" (tap, tap, tap!) "A détruire!!" (tap, tap, tap, tap!) If his honest hammer could have done it the war would have been satisfactorily finished that evening.

Foot and anti-gas helmet inspection, overhauling equipment, and a route march or two to keep our feet hardened for further road work, passed the rest of the time; and on the evening of the 19th we marched independently as a unit via Valheureux and Naours to Flesselles. Even with a moon only four days on the wane and a clear night it was no joke finding one's way through the tortuous streets of the various villages. Naours was full of Anzacs, some of whom had enjoyed—wherever they had got it—an over-generous wine ration, and were lying about in graceful confusion with their empty gilt-necked bottles beside them.

Having failed to extract any intelligible replies from a somewhat bemused sentry, hypnotised apparently by the glimmer of his bayonet, I rode, to reconnoitre our route, up one silent side street; and, at a corner of it, the village church and its graveyard, dotted with white stones, stood out clearly in the light of the nearly full moon shining serenely above the church tower. It was a peaceful sight, curiously suggestive of stage scenery.

Suddenly, to complete the illusion, the quiet was broken by the sound of quaint music; and, silhouetted against the moonlight, a six-foot colonial playing vigorously on a mouth organ, with his sombrero set at a most rakish angle, lurched out of a farmyard entrance into the street. Carried away by a fierce pride in his own tunefulness, like Apollo when he slew Marsyas, he never saw my now somewhat alarmed horse, off which he ricocheted as he pursued his eccentric and melodious career. He looked for all the world like the Pied Piper, and was certainly in a condition entitling him to the necessary retinue of rats.

We got in to Flesselles—choc-a-bloc with troops—at 1 a.m., to find billets few and of the poorest, many of the unit never rising higher than an uneasy rest for some hours in shelter of the buttresses of the church. Four of us were proudly led by the billeting officer to the gate lodge of a château where he had secured one room. Alas! The single bed therein was filled by the adipose body of an unknown French interpreter of another division—none too courteous in his assertion of absolute proprietorship. The landlady, a handsome young woman in a charming *peignoir,* at first peremptorily refused our application for leave to sleep on the floor of the kitchen. Was not her husband home *en permission?* And the first time for two years! The room would be needed to-morrow for his *déjeuner!* He must have every comfort! Did he not deserve it? We agreed with *empressement* that this was indeed true. But I ventured to add:—

"Madame would not make her joy an occasion for our sorrow? Would she turn us, exhausted as we were, out into the street? We—all of us—could perceive by looking at her beautiful countenance that it must be associated with a kind heart!"

That did the trick: the objective was taken: with many expressions of sympathy for our toil-worn condition she helped us to push the furniture into a corner, and we had a sleep of sorts on the floor for three hours. Later, as we, in attempted silence so as not to disturb our amiable hostess, left her door at 4 a.m., she, in the manner of Juliet, opened the lattice of her rose-trellised window, and in charming disarray bade us "bonne chance."

Many moons had slowly waxed and waned when, later, I told this affecting tale with some pride to the then chief of our Divisional French Mission. He followed the story attentively and finally asked:—

"Will you tell me—in French—what exactly you did say to her?"

I told him; and, after a pause, he meditatively remarked:—

"Yes! she *might* have understood it—a little of it anyway!"

His cynicism may have been due to the fact that he claimed descent from Corneille; but I hold it to my credit that until he left us I remained on speaking terms with him—in English.

At 5 a.m. in drizzling rain, which later cleared off to leave a very warm, sultry, summer day, we left Flesselles and trekked, again through picturesque and undulating country, via Villers-Bocage, Coisy, Allonville, Querrieux, La Boussoye, Bodnay and Heilly, to Mericourt-Ribemont, where we had been before in July of the previous year, although now we were in the Ribemont part of the village. The march was again in rear of brigade transport; the pace was as hot as the weather; and the distance covered was twenty miles; so that all hands arrived pretty thoroughly done up.

Our Division was here relieving the 33rd in the attack on High Wood, and in the afternoon two officers left with the bearer sub-divisions to take over the Relay Bearer Post at Mametz and an Advanced Dressing Station at Black Hut in the valley—"Happy Valley"—beyond it; while the rest of the unit moved to Mericourt and there relieved the 101st Field Ambulance in a large barn—the largest I ever saw in France or elsewhere—lit by an excellent pre-war instalment of electric light, in which building they were running their Main Dressing Station. In the 48 hours of their stay they had dealt with 950 casualties; and taking over the show as a going concern, with a steady flow of wounded passing through, was no easy task for our clerks and personnel generally. In addition we had to look after a small château, with huts in its front courtyard, as an officers' hospital; so by evening everyone was up to the eyes in work.

All night and next day the constant stream of wounded from High Wood went on; and in the evening the news came down of the death by shell-fire of three of our men[1] at Black Hut, which post had been completely knocked out by some twenty shells coming over, the survivors of the party falling back on Mametz.

The weather, fortunately, kept fine, and the scene at night was impressive—the steady stream of motor ambulance cars whirring and humming as they came or left, with their headlights, when they passed it, momentarily illuminating the crucifix, vividly white against the greenery of the poplar trees lining the triangle of turf opposite the barn; the cooks' fires silhouetting them against the wall at their work amongst the Soyer's stoves; and the never ceasing gun flashes lighting up the whole horizon. One Wolseley car had been hit *en route* and the driver and car orderly wounded.

By the morning of the 24th work was slightly easier, although the news from the wounded was that furious fighting continued at High Wood, and that the German machine guns were playing havoc, while the artillery fire was heavy and continuous. The M.O.[2] of the A.D.S. came down at night from Mametz with the bodies of our men who had been killed; extricated under fire with great difficulty and risk from the spot where they had been buried by the shells. Their funeral took place next day to ground beside the communal cemetery of Mericourt; and later, two more of our unit[3] passed through mortally wounded, a shell having struck a party who had volunteered to go on foot from Mametz up Happy Valley while a heavy bombardment was on, with dressings and stores in answer to an urgent demand from the Quarry Post near Bazentin.

While the stream of casualties had been steady all day it had not been so heavy; but on the 26th a harder day was put in. For we functioned as an M.D.S. up to

---

[1] Privates McCondich, A. T. Milne and Anderson.
[2] Captain J. S. Stewart.
[3] Sergeant F. Rodgers and Private D. Jackson.

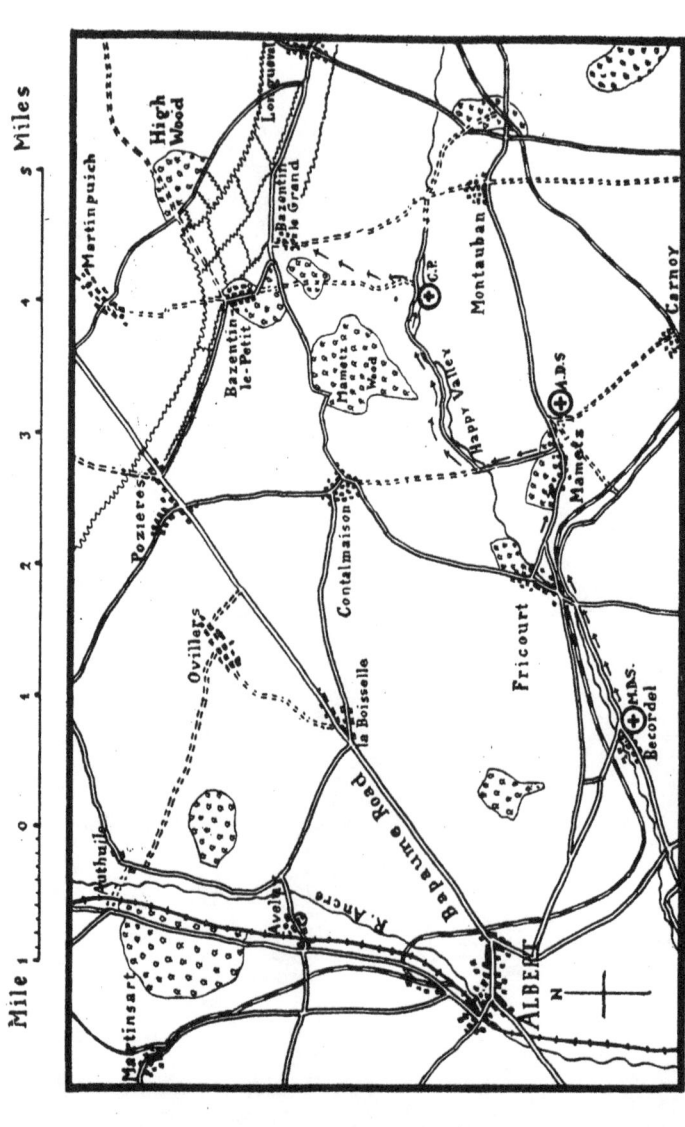

SOMME VALLEY. JULY 1916

12 noon—having dealt with 1,806 cases since we took over—and then, having closed, worked against time loading four motor wagon loads of miscellaneous stores from the château to go to the new Corps Main Dressing Station on the slope of the hill above Dernancourt. That done, with all speed we had to pack up and load our own transport, get a meal served and trek out at 6.30, marching by Meaulte to Becordel, where we camped under canvas by the roadside on the slope of the valley towards Fricourt.

The pace was slow, as the whole district was stiff with troops and guns; all the villages crowded up, and tents and bivouacs on every hand. From our camp at night the entire valley was twinkling with fires in the fine summer night; and a steady cloud of white chalky dust from the unceasing traffic on the road found its way everywhere. Grinding the teeth was easy here, and one bit the dust in the erect position.

On the 28th four more bearers[1] were killed, and, next day, buried in the military cemetery at Becordel, crosses made by our own carpenters being later erected over them.

Each of the three Field Ambulances was now supplying personnel for a 48 hours' spell apiece at the Quarry Collecting Post in Happy Valley, two and a-half kilometres beyond Mametz on the route to High Wood; a most dangerous spot, enfiladed as it was by enemy fire and without proper dug-out accommodation, the only shelters in the quarry being of sandbagged timber, roofed with corrugated iron. But it was a case of Hobson's choice and carry on, although R.E. help was got later to better the conditions generally. Up to this place, however, in spite of the cut-up state of the road and the continuous shelling of it, the Field Ambulance motor cars were running steadily. But, on the evening of the 30th, the corner—"Death Corner"—on the Mametz side

[1] Privates J. Lumsden, A. B. Reid, T. B. Jamieson and R. Donaldson.

of the quarry became quite impassable for cars, owing to shell holes; so horse ambulance wagons worked past it by the field track, and for three days and nights took stretcher cases from the quarry all the way to the top of the hill at Mametz, where they were reloaded in the motor ambulances to go back to the A.D.S. at the File Factory, Becordel—a very nerve-racking piece of work, most gallantly carried out by all concerned.[1]

One of these trips is well described in the words of a horse transport driver; it shows, too, how an experience of this sort was looked upon as all in the day's work:—

"We were working four horses in a team, as it was far too heavy a job for a pair. I was detailed for one of the wagons with another man in the lead. Except for dodging a few shell holes the first twenty-four hours were nothing much out of the way. But the second night got a bit livelier. If I remember aright the 153rd Brigade went over the top that night, so we had our work cut out to keep the Quarry Post clear, and it was made increasingly stiff as there were no wagon orderlies available, and the drivers had themselves to transfer the patients from the horse wagon to the motor. We jogged along not so badly till about 2 a.m., although the horses were beginning to feel the strain, as we were taking four stretcher cases and 'umpteen' sitting cases every trip, all perched in or about the wagon like a lot of monkeys.

[1] Major Bewsher in his *History of the 51st Division* pays the R.A.M.C. the following tribute:—"In this valley the conduct of the Royal Army Medical Corps was superb. Other troops could at least make some effort to make their way out of the danger zone as fast as possible, but the bearers of the field ambulances and the regimental stretcher bearers could not. They slowly pushed their wheeled stretchers from the Crucifix at Bazentin to the dressing station, heedless of the shell-fire and their own security, and careful only to evacuate the wounded with the minimum of discomfort to them. Similarly, ambulance car drivers could not join in the helter-skelter for security on the road to Fricourt. Day and night they plied slowly along the damaged road with their burden of wounded, returning again and again through the valley as soon as their cars had been cleared."

While we were going down the valley Jerry commenced to pop tear shells over and then a big 'Jack Johnson' made a huge hole on the overland track; so we decided, to avoid the risk of capsizing the wagon, that we would have a shy at the road.

"We got to the quarry all right, loaded up and started on our return journey. About a hundred yards from Death Corner a Gordon picket stopped us and told us we should not go any further as the road was being heavily shelled. As, however, we had a serious case on board and the patients were 'windy' (which a man often enough was after he was hit), we decided to push on. At the corner we could not see a yard in front of us for gas and mist, and it was no easy job guiding the wagon through the maze of shell holes.

"Suddenly a great shell burst twenty yards in front of us, and my leader thinking it was somewhat to his left swerved to the right to avoid the hole. As it happened, the swerve took us right into it and the wagon turned over on its side. The leader—a good horseman—shouted to me to try and urge the horses to pull it out and that the wagon might right itself in the process. At the first strain the lead-ropes between the first pair and mine broke; so we made a fresh rope out of some loose wire that was lying about and tried again, but it broke too.

"Stuck in a shell hole, the enemy shelling and the valley full of gas: no wagon orderly and several badly wounded men inside whom we were unable to help—what were we to do? We shouted to some ammunition column drivers going past at the gallop to lend a hand; but they either didn't hear us or thought there were too many shells dropping about for them to stop. So the leader unhitched a horse and rode off to Mametz for help while I stuck to the wagon.

"While he was away I managed to tell a wounded officer inside what had happened and that we hoped soon to remedy matters. He was in a very exhausted state and died a few minutes afterwards; but with almost his last breath he said that if we all pulled through he would see that we got proper recognition for sticking by them.

"Back came the leader no better off than when he left: not a soul at Mametz who could help us. I then went off for a try, and came back with no better luck. When we had about given up hope, one of our own horse ambulance wagons arrived on the scene from the Quarry. They pluckily drew up alongside and we got our cases out of the capsized wagon through the canvas sides and laid them on the ground, while their wagon went off at the gallop for Mametz and came back again for them, loaded up and set off again up the valley. Later on, with a team of twelve horses, we got our own wagon out and started work again. I must say it was a trying experience."

All in the day's work, as I said before: this incident—and hundreds of others like it—remained untold till long after the campaign was over. But all who knew Happy Valley will recognise the severe strain on these two drivers.[1]

For the valley itself was always an extraordinary scene of destruction and desolation. Going down it the road hugged the sharp rise of the hill on the right, into which ran numerous small dug-outs and shelters; while, on the left of the road, flat ground ran for a hundred yards or so gradually sloping up to hill again. On this ground guns were going up with their teams *ventre à terre* at a mad gallop; dead men and horses, and smashed limbers, lay about in every direction; and a torn and twisted light railway shewed protruding strands like hands held up in grotesque protest against the treatment it had received. It was all curiously reminiscent of the illustrated papers; one's prevailing impression was a sense of unreality—*que diable faites-vous dans cette*

[1] Drivers W. Mackie and A. B. McLeod.

galère? War seemed, as the Canadian rhymester puts it,

> . . . the rummiest sort of a go,
> For when it's most real it's then that you feel
> That you're watching a cinema show,

until the heat, the stench from the carcases rotting in the sun, and the shell-fire brought one back to actualities and the job of work on hand.

By 2nd August the Quarry Post conditions were somewhat improved, as four small dug-outs were secured on the roadside beyond it, which accommodated most of the personnel in safety; while the cooks got cover in another and smaller quarry some hundred yards further on.

All the time of our stay our valley at Becordel and that across the ridge north of us had been intermittently shelled and bombed, and the weather had been baking hot. A South African heavy battery, hard at work some hundred yards away, effectually prevented sleep, and the cloud of chalk dust was all pervading. This last often produced curious spectacular effects. To come back from Mametz and meet the horses of gun-teams breast high in a grey-blue cloud of it, only their bobbing necks and heads and those of their riders visible, black against the copper semi-circle of a setting sun, was a sight suggestive of Eastern jinn out on an errand of Ahriman.

We handed over again a few days later to the 101st Field Ambulance and moved back to Dernancourt. There we lay in tents in a field of ripened uncut wheat, like Ruth among the alien corn, on the top of the ridge above the Corps M.D.S. until 10 p.m. on the 9th, when we entrained, the transport having left the day before for Sorel via Cardonette. The train, however, did not set off till 3 a.m., the accommodation for all ranks being cattle trucks; and after a series of short sleeps on the hard and dirty floors, we got to Longpré at 9 a.m., marching five miles therefrom to Sorel. Here, and on the road to it, we smelt the fine, homely, honest smell of peat-reek for the first time in France.

Sorel, a well-to-do and picturesque little village untouched by war, was a welcome sight after our experiences of the past three weeks. Good, cheap, white wine was available at 1 fr. 50 to 2 fr. a bottle, with cider, fresh butter and milk and eggs. Peats—*tourbes*—were the main fuel. The "divots" were smaller than in Scotland and were cut with a longitudinally corrugated spade which left its mark on them; a big, four-wheeled cartful costing 40 frs. The village was on top of a hill, and the wells were of necessity correspondingly deep: the main one was said by a local Munchausen to be 300 feet. However that may have been, in letting down the bucket of our special well too vigorously, some of our men broke the chain, and a busy spell of two hours was spent in fishing for it with a wire rope and a hook; voluble *M. le Maire* and his still more voluble wife contributing much excited exhortation. One worthy in the district made a precarious livelihood by descending on such occasions to recover lost buckets at 10 fr. a journey; but we managed to dispense with risking our money and his life, although our salvage operations resulted in the water being very oily for some twenty-four hours.

Deroy, Dellacourt, Cornu and Succur were some of the commonest surnames in the place; and in my billet, a comfortable, two-storied, old-fashioned country house, was a very fine collection of ancient brass "cruisie" lamps, which again, like the peat-reek, gave a homely touch to our surroundings. Altogether, it was a pleasant "Sweet Auburn"; and my landlady's remark, "La vie est très calme et tranquille ici," was evidently true. I should like to see Sorel again: "a man," as Mr. Markham observes in David Copperfield, "might do very well here."

On the morning of 12th August we set off for Pontremy to entrain, and after a very warm journey via

Abbeville, Boulogne and St. Omer, we detrained at Steenbecque and marched to Blairinghem. All (except the main) roads were narrow and often lined with high hedge-rows: crops—wheat, barley and haricots—were well on and abundant: the peasantry seemed well-to-do, and the ditch or hedge-lined fields, usually small, were well kept and tidy. As was inevitable in flat watery Flanders, mosquitoes were in plenty; but billets for everybody were above the average. At the foot of a large crucifix at a road junction in the village lay a lot of rudely made little wooden crosses about 2 ft. long. Every time a child's funeral passed, it was the picturesque local custom that one such little cross was left there.

Two days later we marched to Eblinghem, entrained for Steenwerck, transport going by road, and spent a night at Lestrades, proceeding next day to Armentières on the Lys near the Belgian frontier. The arrival of the unit there coincided with a sharp shelling of the town by the Huns; but the men, going at intervals in parties of twelve, got safely to their billets at the *Institut St. Jude,* a large Catholic seminary which had already been pretty badly knocked about by enemy fire. An advance party took over the Advanced Dressing Station at the Chapelle d'Armentières brickworks from the 1st New Zealand F.A.; while the rest of the unit were engaged in running the Main Dressing Station at the Maternity Hospital on the Armentières-Estaires road, a small modern building of brick, but with no adequate cellar accommodation as protection against shell-fire.

In the evening the enemy gunners got busy again, and stretcher parties were busy collecting casualties from the streets, 40 in all being dealt with—Scots and New Zealand troops with French and Belgian civilians, a large percentage of the latter being moribund and requiring the last rites of the Church from a neighbouring *curé*. Two sad cases were a mother and daughter, who were mortally wounded by a shell which fell plumb through a two storey building and burst in the cellar of the bootshop they kept in one of the main streets. The shop, a neat well-stocked up-to-date little place, was smashed: the cellar stairs leading from the back shop were blown away, and the stretchers had to be let down and hauled up with ropes through the shell hole, rather a tricky task; but we got them up, although both women were so badly wounded in the head, chest and abdomen that they died next day.

At no time or place was it desirable to be shelled; but to experience it in a town was worse, if anything, than in the open, where at least you could see to a certain extent what was happening. Bad by day it was still worse by night. The thunderous rumbling hubbub of falling masonry echoed amongst the dark and silent streets long after the smashing crash of the shell had died away; while the recovery of casualties from the vicinity of the resulting ruins was often a very risky job owing to the sudden descent of fresh debris.

Even shelling, however, had a humorous side to it. In the street running along to the *Institut St. Jude* a shell landed one afternoon a considerable distance behind a brewer's dray—one of these long, sloping structures on four wheels where the beer barrels lay on two parallel rails. Off went the horses at full gallop: off his perch, too, fell the driver: and off the cart, by ones and twos and threes came the beer barrels. The driver, getting on his feet, started to chase his horses, while nimble Jocks and Anzacs, coming out from their billets like bees from a hive, rapidly rolled the barrels into them. Later appeared dazed Jehu, with his recovered horses and dray, to view an empty street and look in vain for his vanished goods.

We stayed in Armentières till 25th September, and during all the time the town was shelled almost daily by the enemy. Our little hospital was never struck; but

THE SOMME, 1916.

the large French Civilian one immediately behind us, where our M.O.s had to attend surgical cases, was hit several times; while the run of street casualties was always so large that special parties of our men with wheeled stretchers stood by, day and night, for duty at such work. Out of a pre-war population of over 28,000 a large number still hung on in spite of the battering the town was getting, and many shops and estaminets continued open and got good patronage.

Outstanding amongst these was the establishment of Lucienne in the Square of the Church of Saint Waast. Here, with boarded up windows, as shell splinters had long ago ruined the panes, she ran a restaurant whose praise is still in the mouths of men now scattered over the British Empire.

> The city was in ill repair
> And bad for beasts and men,
> Yet who can hear "*Armentières!*"
> But thinks of Lucienne.
> Of all who at her table sat
> The second-loot, the big brass hat,
> She had the ranks and titles pat,
> The nimble Lucienne!
>
> Their names, oft their *petits noms* too,
> Were well within her ken,
> The subtle shades of deference due
> Came quick from Lucienne.
> But big brass hat or second-loot
> Had always the same bills to foot,
> Her items none would dare dispute
> When faced by Lucienne!
>
> *Comment ça va, ma'm'selle*—and where?
> You left the city—when?
> We lost taste for Armentières
> When it lost Lucienne.
> The windows with the shattered glass
> From shells that landed in the *Place*
> Are doubtless whole by now—Alas!
> But where is Lucienne?

A proportion of our transport worked daily under the O.C. Divisional Sanitary Section in connection with the removal of town refuse to the incinerators, of which there was quite a little village in a space behind the cinema show at the Divisional canteen. All over this place there was a continual popping of cartridges which had got amongst the stuff to be incinerated.

"The cartridges keep you lively?" I once asked a man in charge of some incinerators.

"There's nae muckle harm in the cairtridges," said the phlegmatic Jock, "but there was a boom cam in the ither day, an' that's juist gaun a bittie owre far!"

All the same, numerous casualties were caused this way in the course of the campaign; and the unromantic, necessary work of the sanitary squads was never without considerable risk.

One piece of work we carried out here was the timbering, propping and sandbagging of the cellars under the *Institut St. Jude,* into which our personnel had frequently to descend when things were lively; and we did the same for the benefit of some nuns who remained in the cellars under their own part of the building. And at our hospital, in a corner of its front garden where a neighbouring house would likely, in the event of shelling, fall on it and give extra overhead protection, we erected a large thoroughly sandbagged elephant shelter, which we never, fortunately, required to use; although we learnt afterwards that it came in handy for our successors on the first night they spent there.

At the Advanced Dressing Station in the brickfields at Chapelle d'Armentières, the place was also propped and strengthened and the head cover improved with bricks, rubble and sandbags; although, in spite of occasional shelling, life there was fairly uneventful and, as a matter of fact, safer than in Armentières; many of the men even getting "sport" of a kind by fishing for

THE SOMME, 1916.

carp in the small fish pond of a neighbouring and destroyed villa.

One of our sections was detailed to form a dressing station under canvas for the Brigade training camp near Bailleul. The town was then fairly intact, and the greater part of its pre-war population of 13,000 was still there. With its fine old *Place*, its *Hôtel de Ville* of the XVI and its churches of the XVII centuries, its numerous old houses of equal age, and its picturesque lace workers with their pillows and bobbins at their open doors in the back streets, it was always worth a visit. Alas, for its cruel fate in 1918!

On 4th September we took over from the 69th F.A. the M.D.S. at Pont de Nieppe in the school there, along with the A.D.S. at the brewery on the Ploegsteert road—the latter station being a most satisfactory and well-found one in the extensive cellarage of the *brasserie*. We then expected that the 57th F.A. would relieve us at Armentières and Brickfield A.D.S.; but arrangements were changed and they took over instead Pont de Nieppe M.D.S. and the Brewery A.D.S. on the 7th. On this date, too, Armentières got one of the worst hammerings we had experienced, six shells landing on the *Institut St. Jude,* and several near the officers' mess; while one sheered the small tower on the Civil Hospital clean through like a rotten carrot. No casualties resulted to the unit; but there was once more a heavy night's work with street cases, military and civilian.

Towards the end of our Armentières stay the weather was miserably cold and wet, and we were not sorry to hand over to the 103rd F.A. on the 25th September, and trek to La Crêche near Bailleul; thereby missing another heavy shelling of the town in the evening. After the noise of Armentières the little village, rural and quiet, was a pleasant change; and next evening in the gladness of our hearts we held a most successful open-air sing-song round a bonfire in a field there—rather a risky performance, now one comes to think of it, in view of possible attention from air-craft.

Like the rest of the district the village was bi-lingual, Flemish and French. The chief local names in the churchyard were Vanuxeem, Vermeersch and Vandromme, with Becue, Delsalle, Ducrocq, Lombart, Duthilleul, Buidin, Galland and Gille. In one little shop, the owner, a stout old woman, told us that she could understand a good deal of what the men with the *courte jupe* said, but not the language of those in trousers except such as belonged to our unit. The "petticoated men" and our men were north country Scots; the rest were English. So the kinship of our Doric with the Flemish had not escaped her ear.

A week later we left La Crêche at 2.30 a.m. and trekked to Bailleul, entraining there at 5 a.m. for Doullens, whence we marched to Gezaincourt near Candas. Next day, in very wet weather, which got worse as the day went on, we marched in rear of Brigade via Freschvillers and Sarton to Authuie, and then some kilometres further to Bois de Warnimont. Billets were doorless huts in the dripping cheerless wood, the horse lines were in a swamp of a field beside the road, and everybody and every beast was soaked with rain and miserably cold. After a comfortless night we marched to Bus-Les-Artois, taking over some old French hutments there as a M.D.S. from the 132nd F.A., and an A.D.S. in some roadside shelters at Colincamps, a few kilometres nearer the line.

Bus was no great shakes of a place, and the villainous weather made it, with its traffic-cut roads ankle-deep in thick mud like badly made porridge, look worse. And three of us will always remember the reception we got there when we made for our billets and knocked at the door. No answer being forthcoming, we proceeded to enter the little red-tiled kitchen, just as our landlady came in by another door from the back garden. We certainly exuded rain and mud on the hitherto clean floor; but even that could not excuse her lack of welcome to us. Madeleine—she was a married woman, so perhaps I should not refer to her by her Christian name; but I have forgotten her surname if I ever knew it—was elderly, biggish and broadish, with a carefully cultivated vinous complexion that matched her red tiles, and she cut short my polite introduction of myself and colleagues with a shriek of,

"Trois officiers? Jamais! Jamais! Jamais! Toujours *un* officier—un officier, seulement!"

It might have been only "pretty Fanny's way": but how to assuage the *dulces Amaryllidis irae?* While I was explaining—still politely—that M. le Maire had officially detailed this as a billet for three, a third door into the kitchen opened behind us, and Jacques, her husband, attacked us in the rear with a machine-gun fire of "Jamais! Jamais! Jamais de la vie!" To show to what extreme lengths he was prepared to go in defence of his hearth and home, Jacques opened a table drawer and extracted a knife, which he waved melodramatically in the air. The situation had become awkward, and required delicate and diplomatic handling. One of our officers, being a Glasgow man, always carried a large and occasionally full flask; and this—it being luckily that day in a replenished condition—I asked him, *sotto voce,* to produce at once and place prominently on the table. He carried out the ceremony with the profound solemnity a Scotsman always shews when handling whisky; and then in clear, audible tones I asked Madeleine if she had five glasses. The "jamais" storm cleared magically: Madeleine produced a smile and the glasses, while Jacques surreptitiously replaced the table knife in the drawer with one hand, and in a determined, anticipatory fashion wiped his heavy moustache with the back of the other. The *trois officiers* were no longer looked on as brigands, and Madeleine took us under her wing.

Rather too much under her wing, as a matter of fact, for the owner of the flask; he coming later to my room after I was abed, and asking me to get up and speak to the lady, who had invaded his sleeping apartment and was talking voluble *patois* there. I told him sleepily to bear in mind that Jacques was evidently both a jealous man and an expert with a table knife, and that the reconciling flask was now empty; while he pathetically asked me to cease all untimely jesting and to come and charm Madeleine away. But Madeleine declared to me that she only wanted to know whether *monsieur le capitaine* wished an extra pillow; and on my assuring her that in his country one pillow was the invariable rule, she retired. Later I heard my comrade, as an anti-landlady precaution, trying to make up for the keyless condition of his door by balancing a tilted chair under its handle. And a hush descended on the house of Jacques and Madeleine as we all slipped into slumber.

Madeleine, however, improved on acquaintance, and had considerable store of folk beliefs. It was from her I learned that in Artois a cock crowing after dark foretold better weather; and her barometrically-minded rooster, who indulged twice in this habit, was evidently a practical student of local weather conditions, for there was a temporary improvement after each of his efforts.

In Bus we remained for some days, the Division having gone into the line in front of Hebuterne and Colincamps. As it was rumoured that it was to do a push from here, it fell to our lot to go over the trench system and prospect for suitable Advanced Dressing Stations, one such trip starting from Hebuterne at 4.30 a.m. In the darkness we mistakenly ran our "Tin Lizzie" past Hebuterne, and got, by a road heavily pock-marked with shells, to some guns near Foncquevillers. A surprised gunner officer emerging from a dug-out irritably asked us what the dickens we thought we were doing there? Dawn was breaking, the road under observation, and our presence apt to invite mischief. Under the circumstances he advised us to clear out rapidly, which—turning the car with difficulty among the shell holes, while thanking him for the correctness and courtesy of his behaviour—we did.

Numerous fatigue parties worked hard at Home Avenue trench excavating deep cut-outs for Advanced Dressing Stations, which were roofed with iron rails, timber and sandbags; and more work of the same kind was done at Colincamps. But here again—as so often happened—we were altruists and not destined to use them, for in a few days we moved to Forceville, the Division taking over the line at Beaumont Hamel in preparation for the famous battle of 13th November.

CHAPTER V.

Beaumont Hamel, 1916.

There's mud on him? Ay, and there's blood on him!
(Some grub! An' a ration o' rum?)
For we picked him up on the spot where he fell,
And through two kilometres o' compound hell
We've carried him here and we've carried him well.
(Off again! There are others to come!)

"As the season advanced and the bad weather continued the scope of our plan had constantly to be reduced, until finally it was only possible to undertake the much more limited operation of the 13th November against Beaumont Hamel. The brilliant success of this attack, carried out as it was under most difficult conditions of ground, affords some indication of what might have been accomplished had the weather permitted us to give fuller effect to our original plan."—*(Sir Douglas Haig's Despatch of 22nd December, 1916.)*

"BEAUMONT HAMEL," as our then G.O.C. said six years later, "was the first occasion when the Highland Division was able to prove that, given a fair chance, it would certainly be successful against the enemy. Here was a fortress defended by every artifice of which the Boche was a past master. It had several lines of defence connected by subterranean tunnels, and each line defended by several belts of barbed wire. When the Division proceeded there the place had been attacked on at least two occasions, and it still remained intact. When I went to those Divisions that had attacked in order to try to get some tips, I was told, 'You have not a dog's chance.' As you know it rained continuously for several days

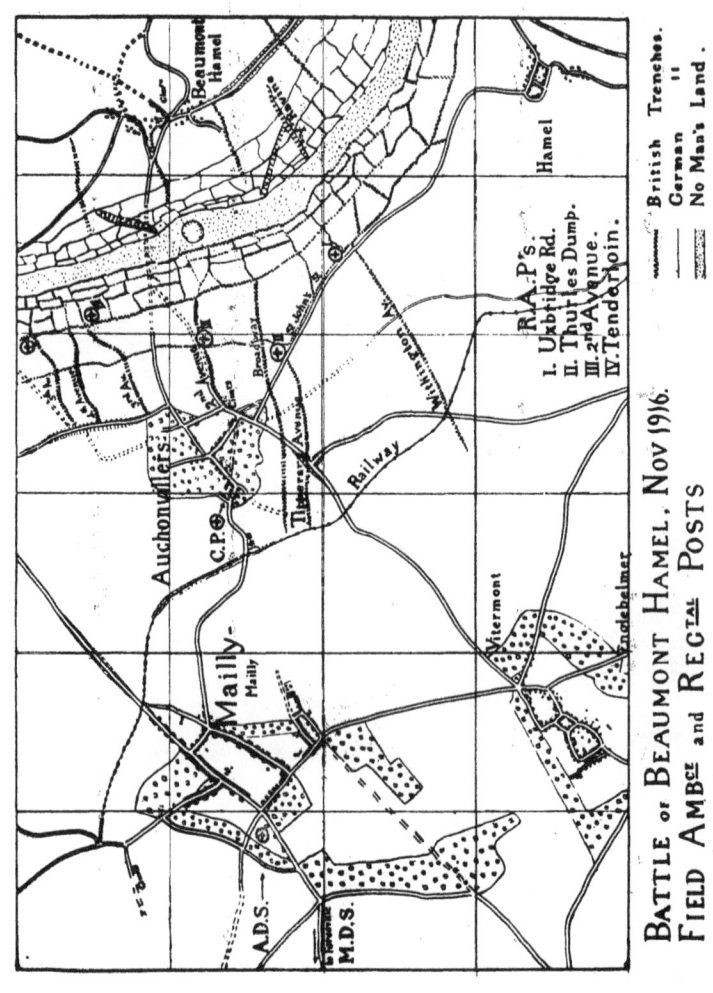

before 13th November. In fact we carried out a raid two or three days before, and the men were so involved in the mud that they could not get on and could scarcely get back. Yet Beaumont Hamel was taken, you might say, with almost automatic precision. We took nearly 3,000 prisoners, and that in spite of very little progress being made on our left. This was the same Division that had fought bravely at Festubert. It had taken over the Labyrinth from the French, which was really over a Boche mine-field, for mines were blown up practically every night. And yet it lost hardly a single trench. It was the same Division that had fought in High Wood on the Somme with great loss. The reason was that elsewhere we were pitchforked into other people's battles, whereas in Beaumont Hamel the Division was able to prepare and fight its own battle in its own way."

So much for the actual battle: let us look at it from the R.A.M.C. point of view.

The previous medical arrangements in the High Wood engagement, where a shifting personnel and a divided jurisdiction of Field Ambulance commanders had been somewhat confusing, were now changed; and a Forward Evacuation Officer was appointed whose duty it was throughout the battle to contrive and supervise the evacuation of all wounded from the R.A.P.s to the Main Dressing Station and Walking Wounded Collecting Station; a more satisfactory method which held good to the end of the campaign.

When we took over the line from the Royal Naval Division on 17th October, the different medical posts were then quite inadequate for the push which we knew to be in prospect; and it was well, from the R.A.M.C. standpoint, that frequent postponements of Zero day took place. For in that time our men, "with necessarily limited R.E. help" (that familiar Staff *cliché*), had to enlarge and add an extra entrance to a Relay Bearer Post at

Tenderloin in White City; to make an entirely new one in Second Avenue Trench and another at Uxbridge Road; to pit-prop and false-roof a Collecting Post at Auchonvillers in the stable of a farmyard there; and to prop, sandbag, and fit stretcher-racks into the cellars of a *brasserie* at Mailly-Maillet as an A.D.S.; all of which entailed on the officer over-seeing the forward work many a weary mile daily, for weeks on end, of trench tramping in the vilest of weather through mud often up to above the knees.

Still, when 13th November came, our preparations were finished and the whole thing was workable. The constant anxiety of a Forward Evacuation Officer was to have good head cover for his men when they were not in action, and to be sure that he had no superfluous personnel at the different posts to invite unnecessary casualties; while equally certain in his mind that he had plenty men to face the work in hand, and that all demands for stretcher-bearers would be met.

Yes, there was always a lot to do before a push, and the experience gained in each had to be duly noted, remembered and used with advantage in the next: *in bello non licet bis errare.* A good surplus of stretchers, blankets, splints, dressings, rations, medical stores and comforts, had to be accumulated gradually at the first Field Ambulance Post behind the R.A.P.s before Zero day. If the weather were wet, as almost invariably happened when a push was on hand, the blankets had to be carried up to the line in bundles wrapped in waterproof sheets, to protect them as far as possible from rain and the soaking, sticky sides of the muddy trenches. Without this precaution they were bound to arrive at their destination hopelessly wet and soiled before they were ever called into use; and as it was quite impossible, owing to the confined space, to have drying accommodation of any kind at such places, this kept us from attaining that warmth and dryness for the wounded so essential in combating shock.

This forward Field Ambulance post was usually the Collecting Post, the furthest up position to which cars could approach with a modicum of safety before the push commenced. As the stretchers, blankets, stores, etc., began to be called for from the R.A.P.s, the M.O. at the Collecting Post had to indent back on the Advanced Dressing Station, and this in turn on the Main Dressing Station, which, again, was in touch with the C.C.S. and the Advanced Depot of Medical Stores; so that cars returning to the front after leaving their wounded at the M.D.S. were always bringing up fresh stores towards the line to replenish the different posts from which they carried back. At an early stage of the battle it was quite possible that the roads would be either totally blocked with combatant traffic or so seriously congested as to make transit an exceedingly slow business; and it was, therefore, absolutely necessary to have a surplus at each stage to refill the medical post immediately in front of it.

The providing of an adequate supply of water was also a problem to be met. It had to be sent up to Regimental Aid Posts, Relay Bearer Posts, and Collecting Posts, in petrol tins, and the supply of these tins was necessarily limited. The Battalion M.O. had always to have a generous stock at his R.A.P., drawn previously by the Quartermaster from the harassed A.S.C. A certain number, if the M.O. was wise, were strictly earmarked for carrying forward when the time came to advance his aid post, and were only used at the original one when the necessity was imperative. On sending back for a refill to the Collecting Post, he was always supposed to return the empty tins, an item in the programme which he frequently forgot; and this omission equally frequently prevented his again getting supplied promptly. For at the Collecting Post a reserve supply had to be kept for their own cases in the event of the tank of the water cart stationed there receiving, as often happened, a punctured wound from shell fragment or shrapnel; or of the supply water-cart being knocked out or held up on its road from the A.D.S. behind.

To provide hot food for the hungry, soup kitchens were usually run as near the communication trenches as possible. In this battle, in addition to the Divisional soup kitchen at Stockton Dump, which we could draw on for supplies, we had a show of our own, generously helped by the Scottish Churches Tent, in our farmyard at Auchonvillers; and there throughout the battle it did yeoman work for wounded, stretcher-bearers, prisoners and all who claimed our hospitality. Besides, by diplomacy, tact and ingenuity, we had accumulated an extra good rum ration, and had further purchased a plentiful supply of canteen chocolate for the bearers.

By the night, then, of 12th-13th November all these things—and many more—had been seen to, and the Forward Evacuation Officer at the Auchonvillers Collecting Post took a final pipe and look over his orders; wondering how far the latter would pan out as expected, and trying to anticipate, with the help of his colleague there, what should be done in the event of any part of the official programme breaking down. Then, with the gas curtains down—for the area echoed all the wet, misty night with the slow and melancholy "Whew-ew-PUNK!" of gas shells—a few hours of disturbed sleep were got on a stretcher, until the hour before Zero made all alert for the work in hand.

At 5.30 on 13th November our furious barrage started, and by 7 a.m. a steady stream of wounded was flowing in, which lasted all day; but evacuation went on well and steadily with no congestion at the various posts. At 11 a.m. and 2.45 p.m. Auchonvillers was vigorously shelled; and we had, for the time being, to carry all the

1

2

Auchonvillers Collecting Post.

1. Entrance to farmyard (arch on left).
2. Entrance to dressing-room in farmyard. (Roof smashed by shells just before battle started.)

Facing page 108.

cases lying in the farmyard, awaiting dressing or removal, inside our already crowded Dressing Room. By the middle of the forenoon German prisoners began passing in large numbers; and a hundred fit men were held up to help to clear the field of their own wounded. These men were fed and treated like our own bearers and worked willingly and well, being docile to a degree; any number up to fifteen at a time going off in charge of one R.A.M.C. man.

Corporal Charlie, one of the best known characters in our unit, had general charge of the Hun auxiliaries, and his management of them and of the language difficulty was admirable. Ordered in the evening to detail twelve men for wheeled stretcher work, in answer to a call for more bearers to go to Thurles Dump, he went to the ruined shed where his command lay; most of them, mark you, smoking cigarettes supplied by their friendly enemies. It was dark by then, and I happened to cross the yard as he began operations. Holding on high a hurricane lamp he shouted:—

"Noo, then, you Fritzes! A dizzen o' ye! Compree?"

"Nein!" said a puzzled voice from amongst the huddle of Huns in the shed.

"*Nine,* ye gommeral? It's nae nine; it's twal' o' ye! C'wa' noo! Look slippy! *You,* Nosey!" (indicating a gentleman well endowed in this way by nature). "An' *you,* Breeks!" (to another, the seat of whose trousers was severely damaged by barbed wire).

He then most appropriately fitted Nosey between the front handles of a wheeled stretcher with Breeks at the tail end, and with a deft shove sent them and their apparatus out of the way; while, again applying his personal method, he rapidly picked out another two. When the tally was complete he turned to the orderly in charge with:—

"Noo, laddie, there's your Fritzes! See ye dinna loss ony o' them!"—and calmly made off in quest of another job.

As a practical linguist he was unique: his French being quite as good as his German. An equal adept was he with penny whistle or mouth organ, or as Rabelaisian raconteur in chief. He was a man of never-failing cheerfulness, and much legendary lore deservedly circulated round him.

Later, going round a dark corner of the farmyard, I collided violently with someone coming from the opposite direction. After tersely commenting on the situation I flashed on a torch light and discovered the corporal, with both arms crossed, like a tombstone saint, over a mass of bulging material inside his tunic.

"What on earth have you got there?" I asked.

"Booms!" came the laconic reply.

"Bombs! What are *you* doing with bombs?"

"Pittin' them in a holie roond at the back."

He had collected about forty bombs from the wounded who had come in, and I was rather glad our collision had not been more violent than it was.

But Corporal Charlie has led me away a bit. All day the run of cases continued and all night of 13th-14th. In spite of the shelling of the evacuation routes there had so far been no casualties amongst our personnel. Morning saw things rather quieter; but in the forenoon, near White City, an M.O.[1] of the 2/1st F.A., one of the most efficient and gallant R.A.M.C. officers in the Division, was killed by a shell, as later was a private[2] of our unit along with two Boche bearers. The good old motor transport, with their usual sang-froid, were now steadily running cars down to Tenderloin Post in White City by the much battered Auchonvillers-Beaumont

[1] Captain H. Begg.
[2] Private Blair.

Hamel road, the route being risky (although no worse than Happy Valley in July); and in any case it was necessary at all costs to ease off the strain on the now thoroughly exhausted bearers, many of whom had their shoulders absolutely raw with the constant friction and pressure of the stretcher slings. Evacuation went on steadily all day and night of 14th-15th.

On the evening of the 14th a batch of some half dozen Boche officers was temporarily left in our charge until an A.P.M.'s guard was available to remove them back. We stuck them under a guard of our own in the much battered part of our building which faced the enemy lines. Shortly afterwards I got a message asking for an interview. On entering their quarters there was much heel-clicking and saluting; and a fat, walrus-faced fellow who spoke semblable English asked:—

"Are you aware, sir, that we are German officers?"

I murmured politely that the fact was obvious.

"Are you aware, sir, that this room is not suitable accommodation for German officers?"

By good luck I remembered what Sam Weller, as boots of "The White Hart," had said to Mr. Perker when the little lawyer remarked: "This is a curious old house of yours." So I gave Sam's reply to the indignant Hun:—

"If you'd sent word you were coming, we'd have had it repaired."

The effect was magical! Walrus-face beamed and translated the remark to his brethren, who all saluted with pleased smiles, while their interpreter observed in the most amiable manner:—

"Do not further apologise!"

I replied that I would not; and, looking in later, found them in very audible enjoyment of some liquid nourishment from the soup kitchen. The incident was happily closed,

And now came the inevitable stage of clearing up the battlefield and searching all possible places where wounded, whether British or Boche, who had not been picked up in the actual battle, might have sought shelter. At daybreak an M.O. and a party were sent to work from Y Ravine towards White City; while another party, including two Jocks with rifles (as the dug-outs with which Beaumont Hamel was tunnelled were not yet clear of whole-skinned Huns), worked across to meet him, an officer of the 6th Seaforths acting as guide. A further object was to search for a wonderful legendary underground Hun dressing station of the Arabian Nights variety, which, incidentally, we failed to locate.

It was drizzling wet and vilely cold, the trenches in places thigh deep in clay and an awful mess of smashed barbed wire, mud, disintegrated German dead and debris of all sorts. In one trench our occupation for half an hour was hauling each other out of the tenacious and blood-stained mud; and during our mutual salvage operations we had evidently made ourselves too visible, as the enemy started shelling. There was nothing for it but to take to the open and make for another trench, which we promptly did; doing a hundred yards in rather good time.

Now, the Jocks and I were of the Julius Cæsar, Napoleon and Lord Roberts type of physique, while our guide was a tall man, whose greatcoat—which for some obscure reason he had put on before starting—blew out as he led us, doubled up on account of the *phut-phut* of bullets, across the open; and it struck me with a great feeling of irritation as we ran that we must be providing excellent comic effect for any of the enemy observing us through glasses, by suggesting an alarmed hen and three chickens on the run. (I had the opportunity of being in a gunner's O.P. near Cambrai in 1918 and seeing four Germans doing a sprint under similar conditions. For once I felt a definite kinship to the Hun: I, too, had been at the wrong end of the telescope.) In the next trench we again set about searching the dug-outs and placarding them, to catch the eye of the stretcher-bearers who would follow, as containing so many wounded for removal; but again the Hun gunners got on to us in an exposed place and we had a second sprint across the open for another trench, where we had to stay below in a *sous-terrain* for an hour till things got quieter.

This dug-out was typical of the many with which Beaumont Hamel was honeycombed. On descending about forty steps one was in a large floored and timbered chamber some fifty feet long; and at the further end a second set of steps led to a similar chamber, one side of each being lined with a double layer of bunks filled with dead and wounded Germans, the majority of whom had become casualties early on the morning of the 13th.

The place was, of course, in utter darkness; and, when we flashed our lights on and the wounded saw our escort with rifles ready, there was an outbreak of "Kamarad!" while a big bevy of rats squeaked and scuttled away from their feast on the dead bodies on the floor. The stench was indescribably abominable: for many of the cases were gas-gangrenous. Any food or drink they had possessed was used up, and our water bottles were soon emptied amongst them. After we had gone over the upper chamber and separated the living from the dead, we went to the lower one where the gas curtain was let down and fastened. Tearing it aside and going through with a light, I got a momentary jump when I caught a glimpse in the upper bunk of a man, naked to the waist, and with his right hand raised above his head. But the poor beggar was far past mischief—stark and stiff with a smashed pelvis. Some twenty other dead Germans lay about at the disposal of the rat hordes. The romance of war had worn somewhat thin here.

When the shelling had eased up and we quitted the place, the wounded firmly believed they were being left for good; although we had repeatedly assured them that in a short time they would all be taken to hospital. But to the end of the campaign the wounded Boche could never understand that he was not going to be treated with the same brutality he had meted out to others at the outset of war; so it was amidst a chorus of shrieks, wails and supplications that we made for the welcome open air, ticketed the dug-out as containing fourteen wounded for removal, and renewed our search in similar surroundings for fresh casualties.

One other memory of Beaumont Hamel is still vivid. Parallel to Wagon Road, and on its Auchonvillers side, ran a *chemin creux* in which were several dug-outs where we—and the Division on our left—had Battalion R.A.P.'s. It had been severely shelled and the sides of the road had fallen in, reducing the cart track to a foot-path knee deep in mud. Going up it one morning soon after daybreak, I saw a headless corpse lying on a stretcher at the path side. From the neck a trickle of blood ran to the feet of a man outside a dug-out who was calmly frying some ham in his canteen lid over an improvised oil-can stove. His mate—fag in mouth—was watching him. What was beside them had ceased to be worth comment. They were surfeited with evil sights. And they were hungry.

On the 16th, Tenderloin in White City became our H.Q. for forward evacuation; and there with two M.O.s and a hundred and twenty bearers we stayed until the 19th, searching all possible locations in the field for any cases possibly missed, and clearing a large quantity of wounded for the Division on our left, who were stunting and whose R.A.P.s could not be cleared without our help. All this time White City and the roads into Beaumont Hamel were distinctly unhealthy, and the weather was vile; while the atmosphere inside our dug-outs—one long chamber with over a hundred and twenty occupants—was almost palpable. A wash was an unknown luxury, of course; but though lousy we were cheerful—even tuneful at times, thanks to the corporal's penny whistle and a veteran gramophone—as our job was nearly done.

By the 22nd our unit had still twenty-four bearers in the R.A.P.s at Beaumont Hamel, twenty-four at Tenderloin, thirty-six in reserve at Auchonvillers, and a tent sub-division at the A.D.S. at Mailly-Maillet; while, in addition, we were running the M.D.S. at Forceville, handed over to us by the 3rd H.F.A., which had left for Puchevillers; so our hands were fairly full. But, on the 23rd, we handed over, and started overhauling equipment in view of our next move.

What Field Ambulance officer does not recall overhauling equipment after a push? The counting of stretchers, blankets, wheeled carriers, etc., etc.; the exploring of Field Medical and Surgical panniers to check missing "unexpendables"; and the inevitable and unanimous finding of all concerned that what couldn't be found had certainly been destroyed by shell-fire! However, on this occasion we had increased and multiplied exceedingly; for we came away from Beaumont Hamel outstandingly to the good in the essential matters of blankets, stretchers, and especially wheeled stretcher carriers; so that the soul of the A.D.M.S. rejoiced within him, until at the first D.D.M.S. conference he had to meet his suffering and blood-thirsty colleagues who had been on our right and left flanks.

Four days later we moved from Forceville to Senlis, and took over a set of hutments on top of a windswept hill above the village from a Canadian Field Ambulance, finding the place—to be quite honest—in a most unholy mess. He was a good man, the Canuck, right enough, and "a bonny fechter"; but he had a way of his own all through the campaign. Our advance party officer was taken round the show by a Canadian *confrère* (in shirt sleeves, breeches and gum-boots) who, on giving an order to a sergeant *en passant*, received the reply:—

"You go to ——, John!"

The officer's only comment was a grieved:—

"Well, now! He shouldn't say that, should he?"— and the matter apparently ended!

Here, then, we stayed for several uncomfortable cold and wet weeks while the Division was in the line at Courcelette;[1] thence for some weeks of severe frost to the Buigny-St. Maclou area near Abbeville, where we were not far from historic Crecy. Later, we were once more at the hutments of Haute Avesnes; and marched thence to Caucourt, on the other side of D.H.Q. at Villers Chatel, to run a Divisional Rest Station and prepare the forward medical posts for the next push, the famous Vimy Ridge battle, where the 51st were on the right of the Canadians.

---

[1] "During December, 1916, and part of January, 1917, the Division was in the Courcelette sector, where things were far from peaceful and hardships were extreme. In February they moved north to Arras and remained there till the Battle of Arras."—(*The Territorial Divisions.*)

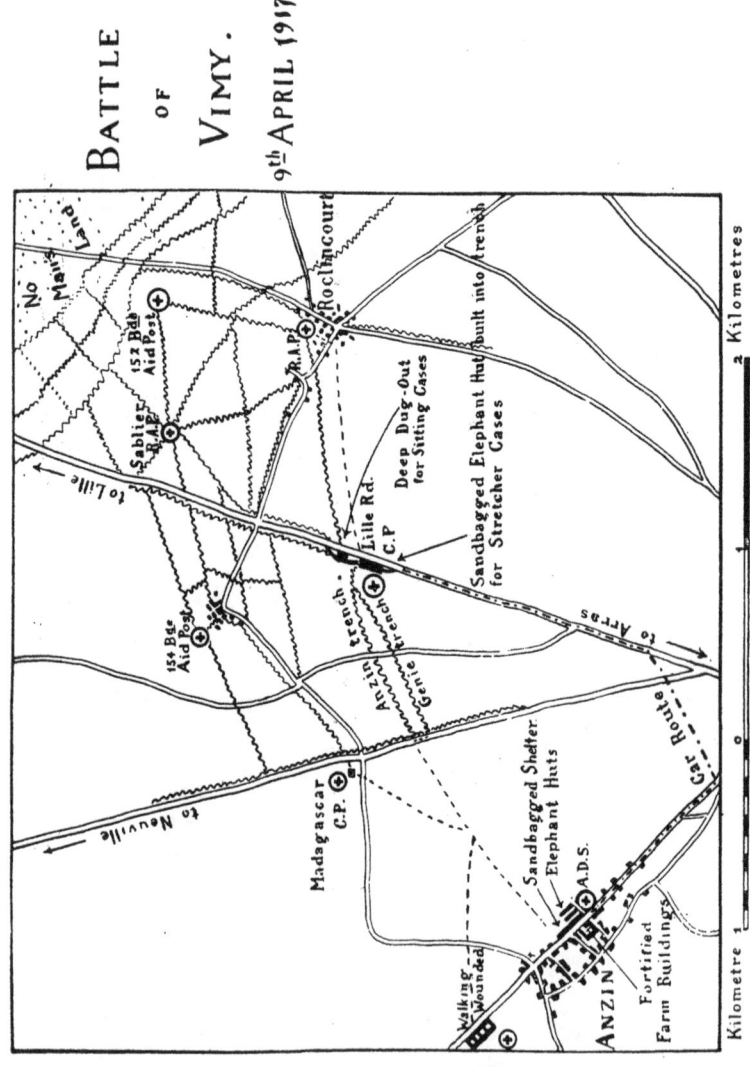

CHAPTER VI.

The Battle of Arras, 1917.

A pair of eyes a-twinklin' beneath a roof o' tin,
A copper nose a-stickin' out above a cheery grin,
Have you met him? Did you know him? agoin' out or in
O' the line 'twixt the dusk and the dawnin'!

"The Battle of Arras commenced on the 9th April, 1917. The 51st Division, then in the XVII Corps, Third Army, attacked east of Roclincourt, north-east of Arras: they were near the left of the line and next the Canadians, whose task it was to seize the main Vimy Ridge. The 51st and its neighbour on the right, the 34th Division, had heavy fighting. Their advance was delayed, not checked. The whole attack on the 9th was a great success. The fighting between the 9th and the 14th is now the First Battle of the Scarpe, 1917. On the 12th the Division left the line, re-entering it on the 15th-16th, and remaining in the battle till the 24th-28th. On the 23rd April our troops made a big attack on a front of nine miles: the Second Battle of the Scarpe. North of the Scarpe the 51st Division were engaged in heavy fighting at Rouex Wood and the Chemical Works. On the 24th the attack was renewed and more progress was then made. For their splendid work on the 23rd the Division was thanked and congratulated by the Corps and Army Commanders. The losses of the Division during April amounted to about 4,000. . . ."—(*The Territorial Divisions.*)

FOR the next impending battle our Advanced Dressing Station and the Walking Wounded Collecting Post were fixed at Anzin on the Arras-Mont St. Eloi road, where some accommodation capable of extension already existed; while at Madagascar, a kilometre across country in front on the Arras-Bethune road, was a dug-out serving as Relay Bearer Post; leaving a Collecting Post—the Lille Road Post—to be constructed another good kilometre nearer the line, in an old trench running alongside the Arras-Lille road. Here, marking off some seventy feet of the trench, we set about deepening it, broadening it, and roofing it with iron "English Shelters," a thinner type of the heavy "Elephant Shelter"; on top of them, again, laying sandbags filled with the excavated earth. Three tiers of stretcher racks were fitted on each side of the interior, the whole available space being about fifty feet by ten, and holding forty wounded; while in the middle, with sandbagged partition walls in case of a hit, was a chamber set apart as a dressing room.

All this meant steady and hard work for the R.A.M.C. fatigue parties of the three Divisional Field Ambulances from the end of February up to the very eve of the battle, as the bulk of the work had to be done in the dark owing to the position being under enemy observation. Steps, too, had to be cut down from the road and fixed with wood; while, at the top of these, the road itself had to be widened and stones hammered in to make a turning-point for the motor ambulance cars. Still, when the job was finished on the night of 8th April and we had gone below for a rest before Zero hour—a retiral that was hastened by a dose of shrapnel from the enemy, as it was moonlight and we had been over trustful in the concealing power of a ground mist—our post had fairly good head-cover and was safe enough, short of a direct hit from heavy stuff.

On our right, some three kilometres away, lay St. Catharine, a suburb of Arras: on our left, the remains of the village of Ecurie: while in front of us, in the dip, were the ruins of Roclincourt, to which, and the trenches, ran a hand trolley line, similar lines running back to Madagascar and Anzin. It was on our programme that these were to be used for carrying back casualties, but the combatant traffic soon knocked this on the head; so we were dependent throughout the battle on hand and wheeled stretcher carriage from the line to the Collecting

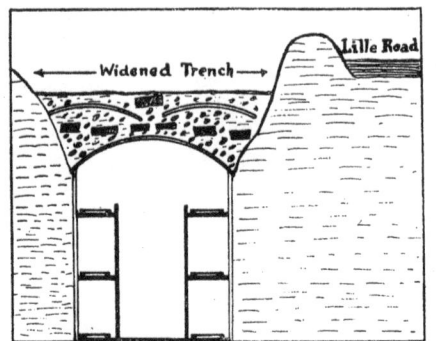

Shows arrangement of stretchers in tiers

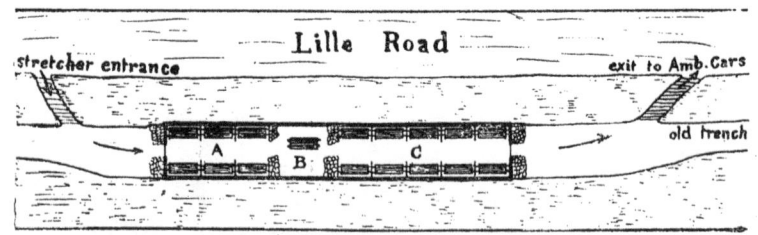

Shows partitioning of the interior
 A. Stretcher cases awaiting dressing.
 B. Operating room.
 C. Cases ready for removal when cars available

Post, and on motor ambulance cars from the Collecting Post to the Advanced Dressing Station at Anzin.

The cars clearing the Lille Road Post had to run to St. Catharine and negotiate a hairpin bend there to get on the road to Anzin, a total distance of some seven kilometres: across country via Madagascar was only about two. A short cut "switch" road from leg to leg of the hairpin had been made some distance from Anzin in preparation for the push; but early in the battle it was needed for guns and ammunition going forward, and our sole car evacuation route afterwards was the longer one.

From left to right our posts in the trenches were Abri Mouton (a specially enlarged dug-out), Sabliers (another dug-out in a sandpit), and a third post in a freshly made dug-out at Fish Avenue, where all the M.O.s of the 152nd Brigade worked together. A further supplementary Aid Post was available in a cellar at Roclincourt. All these had been provided with a plentiful supply of medical stores, blankets, stretcher pillows and stretchers, with an extra chocolate ration for our bearers.

The weather had been for some days wet and cold. This, incidentally, was due—although one might not have thought it—to the fact that it was Holy Week; so the fair daughter of the farmer who was our host at Caucourt informed us. "Le temps est toujours mauvais la Semaine Sainte jusqu'au Dimanche passèe."

At 4.30 a.m. on 9th April, the day of the battle, all hands were roused and the Collecting Post given a final clean up. At 5 the first car was up in readiness, and at 5.30 our barrage started, presenting a weird spectacle of hellish intensity. Day was just breaking, and the dawn was illuminated with the long line of bursting shells, to which the golden rain and coloured S.O.S. rockets of the enemy lent a strangely picturesque variety of colour.

The noise was terrific with the continuous whistling scream—like a furious gale of wind—of the thousands of heavy missiles going over us to the enemy's lines, and the thunderous drumming of their arrival.

At 6 the barrage ceased and the advancing troops were visible from the Lille Road going over the first ridge. But casualties were now coming in (chiefly men hit in the assembly trenches before the advance had commenced), and soon every one was busy—carrying the wounded down to the shelter, dressing them there and loading the cars.

In a nook left between the end of the stretcher racks and the exit from the shelter was set a small collapsible table, whereto were pinned a map of the district and a more detailed one of the trenches, both together making up the board on which you played your own special little game of chess against unforeseen circumstances. A clip took in all the "chits" from the M.O.s at the various R.A.P.s, chronologically arranged as they came in, and marked with the hour of receipt, by the Sergeant Clerk who sat beside you. Each message was supposed to have the hour of its despatch written on it by the sender: fifty per cent of them never had. Many were soaked and barely decipherable—medical handwriting is somewhat peculiar at best, especially when written in indelible pencil which had "run." Many demands were indefinite—"more stretchers," "more bearers," "more dressings": others asked for impossible and exaggerated quantities. Here your knowledge of the sender's mentality had to come in, and you discounted the requests of the M.O. who thought too imperially, and dealt with him on more parochial lines. One M.O., who was a bit "rattled" (and no wonder), might have sent off three messages one after another, all without the hour of despatch stated; and you had to make a shot at which was the latest one (and, therefore, that to be dealt with),

Lille Road Collecting Post.

1. The Trench before we tackled it.   2. The finished product. (Ecurie in distance.)

Facing page 120.

THE BATTLE OF ARRAS, 1917.

as messenger 2 and 1 might turn up in that order after messenger 3.

All the time, too, if you were wise (for it paid you to do it), you were jotting down a running tale of how things progressed, your literary efforts interrupted by visits here and there to lend a hand in dressing cases and loading cars; or by interviewing messengers and supervising the issue of stores in response to indents, and seeing that other indents were going back at once for fresh supplies. Then your map had to be kept up to date as the Regimental Aid Posts changed when the battalions advanced, and all such changes had to be duly notified to the A.D.M.S. Altogether you were the head of a somewhat irritable family, whose nerves, after some hours of it, were apt to get a bit jangled: knowing, too, as regards yourself, that you were the certain recipient of criticism, both from those above and those below you in rank, for all that went wrong; and at the very least expected to remedy the unexpected with the speed of Hermes and the patience of Job. But, above all, your *métier* was to "cock your bonnet and whistle," to be, like Sydney Smith, a "good-humorist," and to preserve throughout all your troubles the placid, enigmatic smile of a Mona Lisa.

Take a look at the map, then, and read the medical account of this battle as it was written down hour by hour for three days in the Collecting Post:—

April 9th.—6 a.m. Ambulance cars bringing in casualties sustained in assembly trenches before advance commenced.

6.45 a.m. M.O. Abri Mouton reports he has thirty bearers and twenty-five Trench Mortar Battery[1] men available, and no demands for them so far. Told to send orderly here to await orders, and meanwhile rest his men till needed. Steady stream of casualties coming in here.

---

[1] During a push the T.M.B.s were at this date usually free to act as stretcher-bearers.

8.10 a.m. M.O. at Madagascar reports twenty-four German prisoners who have been examined by Intelligence Officer available as bearers. No demands yet, so told to hold on to them.

8.30 a.m. M.O. at Sabliers reports things going on steadily and no hitch. Wants ten fresh tins of water. Sent.

8.45 a.m. Some wounded Huns now coming in and plenty prisoners passing back. Work so far well in hand.

8.50 a.m. Satisfactory report from M.O. Sabliers. M.O. Abri Mouton reports only a few cases.

10.30. a.m. Interviewed Tramway Officer and then notified M.O. Fish Avenue that 6 trollies were now free for use from Roclincourt to Lille Road Post, but route will be difficult to work, as all uphill from Roclincourt and trollies will have to be lifted to pass ammunition traffic going forward.

10.45 a.m. All reports show evacuation steady and rapid considering distance from now advanced front line and length of hand-carrying required.

11 a.m. No R.A.M.C. casualties so far. M.O. Sabliers reports wire from O.C. 9th Royal Scots that bearers are urgently needed for No. 1 Co. between new front line and Black Line. Estimated 80 cases. Ordered M.O. Abri Mouton to send T.M.B. officer and 36 men to M.O. Sabliers. Called up reserve Bearer Division of 3rd H.F.A. from Anzin and ordered M.O. Madagascar to hold 50 Huns in readiness. Messages later: orders carried out.

11.14 a.m. Cleared 16 casualties off road right back across country to Anzin by hand-carriage, as Collecting Post choc-a-bloc. Casualties coming in freely. M.O. Fish Avenue asks 36 bearers; sent 36 Huns from Madagascar. Drew 10 for auxiliary loaders here also.

12 noon. Reported to A.D.M.S. on 'phone. Snow now falling heavily.

2 p.m. Notified A.D.S. Anzin to keep all available cars in front area to clear us.

4 p.m. Went round Sabliers and Fish Avenue and

3

4
Lille Road Collecting Post.

3. The Post under snow.
4. The loaded cars leaving for Anzin A.D.S.

Facing page 122.

trenches in front of Roclincourt. At Sabliers saw liaison
M.O. Field Ambulance and M.O.s 7th Black Watch and
4th Gordons. Called at 154 Bde. H.Q. and saw Brigadier
regarding new positions. Saw O.C. 7th Black Watch
and got 24 men from him to assist in clearing the field,
as we have to make the most of daylight owing to extreme
cold and steadily increasing fall of snow. Phoned 153rd
Bde. H.Q. for further parties from Bde. in reserve as
per operation orders. After some delay got parties of
50 each from 7th Gordons and 6th Black Watch. These
parties to search field all night, drawing stretchers from
reserve supply at Sabliers and Fish Avenue. Transferred
all bearers (less two men to look after stores) from Abri
Mouton to Sabliers. At Fish Avenue saw liaison M.O.
Field Ambulance and M.O.s 6th Seaforths, 6th Gordons
and 8th A. & S.H., who reported everything going
steadily. Called at 152nd Bde. H.Q. and saw Brigadier,
who said he was satisfied from his own knowledge that
our work was going on all right. M.O. Abri Mouton
brought back to assist M.O. at Lille Road Post. Abri
Mouton now a wash-out: nothing doing.

8 p.m. Got back by trolley track from Roclincourt.
Track now no use to us owing to snow and constant
ammunition traffic. Phoned report to A.D.M.S.

8.30 p.m. Heavy snow still falling. Collecting Post
acutely congested and 130 overflow cases in open on roadside round about it, owing to no cars coming up. Cars
held up by (1) switch road not available through guns
going up: (2) block on Arras-Lille Road through motor
lorry colliding with gun: (3) all cars on evacuation roads
to M.D.S. going slow through heavy up traffic. Turned
on all available bearers and Huns to hand-carry and wheel-
stretcher the casualties across country to Anzin. Got 50
cases away thus. The long rows of snow-covered,
blanketed figures on the stretchers are a sad sight.
Phoned A.D.M.S. to clear Anzin A.D.S. if possible by
M.A.C. cars and release all F.A. cars to clear Lille
Road Post. All suitable cases in open given hot coffee
and soup, and all spare blankets on them. Hand
stretchers and wheeled stretchers hard at it across open to
Anzin.

10 p.m. Cars have got through again and cases here rapidly diminishing.

12 Midnight. Heavy snow and very cold. Majority of cases cleared.

April 10th.—5 a.m. Still snowing heavily. Steady but lessening stream of cases coming in. Large percentage from dug-outs and shell holes who had been hit early in action: shews field is being well searched and cleared. Many of them enemy cases.

9 a.m. 30 rested bearers now available at Abri Mouton. Brought them here for loaders to relieve Huns who are played out. Huns fed at soup kitchen and sent back to Madagascar.

11.30 a.m. A.D.M.S. up. M.O. Fish Avenue reports his area all cleared.

4 p.m. Reports in from Fish Avenue and Sabliers giving map references of new Regimental Aid Posts. Both report their areas well cleared up. This is borne out by lessening number of cases coming back, and these mostly of the "hit-early" shell hole type. Wrote out detailed report for A.D.M.S. No bearer casualties, and all ranks have worked splendidly.

8 p.m. Things practically stopped: an odd case now and then.

April 11th.—7 a.m. Only 6 cases in through night. Men rested and had 4 hours sleep. First chance since push began.

12 noon. Received report of M.O. 7th Black Watch[1] being killed by stray shell. M.O. from here sent up in his stead. Things now quiet. Several cases of exhaustion and prostration from severe cold have come in.

3 p.m. Received Operation Orders *re* relief here by F.A.s of 2nd Division, to be carried out on 11th and night 11th-12th. Started checking stores at all posts. D.A.D.M.S. 2nd Division with M.O. of 5th F.A. up *re* relief. Cannot get his Ambulances up by time specified. Suggested he should relieve Sabliers and Fish Avenue at 7 a.m. to-morrow, and Lille Road Post and Anzin by

[1] Captain E. J. Blair, M.C.

THE BATTLE OF ARRAS, 1917.

9 a.m. This allows our men to have a night's rest and let the R.A.P.s be relieved by daylight. Agreed.

6 p.m. M.O.s Sabliers and Fish Avenue report their areas all carefully searched again and found all clear of casualties. Some new R.A.P. map references. Sent on to A.D.M.S. Things quiet. All personnel resting.

April 12th.—10 a.m. Relief completed: all routes demonstrated to incomers: receipts signed: unit moved to Acq.

The comic relief at Lille Road Post was supplied by "James," one of our Hun auxiliary loaders. His real name, I suppose, was Heinrich Schneider or something of that sort; but, as he spoke good English, he was appointed interpreter for enemy wounded, and put in charge of his whole-skinned countrymen who were assisting to carry casualties down to and up from the dressing room. He had been—so he said, and there was no reason to doubt it—for ten years before the war a waiter at the Hotel Cecil, hence the temporary name bestowed on him; and his behaviour was certainly a curious mixture of the soldier and the waiter. When spoken to he came sharply to attention (military), with a gentle bend forwards from the waist (Hotel Cecil); while his prompt "Yessir!" almost made one see the napkin over his arm. Stoutish, broadish, and—to us, his captors—affable, he magnified his office with evident relish, and treated his hoplites with true Hunnish high-handedness.

From the entrance to the dressing room I overheard my colleague, who was busy with a wounded enemy casualty at one period of the first day's work, giving James a high moral lesson, in a clear, somewhat professorial style.

"You will observe, James, that here, contrary to the custom of your countrymen in this war, we treat our wounded enemies with the same consideration extended to our own troops,"

"Yessir!"

"Before the war, James, I had travelled much in your Fatherland, and had failed to detect the degeneracy—"

"Yessir!"

"—Which has since, evidently, developed with such alarming rapidity."

"Yessir!"

"Cruelty, on our part, is not made a matter of military routine."

"Yessir!"

"You mean 'No sir,' I think, James?"

"No sir!"

"Ah, well! The case is dressed; summon your comrades."

"Yessir! *Achtung! Zwei träger! Aufheben!*"

And away went James with his compatriots to load the case on a back-going car.

After twelve hours of it, James came to me, saluted, and remarked:—

"Sir, I and my men are exhausted."

"I and my men are also exhausted, James."

"Yessir! But we had no sleep for two nights before this battle."

"Right, James, I shall believe you and relieve you."

So, in charge of a sergeant, James and Co. were sent along the trench to the Divisional Soup Kitchen to have a good feed, and were thence taken below to an old French dug-out, where various worn-out bearers of our own were resting.

Later, it was reported to me that James was missing; and although we made a perfunctory search for him, we could not find him. Two hours afterwards I was passing a small recess blanketed off from the sandbag wall of the dressing-room, in which was a stretcher and some blankets, placed there for my accommodation with kindly forethought by the staff-sergeant, should an opportunity for rest come along. Hearing a stertorous snort, I pulled back the blanket and discovered James sound asleep in my bed, evidently under the impression that his "staff job" entitled him to some precedence. The humour of it tickled me so much that I left him; but his snores gave him away to others before long, and he was "put back where he belonged."

When the time came to hand him and his comrades over to the A.P.M.'s guard, James asked to see me, and giving his salute-cum-bow said:—

"Sir, I trust I have given satisfaction!"

"Let your mind be easy, James: you have."

"Sir, I hope we shall meet again."

"When, James?"

"After the war, sir."

"And where, James?"

"At the Hotel Cecil, sir!"

With which pious hope James solemnly saluted and vanished into the gloom of the trench.

To Acq, then, as aforesaid, we went: mud-stained and very weary. And, as our messroom was not of the roomiest, my fellow-officers decided to dine, with many similarly minded officers of other units, at the well-known "Marguerite's," of whose establishment the song goes:—

> I mind me 'twas in '17
> And Spring, when leaves were turning green,
> We happened where we oft had been,
>   It was a beaten track;
> And there, just off the village street,
> Behold the house of Marguerite,
> Who gave us veal with good *pommes frites*
>   And omelettes at Acq.
>
> Fair was the lass, Ay! passing fair,
> And, as she stood behind your chair
> To press you to her dainty fare,
>   You blessed the maiden sweet;
> Forgot the mud, the blood, the trench,
> The airless dug-out's fetid stench,
> And toasted high the comely wench,
>   '*Votre santé, Marguerite!*

A cheery, rackety crew; gunners, foot-sloggers, A.S.C.—all were there—with a sprinkling of Canadians; clouds of tobacco smoke; corks popping and a jingley piano going thirteen to the dozen; while those who could sing did so, the majority merely contributed a joyful noise. *Dulce est desipere in loco:* "let us eat, drink, and be merry, for to-morrow we die": a somewhat emotional outburst, doubtless, of the nerve-strained. History tells us that throughout the ages the intervals of rest time in war have seldom been lucid: the picture has been stereotyped and the cannikin has always clinked.

> The wine is red and the wit is keen,
> Joy's heel on the neck of Sorrow!
> And we reck no more of the Might-have-been
> Or To-morrow—Oh! Damn To-morrow!

In Acq we remained, resting and overhauling equipment, till the 16th, when we moved to St. Nicolas, on the outskirts of Arras, taking over there from the 28th F.A. an A.D.S. consisting of four parallel tunnels, each some fifty feet long, running back into the hillside, fitted with stretcher racks and capable of holding in all about a hundred and fifty casualties. The tunnels opened on flat ground covered with ruins, some of which had been sufficiently repaired to serve as offices, a dressing-room, stretcher and blanket stores, cookhouses, etc.; while beyond it again the ground dipped to a light railway running parallel to the river Scarpe up the valley towards Fampoux and Rœux by way of Blangy and L'Abbayette, all these places being in ruins. At the last-named was the Collecting Post; and at Fampoux, Three Arches (of the railway embankment), and Athies Lock, were **Relay Bearer Posts**; while the **Walking Wounded Collecting Post** was in tentage about a kilometre up the valley road. Fighting was going on at the famous Chemical Works and a steady run of casualties came in all day.

The roofs of the tunnels, unfortunately, owing to the

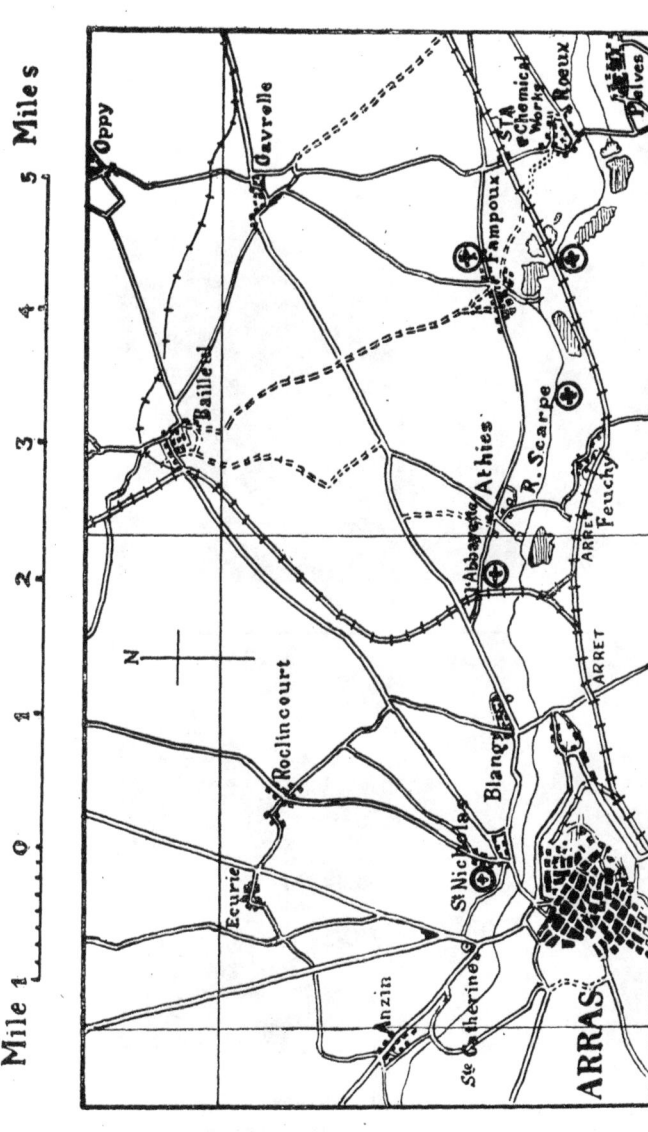

Battle of Arras. April–May 1917.

Medical Posts.

1

2

A.D.S. at St. Nicolas.

1. Roclincourt Road. The small arch to left is the entrance to A.D.S.
2. Inside the arch: the car track to the Dressing Station.

Facing page 129.

persistently wet weather, dripped steadily; and as all ranks were underneath them this did not make for comfort, especially as the water which found its way through was not even clean. At night the unlucky possessor of an upper bunk had to tack his ground-sheet on to the earth roof above him, a precarious protection at best; as in time the sheet bellied out with the accumulated water, and either tore itself from its fastenings, or at the least touch poured out on to the ill-starred sleeper from each end. The tunnels, too, could not be ventilated, smelt like a tomb, and were "fuggy" to a degree; but there were some forty feet of head cover, which made up for many minor deficiencies.

Till the 19th the weather continued vile, and we were busy both with cases coming in (many of them casualties from Blangy and the valley road, which the enemy shelled steadily) and with improving the accommodation—clearing fresh tracks through the ruins, firming up the incoming and outgoing roads for the motor ambulance wagons, and getting up some operation tents for "sitting cases" when space was available. It was always a matter of duty, honour, pride and routine that those in possession should make a place of this sort better than when it had been handed over; and the outcome was that, in some of the sites where unit after unit had worked at the job for months, a wonderfully high standard was attained.

On the 22nd, in view of a new Divisional push the next day, the Bearer Divisions of the Field Ambulances went up to Blangy for distribution to the R.A.P.s (twelve to each) and to the various Relay Bearer Posts. A hundred and fifty extra bearers (from the 5th Gordons and Trench Mortar Battery) were also in readiness, to be sent in relays, as required, by the Field Ambulance cars going up the valley for casualties. Twelve bandsmen also reported for work as loaders at St. Nicolas. All day Arras was shelled intermittently and the valley road steadily.

On Zero day reveille was at 4 a.m., and by 6 the usual steady stream of casualties commenced to come in by our cars, the bearers near the Chemical Works being exposed to very heavy shell and machine-gun fire. One squad of four was carrying a casualty shoulder-high on a stretcher when a shell struck it, knocking the men over in a heap, and carrying stretcher and occupant some ten yards before it burst. The wounded man was blown to bits; but the bearers were unhurt except for the strained neck muscles of the two who had been on the leeward side—a truly lucky escape for them.

German prisoners could always be depended on for marvellous information, and one enemy casualty distinguished himself that day by assuring us that Hindenburg had committed suicide; which, unfortunately, while a cheery bit of gossip, turned out to be untrue.

Between 10 and 11 a.m. over twenty shells landed in our vicinity, one hitting the office of Divisional Signals in the dip below, killing one man and wounding several more; while another landed at our entrance, fortunately at a time when no car was there.

All that day and all night we were busy with casualties, many still coming from the narrow valley road, on which movement was necessarily slow, crowded as it was with the dense traffic of guns and wagons (ammunition, motor, g.s., ambulance and limber). Going up it on a car one would progress slowly for five minutes, then halt for ten, and then on again; and the wonder was (especially at freely shelled spots like the famous broken railway arch at L'Abbayette) that casualties were not more numerous. During our stay here our unit lost one bearer killed in action, one died of wounds,[1] two were wounded and returned to duty, while seven were wounded and evacuated.

[1] Privates J. Sinclair and C. Yells,

A.D.S. at St. Nicolas.

3. Entrance to Dressing Room.
4. Entrance (on right) to one of the tunnels.

Facing page 130.

On the morning of the 25th April, having dealt during our stay at St. Nicolas with 747 cases, we handed over to the 102nd F.A., and on the 26th moved to Agnieres, a small village near Aubigny.

Two days later we moved by Berlette, Berles, Penin, Maizieres, and Gouy-en-Ternois, to Monts-en-Ternois.

It was glorious spring weather, redolent of the promise of even better things to come, and the *coquet* little village, with its red tiled roofs shewing through the verdant leafage, was welcome to our eyes. Truly we could say with St. Francis:—"Praised be God for our Sister Mother Earth, which brings forth varied fruits and grass and glowing flowers." For to us, freshly come from all the desolation of ruined Arras, it seemed no ordinary thing to see a normal countryside with daisies, buttercups, green trees and grass, and the houses whole and untouched by shell fire. A hen and her little fluffy yellow brood, straggling along a side road, came as a wonder seen for the first time; a sight to be followed and leisurely enjoyed, until, doubting the honourable nature of our intentions, the harassed mother hysterically drove us away by a headlong charge. Bliss Carman gives us the spirit of it all:—

> Make me over Mother April,
> When the sap begins to stir.
> Make me man or make me woman
> Make me oaf, or ape or human,
> Cup of flower or cone of fir;
> Make me anything but neuter
> When the sap begins to stir!

And when the bells of the little village church sounded their peaceful call, back to mind came the sonorous lines of Dunbar:—

> Tak consolation in your pain,
>   In tribulation tak consolation,
> Out of vexation come hame again
>   Tak consolation in your pain.

Did they so interpret themselves to the ears of poor M. le Curé, who, crippled with rheumatism, spent most of his time chair-fast in the damp little *presbytère* beside the church, or painfully hobbling about his walled-in and flower-filled garden? I fear me no: use and wont may have deadened their power so to do. He had been called up for service, but was soon invalided out. We ministered to his many infirmities within the limits of our skill and our Field Medical Panniers; but I think he got most help in his physical affliction from the regular rubbings and kindly sympathy of our masseur.

The billets for the men were good (although many preferred bivouacking in the open), while the horses openly rejoiced in, and daily improved their condition by, the unusual nibble of greenery.

Here we remained, then, in the loveliest of weather (the farmers, of course, after the manner of their kind, declaring everything was being burnt up, and expressing polite disagreement should one remark that *le temps est très beau*) until the 10th of May—rejoicing in our environment, resting, overhauling equipment, undergoing a thorough horse inspection by the G.O.C. (for who knew, or loved a horse better than "Uncle" Harper?). Holding football matches, too (did not our unit defeat the 5th Seaforths by 2-0, with Neil Munro, no less, as a spectator?), and open-air concerts, where our orchestra of violins, now a valuable part of our social life, put in some good work with the aid of the padre's harmonium; although "why the dickens don't they specialise more in Scottish music, reels, strathspeys, etc.?" is a critical note in my diary. Then we moved again to our old venue, the hutments of Haute Avesnes; taking over there the vacant section of the Corps Main Dressing Station, and having as colleagues the 12th and 28th Field Ambulances.

St. Nicolas was once more the Divisional A.D.S., this time in the hands of the 2/1st H.F.A.; and an officer with our bearer division was sent there to assist, the rest of our unit carrying on the usual M.D.S. routine until the 30th May. The number of casualties was not unduly high; there was no stress on our personnel; and it was an uneventful stay. On the 13th, in the late afternoon, the ammunition dump at Wanquetin, some ten kilometres away, blew up, and even at that distance was an extraordinary spectacle: huge explosions at intervals sending up sheets of flame and clouds of smoke amidst which shells of all sizes and varieties exploded high in the air. A large portion of the village was destroyed; and the yarn went that the damage was caused, not by the Hun, but by a sentry lighting a brazier in his sentry-box and leaving it unattended.

A good many German wounded went through on the 17th from the 94th and 95th Thuringian Regiments. One was an iron cross man: another, shot through the chest, was a non-commissioned officer though only 17 years of age. Asked what his fellow countrymen were thinking about the war now, he replied, "What care I? Am I to live or die? That alone is of interest to me!" Another Boche had his right arm shattered: shot—so he said—by his officer for not advancing promptly. Two more there were some days later, both of whom came into British hands after lying out for twenty days near their own lines; one vilely septic, with commencing tetanus, the other *in articulo mortis*.

On the 21st our officer with the bearer division took over the front line evacuation, with H.Q. at L'Abbayette: twenty bearers at Fampoux village: forty at Beaver Lock, Fampoux; and a small party at Athies Lock. Evacuation ran from the R.A.P.s either to Fampoux village, whence to St. Nicolas by Ford cars; or to Beaver Lock, and thence on the canalised Scarpe in pontoons to Athies Lock, where the casualties were transferred to cars; an alternative route being by Decauville light railway straight from Beaver Lock to St. Nicolas. As the light railway and the canal were as freely shelled as the road, and as progress on the waterway was, further, a slow-going business at best, most of the cases found their way to the village post and down the valley by car. A road was generally more quickly repaired than a railway.

It was always a tricky old valley. Going round the posts one day with our only Hibernian, things were quiet, the day was fine, and we strolled along the tow-path of the canal engaged in cheerful and improving discourse worthy of "The Compleat Angler." Suddenly old Fritz let go at the landscape, one shell landing in the mud swamp which had once been the opposite bank of the canal. I hastily embraced a large poplar tree on the side away from the enemy, while showers of mud descended everywhere; and then I discovered that I could see no sign of my companion.

"Where are you?" I sang out.

"Where you'd be yourself, sir, if you had any sense at all," came the reply from nowhere I could see.

Much struck by the respectful and practical nature of this reply, I at last detected the top of his tin hat in a neighbouring shell hole, and promptly joined him there: Jerry giving us a quite unsolicited encore, and my colleague a spasmodic lecture to me on the advantages, under such circumstances, of shell holes over poplar trees. And he was quite right, too: he knew his natural history well.

The military cemetery, left at L'Abbayette by the Germans, had some exceptionally well-finished memorials of slatey stone, engraved and even gilt-lettered. One had a well-carved head of Christ on it. Where they got the stones, tools, and opportunity for doing the work was a mystery: but they had a characteristic trick of breaking up the French memorials in the communal cemeteries and using them for their own purposes.

By the 27th our bearers were "out."

CHAPTER VII.

The Battles of the Pilkem and Menin Road Ridges, 1917.

Ye who the deadly days have spent
While cursing in the Salient,
Or crouched in holes to dodge the bomb
And shell-burst of the strenuous Somme. . . .

"The Battle of Pilkem Ridge, at the beginning of the Third Battle of Ypres, commenced on 31st July, 1917, amongst the Divisions engaged being the 51st, then in the XVIII Corps, Fifth Army. They were near the left of the British line, and along with Welsh and Guards battalions secured the crossings of the Steenbeck. The losses of the Division were about 1,600 and they took about 650 prisoners. On the 20th September, along with the 58th Division, they gained the whole of their objectives by mid-day in the Battle of the Menin Road Ridge, with Divisional losses of 1,150. Both Corps and Army Commanders congratulated the Division on its work, the former saying, 'I venture to place it among the three best fighting divisions I have met in France during the past three years.' About this time the enemy published a statement that the 51st was the most formidable division[1] on the Western Front."—*(The Territorial Divisions.)*

ON the 30th May our unit marched by Hermaville, Izel-les-Hameaux, Penin and Maizieres to Ternas, two miles north from our late location of Monts-en-Ternois. Like it, Ternas was a clean village and *assez pittoresque*, billets being above the average and the weather excellent for bivouacking. We stayed there for four days, with the usual foot parades, kit inspection, route marches and equipment overhauling, but with plenty of opportunity for rest and recreation.

[1]The order of *Furchtbarkeit* ("much-to-be-fearedness") was:—1. Fifty-first Division. 2. Twenty-ninth Division (Reformed). 3. Guards Division.

While conversing one day with the "lady of the house" at our mess regarding the number and variety of the troops billeted in the village since the war began—there had been a steady stream since October, 1914, of French, English, Irish, Scots—she trotted out the old belief that breaking a mirror causes seven years' bad luck. But she extended it, also, to include a drinking glass as well as a looking glass. "Ah! Yes! It was indeed true! One of her Scottish officers accidentally broke a glass from which he was drinking. He knew, too, that he would have *la guigne*. *Et voila! Il était tué, lui et son ordonnance!* By the same shell, his servant and he! *Quelle tristesse!*"

On the 4th of June we left Ternas, marching in rear of Brigade via Roellecourt, St. Pol and Wavrans to Conteville, starting early and getting in about noon. It was a truly lovely summer day, but too warm for road comfort. Conteville was a clean and prosperous looking little place, rather reminiscent of Sorel. My billet was in the so-called château where we messed, a comfortable country house with a square garden, and in it a guelder rose tree in full bloom. The neighbouring country lanes were hedged with flowering hawthorn, amongst which it was pleasant to "dander" (and the French have *dandiner*) in the gloaming.

The village church, of great age and well kept, had a special chapel dedicated to St. Benoit-Labre, whose life of poverty inspired the common French saying, "pauvre que Labre!" His chapel, gated off from the rest of the church, was built beside the room in the *ancien presbytère* which he used to occupy on his occasional visits to his uncle, M. Vincent, the then parish priest of Conteville. For St. Benoit-Labre (1748-83) was a *pèlerin*, a religious wanderer to shrines; and in this chapel now lay his image in wax, on a pallet on the floor; a most life-like, or rather death-like, apparition to view in the dusk through the iron bars of the locked gate, clad as it was in a reproduction of the ragged—and I fear during his religious activities, rather lousy—apparel he wore as a pilgrim and when he passed away.

The old presbytery was kept as a sort of museum, containing M. Vincent's writing desk and some other articles of furniture; although the various visits of his sainted nephew must have reduced the house plenishings to a minimum. For on one occasion, *par exemple,* the good old curé had returned home to find that St. Benoit had given away the avuncular table and chairs, and to replace them had dug a hole in the earthen floor of the sitting room; pointing out to his doubtless somewhat astonished relative, eager for rest and refreshment, that if they sat on the floor with their feet in this hole, furniture was, after all, not a *sine qua non!* If King David I. was "a sair saint for the croun," Benoit must have been an equally sair saint for his uncle: but it behoves one, I suppose, to put up with unexpected temporal inconveniences when there is a saint in the family, however queer he may be. And truly he was queer enough. Is it not Anatole France who tells us that when Benoit was presented with an old hat his first act was to drag it in the mud before putting it on, thus making it sufficiently disreputable to match the rest of his clothing? Had R.L.S. ever heard of him? It seems not improbable.

As was usually found in the matter of local history, the village people could tell nothing about him, except that his *fête* was on the last Sunday of June; but the old lady of the château kindly gave me a copy of his "life," which copy I lost, to my great regret, with the rest of my kit library, during the March retreat in 1918. In it were told many eccentric tales of a quaintly religious career; and I think it was on my suggestion (and after a vote) that he was adopted as the patron saint of our mess.

Next day — a day of oppressive heat: perhaps the warmest day we ever experienced in France—we marched through very beautiful, undulating country by Hestrus, Eps, Beaumetz les Aires, Heuchin and Reclingham to Coyecques, a tiring and dusty trek of twenty-six kilometres in all, getting in after over a dozen men had fallen out in the last lap, owing to heat and blistered feet, and been picked up by our ambulance cars. It was a pretty little village, and we stayed there two days; the men enjoying the rest, bathing in a stream near by, and one evening having a most successful smoking concert. Two barrels of stout had been imported for the occasion from St. Omer, and a harmonium once more kindly lent for secular purposes by one of the battalion padres, which again eked out the ever vigorous music of our faithful orchestra of fiddlers.

Three days later we set off by way of Saint Martin-au-Laert to the Château de Givenchy at Eperlecques near St. Omer; remaining there for some weeks under canvas in the fine precincts of the château and running a Divisional Rest Station in the ground floor of the building, the weather favouring us. Bathing was available in the large pond of the château, and a very successful item of aquatic sports was carried out: Eperlecques was certainly one of the places all the men looked back on with unalloyed pleasure. At the close of our stay we moved to the other side of St. Omer to another agreeable venue, the hamlet of Clairmarais on the edge of the forest of that name, in whose vicinity were the ruins of an old abbey.

The district was intersected with canals, big and little; and by these water-ways the inhabitants—mostly market gardeners whose little houses were to be seen dotting the banks—carried their produce to the neighbouring town of St. Omer in boats prowed fore and aft, which, in the narrower canals, they propelled by poles, digging these into the bank with short, sharp strokes very difficult of successful imitation by amateurs. But bigger boats with oars were available for the larger canals, which occasionally widened out into small lakes; and our sergeants, having to proceed some distance to their mess, hauled out and patched up an old sunken hulk of some size, in which, following *l'habitude du pays,* they tore through the water like care-free Vikings.

And the canals had helped to make history. By one of them in 1711, when St. Omer was besieged by Prince Eugene and Marlborough, a humble heroine—*une femme du peuple*—named Jacqueline Robins, saved the city at the peril of her life by successfully bringing into it a boat loaded with provisions and munitions.

The farm of Clairmarais, in whose grounds our transport was parked and our tentage for Brigade sick erected, dated back to 1676. It was built largely out of the neighbouring ruins of the old Cistercian abbey, which (founded in 1140 at the instigation of St. Bernard —whose hermit's cell had been at the near-by hamlet of Scoubroucq — by Thierry d'Alsace, Count of Flanders, and his wife, Sibylle) had harboured in 1165 the refugee St. Thomas à Becket. At what date it had been finally destroyed could not be ascertained locally: some said at the Revolution. A mound in the vicinity of the ruins was stated by one old residenter to contain the bodies of four hundred monks who had been guillotined then. He took a somewhat gory, anti-clerical interest in his tale. "Without doubt *there* stood the guillotine! Between these two pillars you still saw in the field. And their heads had been cut off? But yes! Certainly! To the number of four hundred! It was a good tale, was it not? And of great interest? Ah! There were many such in France!"

And yet a pleasant place it was, leaving memories of strolls in the forest glades of Clairmarais or along the banks of the network of canals. It was sometimes no simple task to retrace one's steps after a waterside walk, for it was easy to get lost owing to the many compulsory right-angled turns caused by the smaller canals joining the larger; but a boat was usually available when in difficulties. On one such evening stroll I saw a small bird—a meadow pipit, I think—who had the misfortune to be foster mother to a cuckoo, flying busily about searching for tit-bits for her imagined offspring. The tiny, active, anxious-minded, little thing had to land on the back of the cuckoo's neck and feed the open-mouthed ever expectant young bird over its own shoulder.

The canals were full of eels, and the people fished for them with large nets fixed round circular hoops at the end of long poles. The dwellings by the bank were picturesque enough, but could not have been too healthy: romantic and rheumatic; water lilies and water rats; an artist's joy and a sanitary inspector's despair. Nor can they have been ideal residences in which to bring up a young family. A harassed mother spanking a small and dripping youngster on the canal bank was asked what he had done. "Ah! The rogue! Was not this the third time he had fallen into the canal to-day?" Provided the child was always successfully rescued, that opened up to the statistician a vista of 1,095 dips per annum, with much physical exercise for *maman!* And this recalls, too, the tale of the matter-of-fact old Scots lady who was shewing a visitor over her garden, at the foot of which was a rapidly running river. "Was this not awkward when your family were young?" he asked. "Na!" she replied: "We didna loss mair nor twa or three *that* wye!"

Rowing slowly on a very warm day up a water-way, several of us landed at an *estaminet* pleasantly placed beneath the shade of a large chestnut tree which stood before the door. Here we had a chat with two French *poilus* home on leave—one from heroic Verdun. They told us that owing to the larger number of the people in the locality being market gardeners, the regiments of the French Army recruited here were nicknamed "Les Chouxfleurs." But, as they carefully and immediately impressed upon us, that did not detract in the slightest degree from their gallantry, and "The Cauliflowers" had given as good an account of themselves as any other soldiers of *la belle France*. We told them—to their interest—that some of our Welsh soldiers had the leek as an emblem, without any serious damage being done to their character for bravery in the field; and we politely drank success to the succulent and popular vegetable that so gloriously signified St. Omer and district.

Near us at Arcques, in the suburbs of St. Omer, was No. 7 (Canadian) Stationary Hospital, under the command of the veteran Lt.-Colonel John Stewart of Halifax, Nova Scotia; an officer who, though in his seventieth year, was full of enthusiasm and energy. One part of his show was an old château where Wellington had stayed in 1815, and a large plane tree in the garden had been planted by the Iron Duke's own hands. In St. Omer itself was the 58th (Scottish) Stationary Hospital, where were many well-known Scottish medicos: Aberdeen, Glasgow and Edinburgh were all represented. I have a pleasant memory of an evening spent there in song, story and laughter.

On the 24th July we left Clairmarais for Lederzeele, and "embussed"—a highly literary expression solemnly and frequently fired off in orders by the staff—for the XVIII Corps M.D.S. at Gwalia Farm on the Poperinghe-Elverdinghe Road. Our bearers had preceded us some time before for the A.D.S. at Essex Farm on the canal bank, a hot spot; and on the evening of our arrival four of them were killed by a shell which crashed into the shelter where they were at The Willows Collecting Post in front of this.[1]

At the Corps M.D.S. we remained for two months, and during all that time the area was persistently shelled by the Huns, and bombed every night it was clear enough for aeroplanes to come over. When we joined, the place was under the command of the O.C. 134th F.A. (who had laid out the station in a most efficient manner), and we had also as colleagues the 1/3rd South Midland F.A., our conjoint estimated accommodation being for 1,000 cases.

This was a land of hops and hop-poles. Our mess was in the tile-floored kitchen of a little farmhouse whose owners lived in the back premises—father, mother, grandmother, two young children and three adult male relatives, one of whom was killed during our stay by a shell which landed in a field on the other side of the road. The kitchen had a wide and high fireplace recess in which was fixed a stove; on the mantel-shelf above it a plaster bas-relief of Joseph, Mary, and the Christ child, framed in an oval frame. On each side was an oblong china plaque bearing a text in Flemish; on one, *Geloofd zy Jesus Christus in Eeuwigheid Amen* (Praise to Jesus Christ in all eternity), on the other side, *God ziet my. Hier vloekt men niet.* (God sees me. No swearing here.) The only other ornaments on the walls were two cheap oleographs of religious subjects. This kitchen was the dining and sitting room accommodation for the officers of the three Field Ambulances supplying personnel for the Corps Main Dressing Station: our sleeping quarters being Armstrong huts—none too weather proof—and tentage in the neighbouring field.

There was only one small shallow dug-out of sorts

---

[1] Privates H. C. Badenoch, W. D. Milne, C. Milne and D. Oliphant. Privates A. Barclay, W. Clyne, W. Duncan and W. Macdonald were also killed in the Ypres Salient,

Ypres Salient—Corps M.D.S. at Gwalia Farm.
1. Receiving Room.
2. Feeding Tent and Nissen Hospital Hut.

Facing page 143.

available on our site; for the deep—and safe—dug-out was an impossibility, as water was usually struck at a depth of five or six feet or even less. All one could do, therefore, against shell or bomb, was to sandbag the huts and tents to a depth of three feet or thereby, and trust to luck that no direct hit occurred. In some cases the ground on which a tent was erected was excavated for two or three feet and the tent sunk in it; while some of the more cautious hut dwellers had a trench dug in the floor, in which, should the spirit so move them, they could uncomfortably and moistly recline when Jerry was soaring skywards.

The large barn of the farm was the receiving room, where all cases on admission were clerked (i.e., entered in the Admission and Discharge Book), given anti-tetanus serum, and sorted out. Thence moribund cases and cases unfit for removal were taken to a hospital Nissen hut; those fit to be fed taken to a feeding tent; those requiring immediate attention to a surgical dressing-room; those who were gassed to special tents where we kept oxygen apparatus, etc. When dressings were done the casualties were taken to the row of large hospital tents, again fed if necessary, and looked after till the Motor Ambulance Convoys took them back to the various Casualty Clearing Stations. Here came in much work for the Dispatching N.C.O.s: head cases and chest cases going to one C.C.S., fractured thighs to another, gas cases to a third, general cases to a fourth, and so on. As the nature of the casualties taken by the various C.C.S.s occasionally changed at short notice, every one had to be alert and on the look-out to see that each class of case reached its proper destination.

To make such things easier of remembrance, a large diagram of the human body was at one time hung up in the receiving room with arrows pointing from each part—head, chest, thigh, etc.—to the name of the C.C.S.

whither each special case should go. The figure being depicted as unclad, bore, very properly and after the manner of statuary, a fig leaf: and one bright morning I discovered that some brighter orderly had duly and appropriately adorned the divisions of the fig leaf with the touching legend "A.P.M."

While here we dealt with the cases from the three engagements of 31st July, 16th August and 20th September; but apart from these had a steady daily run from neighbouring encampments of casualties caused by the perpetual shelling and bombing that went on. On the 7th August I took over command of the Dressing Station from the O.C. 134th F.A. Two days previously, the Hun, who had been sending over high velocity stuff all day, fired a salvo right into the M.D.S. at 10 p.m., killing two of our sergeants[1] (excellent N.C.O.s, valued comrades and old friends) along with a driver of the M.A.C., and wounding 20 others. One shell landed in the evil-smelling farmyard pond as two of us were making for the dressing-room; and from the prone position which was routine on such occasions, an extraordinary rainbow effect could be made out by using the corner of one eye—the other being in close contact with the heel of my colleague's boot—before a malodorous shower of mud and filth rapidly followed.

Once inside the dressing-room, rapidly filling with cases, you were immediately struck by the effects of discipline—the thing abhorred of communists, criminals, cranks, conchies *et hoc genus omne*. The shelling was going on, the huts were of wood and gave no shelter—two orderlies became casualties while at work—and yet the routine proceeded as if things were normal: dressing went on; splints were fitted; Field Medical Cards were duly filled in; each case was taken where it belonged; everyone stuck it and carried on.

[1] Sergeants Robert Ledingham and James Russell.

3

4

Ypres Salient—Corps M.D.S. at Gwalia Farm.

3. Exit from Surgical Dressing-room.
4. M.A.C. loading Cars from Hospital Tents for journey to C.C.S.

Facing page 145.

That night we cleared back to Poperinghe all superfluous personnel—we had a total then of nearly 800 —keeping only those absolutely necessary for the work in hand, as we expected further dirty work. But this precaution fortunately proved unnecessary.

Another scene in that dressing-room was "passing strange." One evening a West Indian Labour Corps camp "got it in the neck" from the bombing circus, and the place was suddenly filled up with wounded niggers. Naturally emotional, and, equally naturally, scared to death, besides—in many cases—being badly injured, the black men made the dressing-room an inferno of shrieks, groans and cries which it was impossible to still. "Hallelujahs" broke out sporadically in various places; one man started a Moody and Sankey hymn, the chorus being taken up in fits and starts by others till a rival tune from another corner bore it down. Outside the bombs kept crashing; we used a minimum of light even though our windows were blanketed, in case of attracting attention; and as one gazed around the dim-lit hall of suffering at the gleaming teeth and rolling white eye-balls of the recumbent blacks on the operating tables and stretchers, the scene and the din, inside and outside, suggested an impromptu revival meeting in the nether regions, and called for the pencil of a Hogarth or a Breughel to do it justice.

And yet, if you could view what was happening with the necessary detachment of mind—which was not always easy—a visit from the bombers was, considered merely as a spectacle, an episode both picturesque and of interest. A clear starry night, perhaps, with a three-quarter moon, and an odd cloud here and there in the sky: everything quiet around us except for the distant gun-fire up the line. Then suddenly, some kilometres away, the sharp characteristic crash of a bomb — a different sound altogether from that of a shell—followed rapidly by several others, always getting nearer and nearer to where we are. Now you hear the broken humming of the 'plane—not the steadier hum of our own aircraft—sounding like a continual *A-woong! A-woong! A-woong!* Searchlights swing up sweeping the heavens in search of him; adventurous anti-aircraft gunners start potting at the sound, and irritable machine-guns are following suit in a jerky manner, as if asking each other, "Have you got him?—Have you got him?—Have you got him?"

Suddenly a beam falls fair on the mark, shewing him up as a golden butterfly against its background of silver. Quickly the other searchlights converge on their quarry, and up the track of each goes a steady stream of yellow luminous tracer bullets, while the *pop-op-op-op-op* of the M.G. is now so continuous and deafening that you hardly hear the Archies pumping away to add new and larger stars to the firmament. Gone! Confound him! He is into a cloud; and the searchlights, hitherto fading into the far distance on high, are now flattened out into mushroom tops as they meet on the cloud and deliberately creep over it, back and fore, up and down, waiting for his exit.

He is out! There he is! One light has just touched and then slid off him. There he is again! And two lights fixing him in the centre of a St. Andrew's Cross! Go it, the Archies!—Good old M.G.!—*Whooce! Crash!* Your sense of detachment goes instantaneously; you are a participant, not merely a spectator, and you prostrate yourself. That one was a bit too close—there are other night-hawks abroad!

Quickly one of the searchlights leaves the original quarry and sweeps the sky for the newcomer, followed more slowly by another beam which has also given up number one. Both 'planes are still bomb-dropping, but the crashes are going further away; the searchlights have lost them and slash the darkness angrily like giant sword blades hacking at random; you get up and dust yourself. Then, finding the spectator next you remains seated and using bad language, you give him an arm into the dressing room. He has a machine-gun bullet through his foot. . . .

I have already said this was a land of hops and hop-poles. It was also a land of spies and rumours thereof. One method said to be employed was signalling by smoke from house chimneys—bunches of wet straw being put on the fire at intervals as per code. The location of our tanks in a wood was said to have been thus given away, with resulting destructive attention from bombers; and it was also said that the spy, caught later *in flagrante delicto*, was obliterated in the mud by an appropriate and lucky tank accident. How many spy yarns there were throughout the campaign!—windmills and church clocks worked to catch the balloonist's eye; men following the harmless, necessary plough and women laying out their innocent white washing, all according to plan for the edification of the watchful enemy flying man. True enough these stories were in many cases: the Boche was—and is—a methodical and wily animal: and those who deliberately choose to forget it are the sons of folly.

Padres abounded at the Corps M.D.S.: barring the Salvation Army I think we had all the known varieties, and several of each at that—Presbyterian (Scots and English), R.C., Wesleyan and C. of E. As they swamped us out of our mess table, we, the sons of Galen, holding only to our proven and divisional spiritual advisers, had to give the rest a long table to themselves. This was popularly known as "The General Assembly," and there they sat and discussed the mess cook and moot points in theology. One was under a cloud: he had buried a Malay in the Chinese cemetery, and later had to disinter him and put him in his proper place at the irate demand of a Graves Commission warrior of Irish extraction: even in death there is no satisfactory blending of Mahomet with Confucius.

The little mess room was, therefore, pretty full, and one day at lunch, after a peaceful forenoon, Jerry pitched a large high-velocity shell[1] on to the other side of the road from us, with an appalling crash that sent in the remains of our already highly dilapidated kitchen windows. It was interesting to see the positions immediately assumed by the lunchers; some chairs with their occupants went over backwards: most of those present got automatically and rapidly below the tables. My own strenuous efforts not to be out of touch with the majority were firmly impeded by some unknown obstacle, which on hasty examination proved to be one of our mess attendants on his knees, with his head (on a charger of cold beef) firmly planted in my abdomen. Glad that the beef was cold and without gravy, I enjoyed the unmerited *kudos* of being heroically erect in my chair as various dishevelled colleagues reappeared from their temporary retirement.

During the pushes German troops from Posen, Danzig and Pomerania, with some Guards, went through our hands. One sub-lieutenant, a sallow, cynical fellow who spoke good English, claimed to be an actor and an assistant of Reinhardt from whom Martin Harvey got his *Œdipus*. Another Hun continued to weep profusely. When asked why these tears, he said it was for joy at being a prisoner! A third, a little chap of about five feet two in height and some forty years of age, was evidently one of the comedians of his unit. His helmet was too large for his head and covered three-quarters of his face. I was attracted to the tent he was in by the laughter he was causing, and found him in the centre of a group of amused orderlies, where he was hopping about on one leg with the other long-booted foot hooked behind it,

---

[1] One of our sergeants, who later inspected the shell hole, very properly described it (in terms which became proverbial amongst us) as "a scandalous affair."

grinning on all around and making obviously playful remarks in his own tongue. When I enquired what he was up to, he said that he was trying to take off his boot. Was his foot wounded, then? No, but his boot had not been off for fourteen days. Unfortunately before I could leave his side he managed to get the boot off, and I decided at once that he was no liar.

Here it was that we first had American M.O.s attached to the Field Ambulances and Battalions, and several of them remained with us to the end. The great majority turned out to be first-rate fellows, although a few had to get over the "effete Yurrup" stage before we took them to our bosoms: a week up the line was usually sufficient to adjust their outlook. But, in spite of little things like that, good chaps they were, and good comrades: their point of view was always fresh and stimulating; they gave us an outfit of terse and vigorous slang which some of us use yet; while the numerous new methods they shewed us of losing our spare cash at games of chance were both surprising and educative.

On the 24th we left Gwalia Farm and marched to Siege Camp, further up towards the Canal bank; to stay there in sandbagged huts and tents for five days, at rest and overhauling equipment. Every night bombers were over and the place was by no means healthy. Football, however, was available for the men, and two matches with neighbouring units were played.

Late on the night of the 27th, during a raid, a bomb was dropped on the road fifty yards from us; a square hit on two g.s. wagons that were passing. In various stages of undress a squad of our fellows made for the scene with stretchers. The smashed wagons and eight mules were all massed in a blood-stained heap from which the quivering legs of the wretched, moribund and mangled brutes stuck grotesquely out. One of the drivers had been blown into a deep ditch at the side of the road, with a compound fracture of the thigh and head wounds: his three comrades—mortally wounded—we had to get out from the heap; no easy job owing to the still kicking legs of the mules. In the middle of our work, too, revolver bullets began unaccountably to sing over our heads. Going round the heap to its other side I discovered a well-meaning (but post-prandially over-excited) gunner officer of a neighbouring division engaged, as he solemnly explained, in trying to put the mules out of their pain. When told somewhat brusquely that there were men in the heap and that he had nearly potted two of our fellows as well, he shook his head, ceased firing, pocketed his "gun" and left us in peace to finish our work.

On each side of the road were numerous horse lines where great damage had been done: confusion everywhere: wounded horses neighing, plunging and kicking: some down and half strangled amongst the ropes, with the line orderlies pluckily trying to get things clear. It was bright moonlight and suitable for the enemy's work. Suddenly another bunch of 'planes came crashing their way towards us—fortunately for us without doing any more immediately local mischief—and there was a general dispersion of the groups of spectators of the previous damage. From the vantage point of the road, which ran at a higher level than the adjoining fields, one could see the rapidly scattering groups of bent figures, with here and there a face, whitened in the moonlight, turned upwards to the sky in search of the terror that flew by night. It was strongly reminiscent of many of the older pictures of the Day of Judgment.

With feelings of relief, then, we got orders to proceed to Proven on the 29th and entrain. With the view of lessening the risk of casualties, the unit, less the transport, left Siege Camp at 6 p.m. and marched to Gwalia Farm, where we temporarily "doubled up" with the 33rd F.A. at the Corps Main Dressing Station. It was lucky we did so, as that night, commencing at 7 p.m., there was a most determined and extensive bombing of the whole area—Siege Camp, Vlamertinghe, Elverdinghe, Dirty Bucket Camp, Caestre, Poperinghe (200 casualties), the Switch Road, all got it in the neck; the performance going on without intermission for five hours to the accompaniment of continuous crashes. At one time there were seven 'planes caught in the searchlights—four of them right over our heads—and the noise of the "Archies" and machine-guns, added to that of the bomb explosions, made up a chorus sufficiently diabolical to stick in the memory. A steady stream of casualties poured into the Dressing Station.

By midnight there were only a few 'planes left, chiefly "returning empties" making for their own lines again; and at one a.m. the unit fell in—with a 'plane again plumb above us, golden in the searchlight's beam—and marched to Proven, preceded an hour before by the transport who had gone through a stiff time, both before they left Siege Camp—where a dud bomb landed beside them—and on the road. The route to Proven—twelve kilometres—was simply stinking with explosive products from the numerous bomb holes on it and beside it; but only an odd bomb or two fell en route, as the night show was practically over; and we got to the station at our scheduled time (3.50 a.m.) to entrain after a cold two hours' wait on the platform. A Soyer's stove was set agoing, however; the men given hot tea and some food; while once in the cattle trucks, a snatch of sleep was got in spite of the fact that there was no straw in them. The route was Hazebrouck, St. Omer, Boulogne, Albert, Bapaume; the weather was fine; and all next day the men sat at the open doors of the cattle trucks, singing, chaffing, and jumping off at every stop to lark about or buy fruit from the omnipresent hawkers.

Getting in to Bapaume—moonlit, destroyed and desolate—at 3 a.m. on the 1st October, we marched to Achiet-le-Petit, where we were accommodated in tents and wooden huts, and again got a few hours sleep. On the 5th the unit moved to Boiry-Becquerelle, with our H.Q. amongst the ruins of a farm beside the Bapaume-Peronne Road; while it also supplied personnel for an A.D.S. at Heninel, and for a C.P. in the caves at Marlieres beside Wancourt. The A.D.S. was old-established and in good order; the caves, roomy and gloomy, also held various parties of combatants, and were impervious to any kind of ironmongery that the genial Fritz could heave over.

Our men were in hutments set in the ruins of a little village, mined and blown to bits by the Hun before he had—quite recently—evacuated it. The demolition work was thoroughly and systematically done: everything was *tout abimé,* even the apple trees had been hacked down to the roots: the scientific Jekyll side of the German had acted as willing gaffer to that of the Hyde brute. This wanton destruction of houses and orchards was characteristic and common; but here the enemy had specially excelled himself in the churchyards, not only in our own village but in the villages round about.

Tombs of any size, especially those with female names on them, had been broken open and the coffins rifled, in the hope that jewellery might have been buried with the bodies. One German ghoul had apparently, after the manner of other people possessed of devils, been actually living in a tomb—his brazier and his filthy blanket were still there—while his leisure time had been spent in operating with a pick on the leaden casing of a coffin he had smashed in. This work of *Kultur* had, however, been interrupted by the British advance before he had finished it.

Another gentle German had dealt faithfully with the

churchyard crucifix. The figure had been taken off the cross and placed on its head at the foot of it. The arms of the cross had been thrust into two of the long leather boots of the Hun soldier. A merry jest, of course, on the part of simple-minded Michael: possibly the work of some earnest Lutheran who disliked Catholic symbolism: the conscientious objector has throughout history a mentality all his own.

And, again, in a dug-out, was found one of the little metal shields so common in French churchyards over the graves of the poor. It commemorated the death of an infant in 1875. The inscription ended, "Thy stay with us was short, O, little one, yet hast thou left us many pleasant memories." Touching enough to the ordinary mind; but the superman had fitted a wooden handle to the shield and used it as a coal shovel. Truly the trail of the beast was over all.

And it was rather a relief to turn for a minute from the *schwein-hund* to a nobler lower animal. Near our huts and in the ruined orchard was an interesting grave, carefully railed off, with a neatly executed wooden memorial at its head. On it the inscription ran:—

> To the Memory
> of
> Billy the Stallion
> Pet of the 156th Heavy Battery
> Killed by Hostile Aircraft
> 12—5—17.
>
> He was only a Blooming Heavy,
>   Only a Transport Horse,
> But if there's a Hereafter for Horses,
>   Billy will not be lost.
>
> For $2\frac{1}{2}$ years we loved him,
>   He fought for us like a Lion,
> So we've Erected this Board to Billy
>   For the sake of Auld Lang Syne.

The hand of the poet was, I fear, like his subject,

"blooming heavy." But the verse was evidently the conjoint output of a committee; and a Scottish member had apparently—and with great originality—supplied the last line. Anyhow, there lay Billy, with some carefully planted chrysanthemums—where on earth had they got them?—flowering on his grave.

In this district we were in the vicinity of the Hindenburg Line, and all the villages were heaps of ruins, in the first instance destroyed by shell fire, as the Boche had advanced, and secondly by mines, before he was driven out.

An examination of the communal cemetery at Boisleux-au-mont, with its military extension, was interesting. The civilian part had been badly knocked about by shells and many of the memorial stones broken. Many more had been appropriated for Hun graves, and the fresh carving on this stolen property was often quite good. A large plain wooden cross about twenty feet high, made of untrimmed tree, was erected to commemorate the dead of one regiment. French and Boche graves containing six or more unidentified bodies were common; in others, to the natural disgust of the French, the Hun had buried his dead along with theirs.

Here one could see, in the midst of all this devilish destruction, the rather sickly sentimentality of the German express itself in the heading "FREUND UND FEIND IM TOD VEREINT" (friend and foe united in death), followed, for example, by "Ici repose le capitaine français M. POINCLOU et un soldat français du 12e regiment. GEM. SAN. KOMP. 52" (a private of the 52nd Sanitary Company). Most of the inscriptions commenced either "HIER RUHT IN GOTT," or "ER STARB DEN HELDENTOD FURS VATERLAND." Their enemies were held to rest in God too; "HIER RUHT IN GOTT EIN TAPFERE FRANZOSISCHE SOLDAT" (here rests in God a gallant French soldier). All the graves were well and tidily kept; and, as they had not to pay for the ground, space was freely occupied. Wherever there was a British grave, our Graves Commission had already erected the little official wooden cross with name plate, while the French ones were marked with the large metal tricolour of the Republic.

It was in Boisleux, too, that we met several French civilians, men and women, who had received a twenty-four hours permission to visit the village and look for valuables buried on their hasty exodus from their homes. The majority of them were women; all were dressed in deep mourning. One, after careful inspection of the heap of smashed bricks that represented her old home, found a piece of the lintel of her kitchen window still in position. Measuring some twelve paces from it she made a mark with her heel, and two willing Jocks started digging for her. At the depth of five feet or so, there, sure enough, was her treasure—a large tin chocolate box sewn up in canvas and containing 4,000 francs, mostly in gold. Another wept and cursed when she found out that the entrance to a deep Boche dug-out ran through the site of her hiding place; and, raking about amongst the debris thrown out at the back, she found the now empty and rusted red tin box that had contained her hoard. A third woman we left anxiously watching the deepening hole one of our men was digging for her; she declared herself sure of the site. We learnt afterwards that she was right, and that she found her money. Getting her friendly Scot to dig again at another spot, some bottles of wine were unearthed; and these, honest and heated man, he willingly accepted as honorarium for his efforts.

One woman who had lost her husband and four sons discovered that the devastated site of her home was now a German cemetery: another—also bereaved—that two Huns had been buried in the ruins of her house, and that a board was affixed saying—in French—that the bricks must not be disturbed as German dead were there. She gave vent to expression of the most intense hate and rage. Who will blame her? And yet our political Pecksniffs roll up the whites of their eyes and ask, in stricken accents, "Why won't the French forgive and forget?"

On the 2nd November the Division moved into the Hermaville area; our own Field Ambulance being located at Montenescourt, a quiet and unpretentious little country village.

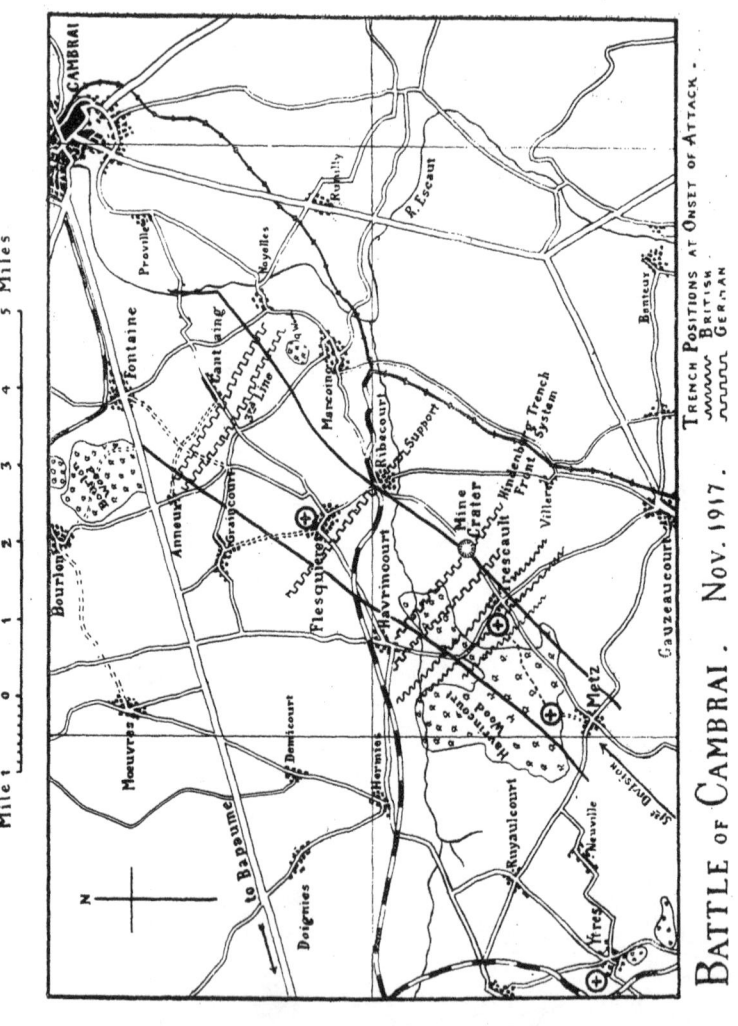

Battle of Cambrai. Nov. 1917.

CHAPTER VIII.[1]

Battle of Cambrai, 1917.

Summer, and leaves a-rustling
O'er the Route Nationale,
With war's traffic hustling
On the Route Nationale.
Winter, and snow a-falling,
Coldness, dread, appalling,
But aye the summons calling
Up the Route Nationale.

"On the 20th November the 51st Division took part in the Battle of Cambrai, 1917, advancing on the left centre of the attack up the slopes of Flesquieres Hill, where very heavy fighting took place. On the 21st they captured Flesquieres village, and later, along with the 62nd Division, Anneux and Cantaing. Later in the afternoon, supported by tanks, they took Fontaine-Notre-Dame. On the following day this village was lost, and on the 23rd the Division again attacked it, but was unable to force an entrance. In the afternoon, during a second attack from the west, several tanks entered Fontaine, remaining till dusk, and inflicting considerable loss on the enemy. The 51st were not in the line on the 30th when the German counter-offensive took place."—(*The Territorial Divisions.*)

ON 15th November, 1917, orders reached our Ambulance H.Q. for an advance party of 50 men, with two officers, to proceed to Ytres and there prepare to take over from the occupying unit. We were rather sorry to leave tranquil Montenescourt, but for some time had suspected that something was in the wind. The continuous arrival of tanks by rail at the depot not far away, and more especially the fitting of each with a huge superimposed bundle some six feet or more in diameter, made up of beams of wood, railway sleepers, tree trunks, etc., pointed to some scheme being hatched; but the tank personnel

---
[1] As I was on leave when the push occurred, this chapter is written by Captain R. T. Bruce, who finished the adventure by becoming a prisoner of war.

were secrecy itself, so no clue was to be gleaned from them.

Ytres proved to be a fairly large, though scattered village, some thirty or forty miles S.W. of Arras. The Field Ambulance H.Q. seemed an imposing affair compared with the one we had left. Evidently the sector was a quiet part of the line, permitting construction work to be done at will. The officer's mess was a lofty and roomy structure of brick, wood and corrugated iron, and they had good billets. Niessen huts comfortably housed the men and provided wards for sick and wounded. In short it was a large and well-equipped M.D.S.

We were hospitably received, spent a pleasant evening and heard more of what was in front of us. A new form of attack was shortly to be made, which, it was hoped, would prove an unpleasant surprise for the enemy. The Highland Division was to have the central position. The main object of the attack would be Cambrai.

About five miles east of Ytres lies the huge Bois d'Havrincourt, half a mile north of the ruins of the small village of Metz. The A.D.S. of the unit in charge of evacuation was situated on the southern fringe of this wood, and consisted of numbers of underground chambers of varying sizes, well concealed by the trees. Clear of the forest, to the east, sloped the hillside, on the crest of which were the trenches our troops were to take over, and about midway in the trench system were the remains of Trescault. This was the ground we had to reconnoitre, and we seized the first opportunity to do so.

Motoring as far as Metz, we walked to the wood and inspected the accommodation at the A.D.S.—none too ample. Thence a guide took us to the trenches. A fair road runs from Metz to Trescault, which could be used at night but was under observation by day. Our route was, therefore, through the forest, following a narrow gauge line which skirted the dressing station, threaded the trees

BATTLE OF CAMBRAI, 1917.

and emerged at the eastern side, running as far as the Metz road.

At this point we left it, climbed the slope on the other side of the road, and very soon afterwards dropped into the first trench. Not much time was required to examine the front. The trenches were deep, good and well supplied with dug-outs, but the sector was a narrow one, and we were chiefly interested in the possibilities of Trescault as regards a Dressing Station or Collecting Post. We decided that it would do. The Field Ambulance would come up to the Bois d'Havrincourt and there open out as a M.D.S., the A.D.S. being in the line. In Trescault we discovered a large dug-out, very deep down and with two shafts of access, one served by a winch, the other by fairly good steps. It was right on the main road and there were one or two outlying dug-outs for our men.

Our A.D.M.S. turned up at Ytres and I was told that I was to be bearer officer for the Division during the attack, the date of which was uncertain. The news was received with mixed feelings, as my leave was due!

The following days at Ytres were full of interest. "Days" is hardly the correct word. Secrecy being essential, all troops, guns, tanks and transport had to come up by night. The general idea was to conceal as large a force as could rapidly be assembled and successfully hidden, and hurl the lot at the unsuspecting Boche. There was to be no preliminary advertising of the attack by weeks of wire cutting as formerly done. The enemy was not to suspect the necessity for bringing up reinforcements. It was a new experiment and the tanks were to have the honours of the day. They were to go first, to crash through the uncut wire and to make lanes for the following troops! So by day all was kept as normal as possible—just the right amount of artillery fire; no special movements of men; no signs of any stir.

Night, however, ushered in a very different order of things. Troops, guns, tanks and transport of all sorts poured in unceasingly. One could hear the countryside hum with traffic. Late one evening, sitting in the mess, I was attracted by distant, but at the same time unusually loud, clanking. Tanks were evidently coming up in numbers, and I succumbed to the temptation, wet and dark as it was outside, to sally forth and seek them out. Lanes and fields were in a horrible state, and I had only my ears to guide me, but half-an-hour later had the luck to trip over the broad tape laid down as a guide to their route. And just in time. Shortly there loomed up quite a procession of the huge, unwieldy monsters, each bearing its mammoth burden on its back and preceded by an officer who occasionally flashed a torch to enable him to follow his tape. It was a weird procession.

On the 19th November we moved into the wood, selecting a tiny dug-out which boasted two wire beds. The rest of the unit was expected late that evening and there was much to do in the way of preparing the billeting arrangements. Where all the men were to sleep was a puzzle. Tarpaulin bivouacs would have to be used. The day soon passed in this way and in prowling about the confines of the wood, noting how alive the whole place had become since our first visit. Tanks along the edges, fresh batteries everywhere, and all cunningly concealed.

In the evening I sallied out to meet the Ambulance, striking across country for the Ytres-Metz road. I failed in my object, as the unit had, unknown to me, been ordered to come by a different route, but I was held spell-bound by the spectacle the road presented. It was one solid mass of troops, all making in the same direction, but apparently hopelessly mixed up. Troops, guns, limbers, g.s. wagons, etc., etc., even a stray tank in difficulties and obstructing the traffic! Military police at various points were driven frantic trying to keep the

BATTLE OF CAMBRAI, 1917.

stream flowing. The tank had evidently wandered from its rightful place in the open and was proving a tremendous obstacle. And all around one heard the *clank, clank* of the engines and saw the continuous flashes of torches in the hands of the guides. It appeared impossible that the Boche should fail to spot the activity. Till one reflected on the width of "No Man's Land" in these parts—said in places to be fifteen hundred yards—one imagined the enemy could not help seeing the lights or hearing the row. But there were no signs that his suspicion was aroused; no unusual strafing or shelling of Metz or the wood.

The Field Ambulance arrived late and tired and all were got under cover somehow. Next day was devoted to settling down and making hurried arrangements for the attack. There was much to do. Offices had to be planned, "wards" arranged for the dressing of the wounded, tent sub-divisions allotted their duties, bearers equipped, cookhouse built and feeding schemes matured, stretchers and blankets piled and a thousand other things attended to. We now learnt that Zero hour was at dawn on the 21st. Not much time to perfect one's plans! My men were to assemble that evening and be marched by me to Trescault, there to occupy the A.D.S. which was to be my H.Q. during the first stage of the battle. That the attack must be made immediately had become obvious. Masses of men were everywhere concealed; tanks lurked in bunches; batteries littered the open. The Boche could not possibly remain in ignorance of what was afoot. The narrow gauge line running past the Main Dressing Station on the edge of the wood, which we hoped to use next day for the evacuation of the wounded, suffered cruelly from the arriving tanks. Squads of our men were kept busy repairing it each time a monster crossed the rails. But, apart from the military activity around, it was strangely quiet. Hardly a shell appeared to be coming over, and our own guns kept up only a desultory fire. It was the calm before a storm!

I had but vague information to go upon as regards the disposition of the enemy trenches or the lie of the land. I was ignorant of the arrangements made for our Brigades, or which were to open the ball. I knew our own position. Roughly, it lay along the crest in front of us, with Trescault about the middle of it. Far to the left of our front the ridge made a half circle towards the north, and the village of Havrincourt could vaguely be made out from Trescault, but the attack on this was to be shared by the Division stationed on our left. In front, the view across "No Man's Land" was merely of undulating country. Two series of Boche trenches were concealed there, one a part of the famous Hindenburg Line. I learned that this immensely wide and deep trench was expected to give trouble to the tanks and this was why they had been supplied with the bundles. On reaching the trench each was to shed the bundle off its snout by loosing the chains in the interior. The bundle, it was hoped, would fall to the depths and provide a stepping-stone for the tank to cross by. Beyond these trenches there was, according to the map, more undulating country, then a ravine running crosswise with an embankment and railway line, and beyond these a somewhat steep slope with the village of Flesquieres on the crest. There was only one main road, from Trescault to Ribecourt and from the latter to Flesquieres. Ribecourt, I was given to understand, was not in our area, and this road, for all I knew, might be barred to us. The Highland Division would advance rather to the left of it, the main direction of the attack being almost directly north-east, towards Cambrai.

Late in the evening of the 20th my men paraded in the intense darkness under the trees. They comprised the effective bearer strength of the three Field Ambulances, and I was to be reinforced at the A.D.S. by drafts from Trench Mortar Batteries and other odds and ends, so that a large body of men would be available. Previous experience proved the necessity for this. There is no more exhausting work than that of the stretcher-bearers and it is almost impossible to have too many in a push.

Soon we moved off, and I marched, with trolley line as guide, through the wood, across the open to Trescault road, and reached the A.D.S. within the hour. Once there, I set about drafting off the various parties of bearers to their respective Aid Posts and made all arrangements possible for the comfort of those remaining. Seeing the "carry" was likely to be a long one, should the attack prove successful, it was essential to have a large body in hand at H.Q.

M.O.s of Battalions had been made aware that Trescault was my H.Q., to which they could apply for supplies, and intimate to me there any change in the position of their Aid Posts. My duty would be to keep personally in touch with them, so that I would have not only the organising, writing and planning to do at Trescault, but this job also, while the Aid Posts, in all probability, would be rapidly advanced! It sounded impossible to do both adequately, and I feared that in the attempt to do it I might fail to effect either.

One gets little sleep under such circumstances and I did not need the crash of the guns to waken me. How astonished the enemy must have been on the morning of the 21st when unsuspected pandemonium broke loose! Our guns were in full blast by 6.30 a.m. and the noise was truly devastating. They must have been firing largely by the map, because there had been few opportunities for registering targets. But fire they did, and that most heartily. I was off at the earliest possible moment for the front line, eager to view the sight, accompanied by a sergeant of our own Ambulance.

The tanks, I knew, must already be in action. All night long they had been creeping, each to its allotted place, in No Man's Land, the scheme being that dawn breaking was to disclose one long line of them, far as the eye could reach. When Zero came every engine would be running and the leviathans would move slowly forward, mowing down, or crashing through the uncut wire and making lanes for the following battalions, every company of which knew exactly which tank or tanks they were to accompany.

We made our way along the front line trench to a commanding spot; but so feeble was the Boche response to our barrage that we were able to climb out into the open and join the second line troops waiting orders to advance. Dimly in the distance one could see the long line of tanks, and even, here and there, minute objects representing the men behind them. They appeared stationary, so slow was the progress. Most of the shelling was well forward from our position, and no doubt directed at the advancing troops and tanks. I was told that practically every tank had reached its position on time, and at Zero hour every engine started up. A wonderful feat! We pressed forward for a short distance to try to learn the hang of the land, but I judged I should first return to the A.D.S. Here I found our D.A.D.M.S. eager for news, and supplied him with a guide to our old front line. Wounded had already begun to trickle in, and some shrapnel was bursting over the station, but we were escaping wonderfully. I started out at once with the sergeant and an orderly to explore the forward area.

Keeping more to the left, we had barely cleared Trescault quarry and the trenches when I ran up against the M.O. of the 5th Gordons, who told me his Battalion H.Q. was moving forwards and he was on the look-out for a forward Aid Post. So he and his orderlies joined my party and we soon found a narrow lane running in the direction we wanted. My desire was to go forward as far as possible in the middle of the divisional area, so that I could pick up a good idea of the country. On our right we occasionally had glimpses of the Ribecourt road along which wounded could be seen passing. It was a relief to be in the open, and an interesting journey. Few shells came our way. Our own guns had quieted down and one could hardly believe a battle was in progress. The first object of interest to present itself was a deep quarry which had evidently been found useful by the enemy. Ladders led down to its depths and galleries ran round the walls, giving entrance to various roomy dug-outs. The place seemed eminently suited for a Relay Post, and I at once sent back orders for a party of bearers to come forward and occupy it.

A couple of hundred yards further on we came on the Hindenburg trench, immensely wide and deep. Stuck on the parapet of it, inextricably jammed though not much knocked about, were three abandoned tanks. Together they made a splendid landmark for the quarry Relay Post. One glance at the trench made us realise the wisdom and forethought of the bundles on the tanks. Even with their help I marvelled that they could cross at all.

We had met few wounded, and there had been a pleasant absence of "horrible spectacles" as we crossed what had been No Man's Land. Evidently the first line had been captured with ease and small loss, and our hopes were high for the success of the day. That the tanks had succeeded with the wire was obvious to us the moment we left the trenches. The lanes in the wire we walked through were splendid. Reconnoitring further we came in due course to a second series of trenches. Parties of German prisoners were pouring back and the shelling here became more serious. We were glad to find a communication trench running our way and congratulated ourselves that we were in it. Suddenly I caught sight of a Red Cross on the trench wall, and at the same time spied a Boche prisoner wearing a brassard. We collared him at once and made him guide us to the "Sanitats," which proved to be a capacious, two-roomed dug-out further down the trench. The 5th Gordons M.O. pounced upon it for his new Aid Post and I made a note of the map reference for despatch to the A.D.M.S. At least I now knew where one advanced Aid Post was situated!

Leaving him, my party hurried back to Trescault, where I plunged up to the neck in work. The scene was a busy one. Wounded were pouring in and all were hard pressed to cope with them. German prisoners were working the winch, and the ambulance cars were loading at the A.D.S. itself. Only occasional doses of shrapnel were being administered by the enemy. I found any number of chits from M.O.s all asking for more bearers, blankets, stores, etc., and notifying me of the positions of new advanced Aid Posts. These had all to be answered as satisfactorily as possible, parties of bearers made up and sent off with stretchers, supplies and a note from me *re* the Relay Post. In addition, all information possible had to be sent to the A.D.M.S. I had, besides, to report to the acting O.C. Field Ambulance that the advance of our troops was so rapid that either the A.D.S. and our car depot must be pushed forward or there would be a colossal carry for the bearers.

Word now reached me that our only main road, that leading to Ribecourt, was impassable for cars because of a huge mine exploded by the enemy. With another M.O. I made for the spot to see what was what. There we found a gap of forty or fifty yards in the road! No car could circumnavigate it, and the engineers stated that it would be some time before a bridge could be constructed. We

At Trescault.

Bringing Wounded up from a Dug-out on Slides by Winch, 1917.

(Imperial War Museum Photograph—Copyright Reserved.)

agreed that the only thing to do was to bring the cars to the proximal end of the gap and have a party of bearers posted at the distal to help carry the stretchers around the crater. Possibly the Fords might be manœuvred round it, and, if so, they would at least take some of the burden off the bearers' shoulders. Fortunately there was any number of prisoners by this time and they were freely used to bring in the wounded. Still, the scheme was only a makeshift and not at all satisfactory. Our troops were fighting beyond Ribecourt, which village was fully two miles from the car depot at Trescault!

Evening came on and I was tired enough. With an early start, so much worry, walking and work, and so little food, I was glad to get back to the dressing station. The news, on the whole, was good, but the Highland Division was held up below Flesquieres village. This occupied a commanding position on the crest and our troops had failed to storm it, a German officer having earned fame by the number of our tanks he had knocked out with direct hits. On the other hand, the Divisions on either side of us were well in front and a big haul of prisoners had been made.

Towards the small hours of the 22nd I tried to get some sleep in the dug-out, but, tired as I was, it was impossible. All hands were hard at work dressing the wounded which still poured down our shaft, and the resulting groans and yells, coupled with the tramp of heavy feet, effectually kept me awake.

I rose as daylight began to appear. There was no chance of a shave or wash and but a pretence of a breakfast. Necessary work completed, I determined again to go forward and, if possible, see for myself how the evacuation of wounded was progressing. This time I struck a shallow ravine rather to the left of the previous day's route. From fellows I met I learned that the good old Highland Division, refusing to be held up by any village, height or no height, had attacked in the night and were now firmly lodged in Flesquieres itself. News from Ribecourt road was bad: the R.A.M.C. were finding it next to impossible to keep up with the rapidly advancing troops. However, I proceeded on my way, crossed the Hindenburg and second line trenches and reached the Railway Ravine. Here Flesquieres could be plainly seen, and I made a direct line for it, over the embankment and up the hillside. Before noon I was in the village. What a spectacle of messed-up tanks and mutilated bodies presented itself! There were trenches all along the crest, and in a deep dug-out below one of these I found the O.C. and a cheery crew of the 5th Gordons. They were in great form and gave me a hearty reception, and all the news. It was a splendid dug-out, well stocked with food, solid and fluid. I drank their healths and passed on to explore the village for a possible dressing station. This soon presented itself in the shape of a huge, though battered building, once a monastery, apparently. Two courtyards, with buildings around. Just the place and situated on the main road! All we had to do was to get our transport past the mine crater! But a biggish "all!"

So off once more on the return journey to report. This time I went by Ribecourt and was held up a long while, for my pains, by our cavalry streaming forwards. But at length I got through and down the slope to the crater and so to Trescault. There I learned that part of the transport had now got as far as the hollow below the crater, and that I must have missed it by circling round the far edge on the other side. As there were no fresh orders for me I had just to carry on. I sent back a report on the possibilities of Flesquieres and set off there again. It worried me that we had no forward post and I thought that a nominal A.D.S. would be better than none. If the Fords managed to get round the crater they must

BATTLE OF CAMBRAI, 1917. 169

come through Ribecourt and would find us a mile further on. It was dark long before we reached our destination, at which we arrived very exhausted and covered with mud. Although I knew the way so well, we missed it in the dark and floundered miserably for a long time in what seemed a maze of lanes and cuttings. At least we now occupied a forward post. Soon messages found us from the battalions in front, all bringing urgent requests for bearers and supplies. Fortunately a Ford, well loaded, had now got over the road obstacles and we spent most of the night making up and sending forward bundles of dressings and medical comforts. A few wounded trickled in, but there was ample accommodation for them. Towards morning I dossed down on the stone floor and managed to get some badly-needed sleep.

On the morning of the 23rd I was up very early: stiff, dirty and uncomfortable. No shave, patchy washing and haphazard feeding these last days. The monastery buildings, or whatever they were, of Flesquieres failed to cheer one in the thin morning light. A huge courtyard surrounded by large but much shelled stone buildings and outhouses. Those sufficiently intact were soon adapted to the various purposes of a Field Ambulance, and the unit, which had been coming in during the small hours, was already settling in; the men and N.C.O.s in one block, wounded in another, officers in a third. A good deal of shelling was going on, and it struck me that the prominent buildings we occupied were not so desirable as I had thought; all right if our advance continued and Cambrai was captured, but bound to be pounded to pieces in the event of a hold up or reverse. However, it was the only possible spot available.

After a scratch wash up and breakfast, I decided to do a tour round the Battalion Aid Posts and see how the medical arrangements were working. The various M.O.s had kept in touch with me and I had marked on the map the position of the R.A.P.s given me by them, so there appeared to be no special difficulties ahead. One of our padres[1] accompanied me and we set off together, soon leaving the village of Flesquieres behind. An open country stretched before us, and we trudged along a good enough road, here and there gaping with nasty shell holes. It led in the direction of Fontaine, a large village some kilometres short of Cambrai, on the Bapaume-Cambrai road. Passing the small Bois de L'Orval on our left, we soon came to the farm of La Justice, where was the first Aid Post, and I spent some time ascertaining and noting the inevitable wants of the M.O., who had a room full of wounded and no means of evacuating them. So far there had been little in the way of shelling to trouble us and the walk had not been unpleasant. On the outskirts of Flesquieres we had passed a derelict tank, with two headless bodies lying beside it.

Pickets of the 7th Gordons were digging themselves in to left and right, and further forward were the wagon lines of the R.F.A. in the shelter of the spinney. The guns were halted on the further side to the left. Near to La Justice the road ran between a row of holes, breast high and manned by a Lewis gun section who were able to give us some hazy notion of the actual Front. At the Aid Post the padre picked up a German dictionary left by the retreating troops. There were many Germans amongst the wounded, one an abdominal case in a serious condition.

This job over we passed on our way. The direct route to Fontaine, where I believed I would find the 5th Gordons, was straight forward by the road we were on; but as an Aid Post was indicated on my map at Anneux, on our left, I decided to deviate there in the first place and make fresh plans at that spot. Anneux was only about half a-mile distant, the morning fine, and there appeared

[1] Rev. Andrew Grant, M.C.

BATTLE OF CAMBRAI, 1917.

to be a reactionary quietness in the matter of shelling. Some shells were falling in the dip between Anneux and Fontaine, but none at all near us. Half way to Anneux we met a 7th Argyll, who had been sent back in guard of prisoners, resting in a sunk pit by the side of the road on his way back to his battalion, which he said (with a sweep of his hand including Bourlon Wood and Fontaine) "were holding that ridge!" The ruins of Anneux seemed quite deserted, but we discovered some West Riding Yeomanry leisurely examining two mine shafts. They had no clear idea how things were in front of them, did not belong to our Division, and knew little of their own! As we afterwards learned, there existed a gap between the 51st and the Division on its left (62nd I think), and we had unwittingly struck this hiatus; nor could these men give us any idea of where the enemy were. All the information they could give was that it might be unwise to go across country to Fontaine from where we were, because a sniper frequently got busy in that direction.

The padre and I consulted what to do. It seemed to me that the large forest, the famous Bois de Bourlon, on our left front must be in our hands as it dominated both the Bapaume Road and Fontaine. Unless we held it I failed to see how our troops could be in Fontaine. Our choice of routes to the latter place was between the main road, which skirted the Bois de Bourlon less than a mile north of Anneux, and directly across the country over which the sniper was said to be busy.

Everything being quiet, and the road not appealing to us, we decided to chance the sniper, and therefore followed a track made by a tank and proceeded across country in the direction of Fontaine, some three or four kilometres distant as far as we could judge. Occasional shells threw up large pillars of earth on our right, but not near enough to be alarming, and the walk was really quite enjoyable, the padre being in his usual good spirits. My idea was gradually to bear to the left towards the main road and strike it shortly before it passes into Fontaine. We dropped into a sunken road which soon emerged into the open flat and was there newly metalled, but the stones not pounded in or rolled in any way. Like all the German construction work it was extremely well done and had bricked edges.

We still walked through quiet, but pretty scenery, and were troubled very little by shells. If there were a sniper he took no notice of us. As we were nearing the road, however, our steps were arrested by shouts coming from our left. The padre said he saw some men he took to be West Yorks on account of their short coats and woolly jackets. We halted, listened, and again heard the shouts, coming apparently from the edge of Bourlon Wood quite close to us. I could see nothing.

Thinking it possible that some wounded might by lying there and that my Red Cross brassard had been recognised by them, I suggested to the padre we should slant in the direction of the shouts and ascertain what was the matter. I had my Zeiss glasses with me but failed to discover anything suspicious, though, perhaps, the scrutiny was careless owing to neither of us imagining the enemy was so near as he turned out to be! On getting close to the main road we were hailed by unmistakably Boche voices, a number of soldiers with rifles at the present sprang into view on the edge of the wood and we were fairly caught! Escape was out of the question. The sunken road was too far behind us, neither of us particularly fleet of foot, and we would in any case have been riddled with bullets before we had gone fifty yards. "Hands up" we were ordered, and hands up it was till we reached the wood. Here we found quite a large party of men under an officer ambushed at the edge of the wood in a well-engineered earthen redoubt, with loopholed banks and a number of light guns. On our arrival we were lightly searched for arms by the officer, questioned as to who we were and placed under guard. As the padre said, the scene was like one from a brigand story. Lines of soldiers, like posts in a fence, each standing in a cut of his own length held the fringe of the wood, and extending as far as we could see.

But our halt there was of short duration; two very young lads, with open and cheerful countenances, were placed in charge of us, given their orders, and we were marched off through the wood in a northerly direction. I don't know how the padre felt, but for my part the shock was pretty great and I felt most horribly depressed. It had come on so suddenly. At one moment we were free and having a walk which was enjoyable enough considering where we were and what was afoot; the next we were prisoners. We had suddenly dived behind that impenetrable screen before which we had moved for nearly three years. It was an unexpected plunge behind the scenes! My guard was a mere lad, I should think about nineteen, most likely a farm labourer from some quiet country spot. There had been at first unpleasant glances all around us at the fort, but once it was known it was a case of "Artzt" and "Pfarrer" these changed to good-humoured amusement! Depressed as I was, I found the march to Bourlon village, to which we were conducted, intensely interesting. What first attracted my attention was the extent to which the Boche used the trees as look-out places and sniping posts, stout crow's nests being visible high up the stems of many of them. No wonder there were reports of sniping over the ground we had crossed!

The *Bois* consisted of stout and very tall trees, closely set together, with paths and clearings, and here and there a road cut through. The crow's nests must have been ideal spots to snipe from, but nasty for the occupants during shelling! The wood proved to be full of Boches — in dug-outs, trenches, behind roads, in bushes, etc.

Through this wood we were guided and, in half an-hour or so, reached the railway station of Bourlon village just to the north.

Here, apparently, was a H.Q. of some sort. We were kept on the station platform while our arrival was reported, and soon there emerged from the station buildings an officer of some rank, a colonel, or brigadier, perhaps, who immediately set about questioning us eagerly. His main object was to extract from us the Zero hour for the day. He said in broken English:— "When the attack? One o'clock? Two? Three?" Of course there was nothing doing with us, nor did we ourselves know anything about it. The time of our capture must have been about 10 a.m., and so far as we knew our troops might not be going to attack at all. We had started on our tour too early for the news of the day's doings to have leaked out.

Suddenly, while we were being questioned on the station platform, there came the scream of a shell and we got our first sight of how a British shell explodes! Most satisfactory it was too! Another, and yet another, followed in rapid succession, each falling nearer and nearer to where we stood. It was quite obvious they were meant for the station. My own mood was such that I felt I cared not a single jot. For the first (and only) time I did not care if it snowed shells! But with the Boche it was not so. Where there had been quite a little crowd around us—officers, soldiers, guards, orderlies, etc.— there was soon only open platform. Every man Jack, even our guards, bolted to the buildings and no doubt went rapidly below ground. So comical was it, that my first thought was "Why not do a bunk?" But a moment's reflection made me realise the hopelessness of it. We would have to hide until dark, make our way through a huge forest crammed with Germans, and chance being shot at. For two elderly non-combatants any such adventure would have been merely silly.

The next incident to happen was the arrival right above us of a British aeroplane. Whether it was to observe the shooting we were unable to say, but we hoped no bomb was coming our way. In any case the shelling stopped, the 'plane disappeared and the officer and crowd emerged once more. After much more talk, a motor lorry passing along the road near us was hailed, and we two prisoners directed to climb in. The padre with one guard disappeared into the interior, while I was soon perched in front between the driver and the other. The lorry had evidently conveyed small arms ammunition to the front and was returning empty.

The drive, however, was not to be uneventful. Shelling was in full force once more and our driver was of the "windy" species. The road was fairly good, quite straight, lined with tree trunks and, though none too wide, was of good enough surface for the speed we were travelling. What disturbed me more than the shelling was the driving! The padre was inside and missed our erratic swerves, but I had the full benefit. Our driver was much more interested looking backwards to see "where that one went" than in attending to his wheel. Once we missed a tree by inches! I found my few words of German flowing back to me, and these I used in the most energetic fashion, while more than once I could not help grasping the wheel to try to prevent a disaster.

Happily the danger of this grew less as we made our way back from the line, and the drive became really interesting, despite the shocking smell of the petrol, benzol, or whatever it was that propelled the machine. There were Boche troops and guns to look at, the myriads of notices stuck about, etc., etc. It was chilly without an overcoat, however, and I for one was not sorry when the engine, which for some time had given trouble, gave out altogether, and we were ordered to get down and march along on foot. Of course we had no idea of our destination. We got out at a crossroads, and, after a march of some miles, reached Sailly Lestrem, a good sized village. German guns were blazing away all along that road in the direction of Fontaine. Although we were unaware of it, Fontaine was being heavily attacked, and, as we afterwards learned, was captured during the day. Had we reached that spot as we intended before our capture, there is small doubt that we would have participated in the disaster, and not unlikely in unpleasant fashion!

At Sailly we were marched into an imposing house in a garden, probably a Brigade H.Q. Here a photographer was taking a group of orderlies in the doorway where we were halted. The padre believed that we were included, but we tried to dodge the compliment. Inside, we were again questioned, but only in a perfunctory way. Lunch was on the table and one Boche officer was loudly partaking. Another was poring over a map at the 'phone. We were not offered food, though very ready for it. An officer then buttoned on his coat and beckoned us to follow. A fine touring car awaited him and into it we all got, the officer saying to us, "Gentlemen, you are my prisoners." For half an hour we bowled easily along. The car was a good one (though the spirit again smelt vilely), and I was much charmed with the musical whistle employed in lieu of a horn.

From accounts given to us by other officer prisoners later on we realised how fortunate we were to be driven. Possibly the fact of our being non-combatants and not in the first bloom of youth had to do with our luck in this respect! We were taken to quite a large château about ten miles distant, evidently newly taken on as H.Q., as

BATTLE OF CAMBRAI, 1917.

the telephones were in the course of being installed. We learnt later that Cambrai had been evacuated hurriedly, fearing its capture by our troops, and this was one of the fresh H.Q. Lunch was being served, and we did not know whether we hoped to be offered any or not. We were frightfully hungry, but also very dirty, and cut poor figures as British officers. I was unshaven, and both of us were wearing the oldest of breeches and tunics, much disfigured by the muck picked up during the battle. However, there was no invitation and we remained hungry. I had no idea what time it was, as my watch had broken down and been left by me at Flesquieres. More perfunctory questioning, and we were conducted to what was possibly Corps H.Q., and then to the office of the Intelligence Department, where a long wait ensued, fortunately beside a nice stove! Then came the real questioning, and for this we were taken separately — I suppose to see if our answers tallied. The questions were put abruptly, not to say roughly, but there was no real impoliteness. Of course every attempt was made to extract information, but on our denial there was no exhibition of "frightfulness." Some amusement was caused by my refusal to give Division, Brigade, Brigadier's name, etc., seeing that the information was plastered over my uniform and helmet, and when I refused the name of my Brigadier I was told "He is Pelham Burn and he goes on leave next week!" They knew more than I did!

Apart from attempts to extract information, we were asked all sorts of informal questions, here as everywhere else where we were questioned. How long did we think the war would last? How did our men like it? What did we think of the U boats?, etc.

We had to hand over all written matter in our possession, my fine field glasses, maps, etc. I tried to keep my business book, which, as I pointed out, contained nothing but family and personal business entries, but it was no use. The padre, similarly, lost his cheque book, private letters and other odds and ends, his Sam Browne belt, prayer book and other religious books. Our watches, pocket knives and money were not touched. Two new guards now took us in charge and marched us to the Town Major's, where a chit was given us for a meal! This was afforded at what seemed to be a newly opened soldier's club kitchen, a beautifully equipped and spotlessly clean apartment.

There we ate soup, bread and sausage, and were removed later to the guardroom, a long, large, wooden hut with a stove at one end, four wire beds on each side of the room, some forms, a table and half a dozen soldiers. They were decent fellows, quite ready to be amicable, and set us down by the fire and tried to talk to us. One, a Pole by his name, told the padre he too was a Catholic. My scanty knowledge of the language here began really to be of use. I suggested "How about beer?" They were visibly cheered by the question, and said it could easily be got. They had to pay for it themselves, however, as our French money was of no use! This was at Marquette, a small village north of the Sensee Canal and due north of Cambrai. Here we remained until early evening, occasionally talking to the men in the guardroom who were, of course, keenly interested in us and all we managed to say to them. I, too, was interested to see their military routine going on. Every now and then a soldier got up, buckled on his equipment and disappeared, while others, whose spell on guard was over, returned to the comfort and ease of the guardroom. Their politeness of manner and instinctive avoidance of offence nearly equalled that of our own men in similar circumstances. . . .

So much for the first impressions of a prisoner of war! . . .

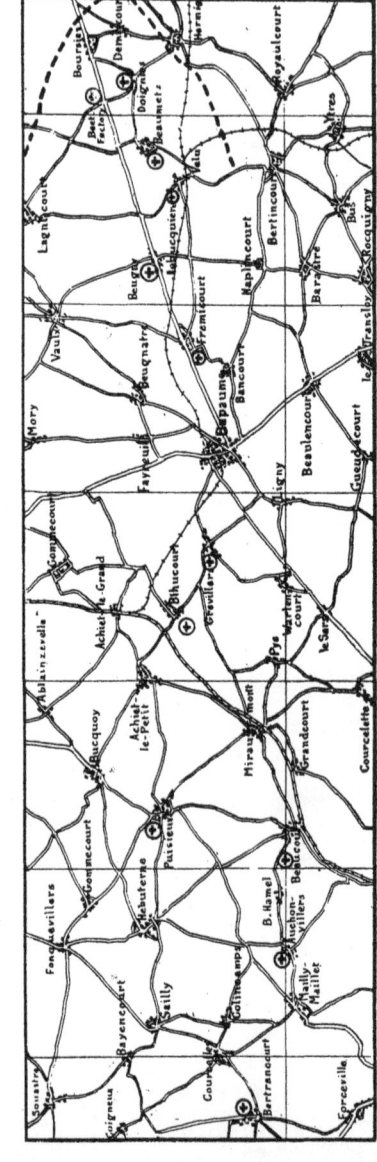

Medical Posts during the Retreat, March 1918.

Facing page 179.

CHAPTER IX.

The German Offensive, 1918.

*"Good old 51st!
Sticking it still!
Cheerio!"*[1]

"*21st March.*—On the Third Army front our line in the Flesquieres salient had not been heavily attacked and was substantially intact. Beyond this sector fierce fighting took place around Demicourt and Doignies, and north of the village of Beaumetz-lez-Cambrai. In this area the 51st Division was heavily engaged, but from noon onwards practically no progress was made by the enemy. . . .

"*22nd March.*—A very gallant fight was made by the 51st Division in the neighbourhood of the Bapaume-Cambrai road, against repeated attacks. . . . In the neighbourhood of Beaumetz the enemy continued his assault with great determination, but was held by the 51st Division and a Brigade of the 25th Division till the evening. Our troops were then withdrawn, under orders, to positions south of the village."—*(Sir Douglas Haig's Despatches.)*

"During the next few days the 51st Division fought many critical rearguard actions. It was thereafter taken out of the line. Its total losses since the morning of the 21st were over 4,900."—*(The Territorial Divisions.)*

By the 3rd December, 1917, the Division, after a rest in the neighbourhood of Baisieux, had taken over from the 56th Division a sector of 6,000 yards astride of the Bapaume-Cambrai road, from Betty Avenue, Demicourt, on the right, to The Strand on the left; Boursies on the Bapaume-Cambrai road being about the centre.

Our R.A.M.C. Advanced Dressing Stations were dug-outs at Doignies on the right, and Beetroot Factory (where the *sous-terrain* ran under the *Route Nationale*)

---

[1] Message from the enemy, written on small white balloon sent over.

on the left, with the Main Dressing Station at Beugny and the Divisional Rest Station at Bihucourt. As Forward Evacuation Officer, my residence was one of the dug-outs in Doignies, where we had an uneventful enough stay for three weeks.

The village—what was left of it, anyway—was shelled daily, with an occasional bombing by way of variety. But the men were ensconced in two deep dug-outs; while a sandbagged shelter off the trench served as officer's messroom, with a two-bunk dug-out opening off it again, into which one descended for sleep at night or for safety by day when more head cover was desirable. In the evening when nothing else was doing we read the awful magazine rubbish that passed for literature in war time and such places, or entertained angels unawares—gunners chiefly—who gave us much mixed news in return for our hospitality.

One fine afternoon we were greatly cheered by a well-informed caller telling us that the Hun was mining the village and that we might all go up at any time. That same night the A.D.S. was vigorously plastered with shells, and Jerry got on to a dump behind us which went aloft with a terrific concussion. It also spoiled our frugal dinner; as our messman, bringing it in on a tray, most excusably lay down on the top of it through one shell landing on the parados of the trench three yards away. What he rescued of our meal was not appetising, and my diary comment that night of "this place is pretty rotten altogether," was, I believe, justifiable. But next morning, it being Christmas Day, that same chap was out bright and early and had our messroom decorated with ivy which he had got off a ruined wall in the village—"just to make it a bit more seasonable like." Good lad! Optimism was always an outstanding asset in war.

The following day an English Siege Battery officer blew in to say his people "were killing their pig in view of

the festive season." Their *pig?* O, yes! For some time
they had been carrying two grunters about with them;
but lately some Americans had stolen, killed, and eaten
the better of the two; vigorously denying, when taxed
with the offence, any knowledge whatsoever of the matter.
St. Serf, I suggested, would have been the most useful
man to get as umpire in such a case, for one remembered
his success with the sheep-stealer. This evil-doer also
denied a similar charge, and persisted in his denial, even
when confronted by the accusing saint; but

"The sheep then bleated in his wame"

(according to "Wyntoun's Chronicle"), which effort, of
course, completely gave the show away. But a modern
Yank was probably far beyond being got at by such a
borborygmous miracle. My English friend, however, was
not interested in the reference:—"Never heard of the
blighter! Damn these gum-chewers, anyway!"

On the 27th I was called back to Divisional Headquarters to act as A.D.M.S., owing to Colonel C. C.
Fleming, D.S.O., who had come out with us in that
capacity, having died of wounds sustained during a
bombing raid at Fremicourt the previous evening. His
death caused widespread regret amongst the R.A.M.C.
of the Division, with whom he was deservedly popular
owing to his genial, kindly disposition. Later on my
appointment was confirmed at—as I learnt afterwards—
General Harper's request; and it then fell to me to set up
business as a prophet in my own country, a proceeding
that we have good authority for recognising as being not
without risk. But I had the good luck to fall heir to a
most active and efficient D.A.D.M.S.[1] and an ever reliable Q.M.S.[2] with—what I never had—an encyclopædic
knowledge of all Army Forms. Nor can I pay a sufficient

[1] Captain A. Ramsbottom, M.C.
[2] Q.M.S. James Stables, M.S.M.

tribute to the unforgettable loyalty and good fellowship of all the M.O.s in the Division, Field Ambulance and Regimental, which made my job of work a constant pleasure up to the last.

Our Divisional Headquarters, set in hutments amongst the ruins, were at Fremicourt, a few kilometres from Bapaume. A short distance up the Route Nationale to Cambrai was Beugny, also badly knocked about. In the ruins of the church there, amongst all the broken symbols of religion, was a tablet let into the wall, behind what was left of the altar, to commemorate the rebuilding of the church in 1878. The *curé* of that day had indulged in a gentle innuendo against his wealthier parishioners, for the last paragraph ran:—"Les riches ont donné et les pauvres ont été généreux." A nice distinction!

Interesting visitors we had occasionally. In the earlier part of the year various U.S.A. officers were at D.H.Q. for instruction. One was Major-General Alexander, by descent a Forfarshire Scot, his folk having left there in 1717, after being mixed up in the '15. Since then they had been Marylanders. A fine, bluff, hearty man he was, who had seen a lot of service in the Philippines and Mexico. Another was Colonel Stimson, who had been Secretary of State for War in Taft's Cabinet. He had a good tale about an Alabama regiment which, on landing in England, was played from the quay to its quarters by a well-meaning British military band enthusiastically pumping out "As we went marching through Georgia!"—a very much mistaken compliment which the new arrivals took uncommonly badly! On another occasion we had a visit from four French journalists, representing the *Matin*, *Journal*, etc. One had the *Medaille Militaire*, the *Croix de Guerre* and a wooden leg, all gained in the war.

Going about the area it was always worth noting the different nationalities—European, African, Asian. The

French Algerians, picturesque fellows in blue tunics with red trousers (old French infantry uniform) and red fezzes, were busy putting up temporary sectional houses for the returning inhabitants. One day a lot of these Africans ran *amok*, as they objected to living in such a freely bombed area, and had to be rounded up with revolvers by the Divisional gendarmerie. (Their objection was not without reason: one bomb that was dropped behind our Divisional Rest Station at Bihucourt made a hole 30 feet in diameter by 20 deep.) On our part we had Chinese and Indian Labour Companies. The Chinese were a cheery, chattering crowd, but vicious when roused. An R.C. padre told me that in his area ten of them attended mass regularly and could recite their prayers in Latin: converts of some Catholic mission. The Indians always looked the picture of misery in cold or wet weather.

Walking behind a man of a Labour Company on the Cambrai road one day I read this interesting inscription on his gas helmet satchel:—"Peter Dean. This is mine! Stolen goods! PUT IT DOWN!" Peter had, after much experience, evidently lost faith in military mankind and methods, and set about putting his house in order on purely individualistic lines.

Gymkhanas were held at intervals — betting by totalisator—on a slope behind Fremicourt, in full view of Bourlon Wood: hurdle and flat, with occasional bareback mule racing for Hindu R.A. drivers and ditto for Jocks in kilts!

Divisional baths at Beugny, Lebucquiere and Fremicourt dealt weekly with 11,000 men. The Foden Lorry Thresh Disinfector, in constant demand, toured the district regularly, the merry merchant who drove it sleeping (for warmth and head cover from Hun ironmongery) inside the steam chamber! He was pre-eminently and to the end a civilian in khaki, and his highest attempt at a military salute never rose beyond touching his cap with one finger and the bestowal of a friendly grin on those he favoured. When you had thoroughly gained his approbation, he usually dispensed with his meagre acknowledgment of differences in rank. We meet him again.

Medical work remained of the routine nature usual in trench holding until March, when it became evident that an attack by the enemy was impending. On the 11th our Divisional G.O.C., Major-General Sir G. M. Harper, K.C.B., D.S.O., was promoted to the command of the IVth Corps.[1]

Up to now all our R.A.M.C. experiences had consisted of attending to casualties while "sitting tight" in trench warfare, taking part in pushes, or in the more rapid advance of Cambrai. But here we were for the first time to face the far greater difficulties of evacuating wounded during a retreat.

On 21st March the long expected storm broke, and broke with hurricane fury. The enemy's barrage commenced at 5 a.m., extending from "the front line to Paris." In our sector Doignies, Beaumetz, Lebucquiere, Velu, Fremicourt, Beugny and the Bapaume-Cambrai road were all heavily shelled. At Fremicourt, the first shell fell in D.H.Q., killing a signaller, and the wooden hutments had to be rapidly evacuated in favour of a large

---

[1] "Though his promotion came as no surprise, and was indeed confidently expected, the departure of the General came nevertheless as a severe blow.... General Harper's personality was one which won for him the genuine affection of all ranks with whom he came in contact.... It can safely be said that the Jocks regarded 'Uncle' or 'Daddie,' as the General was known to them, not merely as a commander in whom lay the origin of their success, but as a friend who had their constant welfare in mind.... General Harper was succeeded as commander of the 51st Division by Major-General G. T. C. Carter-Campbell, C.B., D.S.O., Scottish Rifles, who remained in command until after the armistice.... He could not have been more unfortunate in the period in which he took over command of the Division than he was. Within a few days of his arrival tremendous losses were sustained in the German offensive in March, only to be followed by a further engagement in April, with an almost equal number of casualties."—(*History of the 51st Division.*)

THE GERMAN OFFENSIVE, 1918. 185

and deep dug-out. "In rear of the Divisional area, places such as Bapaume, Albert, Frevent and St. Pol were all shelled by long range guns, while Paris was engaged by 'Big Bertha.' "[1] The bombardment lasted with its original intensity for four hours.

21st March: First Day of Enemy Offensive.—When the enemy offensive began the medical arrangements for the evacuation of Divisional wounded were on the following plan.

The Forward Evacuation Officer at the time was the O.C. 2/1st Highland Field Ambulance, whose personnel was supplemented in the routine way by the bearer divisions from the other two Field Ambulances. His headquarters were at Gropi Camp, Lebucquiere. Advanced Dressing Stations were situated at Doignies and at Beetroot Factory on the Bapaume-Cambrai road, with Relay Bearer Posts at Beaumetz and Demicourt. The bearers of all three Field Ambulances were employed in the evacuation of wounded under his orders, and distributed so as to give:—

- 8 bearers at each Regimental Aid Post.
- 50 bearers at Beetroot Factory A.D.S.
- 30 bearers at Doignies A.D.S.
- 30 bearers at Relay Post, Beaumetz.
- 20 bearers at Relay Post, Demicourt.
- 20 bearers at Relay Post, Level Crossing, Lebucquiere.

The remainder were held in reserve at Gropi Camp, Lebucquiere.

The tent division of the 2nd Highland Field Ambulance was employed at the Divisional Rest Station, Bihucourt: that of the 3rd Highland Field Ambulance at the Corps Main Dressing Station, Beugny: while that of the 2/1st Highland Field Ambulance was employed at

[1] *History of the 51st Division.*

the Advanced Dressing Station, as its O.C. was Forward Evacuation Officer.

All motor ambulance cars, less one car which remained at the Rest Station, Bihucourt, and all horse ambulance wagons, were parked at Beugny; from there to be distributed as required under orders of the Forward Evacuation Officer. Wheeled stretcher-carriers (collapsible Miller-James type) were parked at Gropi Camp, Lebucquiere, and at Main Dressing Station, Beugny, to be sent up in cars when wanted.

A Corps Main Dressing Station was established at Beugny, to which were to be sent all cases except those urgently requiring evacuation direct to the Casualty Clearing Station from the Advanced Dressing Station. Evacuation from the Main Dressing Station was by Motor Ambulance Corps right through by road to the C.C.S.s at Grevillers; or by the light railway to a detraining centre at Bapaume, from which place M.A.C. cars conveyed patients to the C.C.S.s. A Walking Wounded Collecting Station was established in marquees at Beugny, beside the Corps Main Dressing Station. Horse ambulance wagons were available at Beaumetz, and road junction of Nine Elms Road with main Cambrai Road, to pick up walking wounded and convey them to their Collecting Station.

In the event of a retirement the arrangement made was that the Advanced Dressing Station, Doignies, was to fall back on Gropi Camp, Lebucquiere, leaving a Collecting Post at Beaumetz Relay Bearer Post, to which cars were to run as long as possible. Doignies A.D.S. was then to become a Regimental Aid Post, and casualties from it were to be evacuated to Beaumetz by wheeled stretcher and hand carriage. Similarly, the A.D.S. at Beetroot Factory was to fall back on Beugny, Beetroot Factory becoming then an R.A.P. A Collecting Post was then to be established at Nine Elms, to which cars were to run as long as possible. Cases from R.A.P.s were to be taken there by wheeled stretcher and hand carriage. The Corps Main Dressing Station at Beugny was, on retreating, to fall back on huts at Loch Camp on the Bapaume-Cambrai road near Fremicourt.

For three months before the action commenced construction work had gone on steadily at the two Advanced Dressing Stations at Beetroot Factory and Doignies, with the view of strengthening them and increasing the accommodation. A new sloping entrance to Beetroot Factory dug-outs—which ran in beneath the Bapaume-Cambrai road—had been completed, and the dug-outs themselves enlarged. At Doignies, where the accommodation had consisted of only two deep dug-outs, a new elephant shelter for an extra 20 lying cases was constructed, sunk in to the side of the trench and covered with iron rails, bricks, etc., so as to leave a "bursting space" for further safety. A good supply of blankets, stretchers and medical stores was always maintained in each post; in the anticipation that, had our troops to retire and cases to be left in the enemy's hands, our casualties would to a certain extent benefit by this supply.

It was also fully anticipated that the routes Beetroot Factory to Beugny and Doignies to Beaumetz would be extremely difficult to work; but the absolute occlusion of these routes by the intensity of the initial enemy fire put the Advanced Dressing Stations completely out of action at once and finally. All personnel there became casualties, while the cars and motor cycles in use were destroyed by shell fire. One medical officer made an attempt to work across from Beaumetz to Beetroot Factory, but found it quite impossible and returned to Beugny. Another M.O., newly reported for duty from England, and detailed for Doignies, managed to get through the barrage after the action commenced, guided by our gallant and indefatigable senior chaplain,[1] only to be taken prisoner there in his company.

After the action began no cases were evacuated from Beetroot Factory and no messenger or car got through. Similarly, no cases were evacuated from Doignies; but in response to the only message that got through from the M.O. in charge there,[2] dated 12.30 p.m., an attempt was made to send up three horse ambulance wagons from Beaumetz by the fair weather track to Doignies. The message had stated that a steady stream of casualties was arriving; that a large amount of gas shells had been thrown over; that the Advanced Dressing Station had received several direct hits, but that no casualties to the personnel had been so far sustained. After proceeding about half way under very heavy fire the drivers came in full view of the hordes of advancing field-greys, and saved the wagons by galloping back to Beaumetz.

At 11 a.m. the Forward Evacuation Officer[3] was killed by a shell at his headquarters at Gropi Camp, Lebucquiere, while getting his men into a sunken road for shelter, and the same shell mortally wounded one of his officers,[4] who died two hours later at the Main Dressing Station, Beugny. The duties of Forward Evacuation Officer were at once taken over and ably conducted throughout by the second in command of the 3rd Highland Field Ambulance.[5]

As all telephonic communications had now broken down, various attempts were made by motor cyclists and runners to get in touch with Doignies and Beetroot Factory, but without effect. One motor cyclist got within sight of Doignies about 12 noon, but through field glasses could see no sign of movement there.

[1] Rev. Patrick Sinclair, D.S.O.
[2] Major J. S. Maconochie, M.C.
[3] Lieutenant-Colonel James Robertson.
[4] Captain B. G. Beveridge, M.C.
[5] Major J. Martin Smith, M.C.

THE GERMAN OFFENSIVE, 1918. 189

Meanwhile the staff at the Main Dressing Station, Beugny, the Relay Posts at Beaumetz and at the Level Crossing, Lebucquiere, and the Medical Inspection Room of D.H.Q. at Fremicourt, were fully occupied with local casualties due to the continuous and heavy shelling of the area. Early in the morning the Corps Main Dressing Station and Walking Wounded Collecting Station at Beugny, the latter of which was in the hands of a party from an ambulance of the 25th Division, came under heavy enemy fire. Both institutions consisted only of huts and tentage with no deep dug-outs or other reliable cover, and a medical officer of the 25th Division was killed.

In the afternoon the M.O.s of the 6th and 7th Black Watch were reported missing, and as the M.O. of the 7th Gordon Highlanders was ascertained to be at a new R.A.P. a kilometre to the right of Morchies, an additional M.O. was ordered up at night from Beugny, with bearers, to join him and help to carry on the medical work of the three battalions in that area. Through the night this R.A.P. was vacated and moved to a deep dug-out at Chaufour's Wood, whence the cases were carried to the Highland Division Soup Kitchen site, between Beugny and Beetroot Factory, and then trollied along the light railway and met by cars on the Cambrai road. These two officers remained at this post till the enemy were within 300 yards of them, and managed to evacuate all their cases. In the late afternoon also, three cars were got up by Hermies to within 100 yards of Demicourt, and evacuated cases from battalions on the right, which had side-slipped there owing to the Doignies-Beaumetz road being impracticable. An R.A.P. at the old Relay Post in the Sunken Road at Beaumetz was also got in touch with, and cases there taken to Beugny. A Ford car was knocked out at Lebucquiere at 4.30 p.m.

At 5 p.m., as the Main Dressing Station and

Walking Wounded Collecting Station at Beugny were again being freely shelled, these were moved back, according to the arrangements previously made, to Loch Camp at Fremicourt, some three kilometres nearer Bapaume on the Route Nationale, the details of the 2/1st Highland Field Ambulance at Gropi Camp, Lebucquiere, also moving there; while a party of the 77th Field Ambulance of the 25th Division accompanied them to carry on the Walking Wounded Collecting Station. The Forward Evacuation Officer remained with a party at Beugny to conduct an Advanced Dressing Station as long as possible, and to maintain touch with what R.A.P.s he could locate, by cars, cyclists or runners. An officer and party were also left at the Level Crossing elephant shelter, Lebucquiere; and an N.C.O. and 10 bearers at Sunken Road, Beaumetz, with the same end in view.

A continuous stream of local casualties continued to be dealt with at all these posts. During the night enemy fire slackened considerably, and cars managed to run well forward on the Cambrai road to the Soup Kitchen and Nine Elms, beyond Beugny, clearing numerous cases from the line and local casualties from the roads and encampments.

22nd March: Second Day of Enemy Offensive.— At 1.25 a.m. and 3.55 a.m. the Main Dressing Station reported that the Motor Ambulance Convoy service was unable to cope with the very large number of wounded requiring evacuation; and that sufficient blankets were not available from the Casualty Clearing Stations[1] at Grevillers, as these were moving back and that to do this the M.A.C. was called on to help. All horse ambulance wagons, with some motor ambulance cars obtained from the 57th Field Ambulance, were therefore turned on to clear the M.D.S., and its casualties

---

[1] Casualty Clearing Stations had no transport of their own.

were also evacuated by Decauville railway to the detraining centre at Bapaume. By 5 a.m., as wounded were coming in steadily and in very large numbers, the Main Dressing Station still reported the M.A.C. service inadequate for rapid clearance. This delay, however, was inevitable owing to the double duties of the M.A.C., the great congestion of traffic on the evacuation routes, and the consequent holding up of the car service.

At 10.30 a.m. the progress of evacuation, though still somewhat slow, was held to be as satisfactory as it could be under the extremely difficult circumstances prevailing.

At 11 a.m. the positions of the Medical Posts that could be definitely ascertained were as follows:—

Regimental Aid Posts.—Beaumetz.
Collecting Posts. — Chaufours Wood, Beugny, Lebucquiere (Level Crossing).
M.D.S., H.Q. of Ambulance Evacuating Line and W.W.C.S.—Loch Camp, near Fremicourt, on Bapaume-Cambrai road.
Casualty Clearing Stations.—Nos. 3 and 29, Grevillers (engaged in moving back).
Divisional Rest Station.—Bihucourt.

Owing to the continued and increasing shelling of Beugny the Forward Evacuation Officer was now ordered to fall back on Loch Camp, and to keep on running his cars up the Cambrai road as far, and as long as, he could.

At 1 p.m. Divisional Headquarters moved back from Fremicourt to Grevillers. At 4 p.m., as the Loch Camp Main Dressing Station (merely a collection of huts without dug-outs or other shelter) was getting sharply shelled, the 3rd Highland Field Ambulance was ordered to move back to the site at Grevillers vacated by No. 29 Casualty Clearing Station, to deal with lying cases; while the site of No. 3 Casualty Clearing Station was taken over by an ambulance of the 41st Division as a Walking Wounded Collecting Station. The 3rd Highland Field Ambulance opened a Main Dressing Station at 7.30 p.m., and very soon had over 500 casualties dumped on it by ambulance cars of other Divisions, who were unaware that the C.C.S.s had closed down and were on the move. The Forward Evacuation Officer remained behind with a party and cars at Loch Camp to run an Advanced Dressing Station as long as it was feasible. At this stage, too, the A.D.S. at the Level Crossing, Lebucquiere, was vacated by 51st Division personnel by arrangements made with the A.D.M.S., 19th Division, the personnel retiring to Loch Camp.

In response to a message from a new R.A.P. of the 7th Argyll and Sutherland Highlanders in front of Velu, cars were run up there to evacuate cases, but failed in the darkness to find the place. A Brigade staff officer stated that everybody was supposed to have gone. The M.O. 4th Gordon Highlanders, however, was got in touch with in the same vicinity and his cases evacuated. Later, the other location was got at and also cleared.

At 8 p.m., as the Loch Camp area was again being heavily shelled, the Forward Evacuation Officer was ordered to fall back on Grevillers, leaving cars and a small party to continue clearing the Cambrai road. The 2nd Highland Field Ambulance reported from Divisional Rest Station, Bihucourt, that it had been dealing all day with casualties from the 40th Division, which had found their way there via Sapignies, that the site was now coming under steady shell fire, and that it had sustained several casualties.

23rd March: Third Day of Enemy Offensive.—In the morning definite information could be got regarding the position of only three battalions, viz.:—7th Argyll and Sutherland Highlanders in front of Velu, 6th Seaforth Highlanders at Lebucquiere, and 6th Gordon Highlanders at Middlesex Camp.

THE GERMAN OFFENSIVE, 1918.

As M.A.C. cars continued to be insufficient to clear Main Dressing Station, Grevillers, over 150 cases had accumulated; and as the area was being shelled, 20 extra cars were got from Corps and put on the route, while four lorries, also from Corps, were sent to Grevillers to salve all possible medical stores there for removal to Corps H.Q. The M.A.C. was still having very heavy work owing to the extra task of assisting in moving and clearing the C.C.S.s to positions further back. At Grevillers the Main Dressing Station and the Walking Wounded Collecting Station were quite evidently soon to be shelled out of their present site owing to the presence of batteries in their immediate vicinity, which brought the enemy fire unpleasantly close, while the area was also being bombed. As the 2nd Highland Field Ambulance reported 5 killed and 8 wounded at the Bihucourt Divisional Rest Station from shell fire, it was ordered to move, after it had cleared its cases, to Puisieux.

To adjust the medical arrangements to the movements of troops the Forward Evacuation Officer was sent to reconnoitre Bancourt for a Collecting Post to take cases from the battalions in front. He got in touch with the M.O. 7th Gordon Highlanders; and a party of bearers with stretchers and dressings went up with a car to evacuate cases. He could not then find Brigade Headquarters, but they were got later and the location notified. The M.O. 4th Gordon Highlanders was also got in touch with and supplied with much-needed dressings and stores.

At 6 p.m. the Main Dressing Station was being better cleared by the extra 20 cars put on; and as shelling of the vicinity of the M.D.S. was continuing, the transport lines of the 3rd and 2/1st Highland Field Ambulances were now moved further back on the Grevillers-Achiet-le-Petit road. Five horses had been killed and one driver wounded.

The chief difficulty all day was the unavoidably slow evacuation of the wounded by the M.A.C. cars, whose work was much impeded both by the congested state of traffic on the roads and by the extra work thrown on them of assisting the retiral of the C.C.S.s.

24th March: Fourth Day of Enemy Offensive.—At 8 a.m. cases were still being brought in steadily; but the greatest difficulty was experienced in keeping in touch with the constantly changing R.A.P.s of the retreating troops. It was now definitely ascertained that the medical officers of the 6th and 7th Black Watch and 4th and 5th Seaforth Highlanders were missing, believed prisoners; while, later, the medical officer of the 8th Royal Scots and the medical officer of the 7th Black Watch (who had just returned from leave and rejoined his battalion) were wounded and evacuated.

As the Main Dressing Station at Grevillers was now rapidly becoming untenable owing to shelling and bombing, orders were sent to the 2nd Highland Field Ambulance at Puisieux to fall back on either Beaucourt or Miraumont, after a site had been prospected and chosen, and to open as Main Dressing Station. The 3rd Highland Field Ambulance was ordered to close down the Main Dressing Station at Grevillers whenever it had cleared all its casualties; and, failing a sufficient supply of M.A.C. cars for evacuation to C.C.S., to get rid of surplus cases by horse ambulance wagons and motor lorries to the new Main Dressing Station, Beaucourt, where the 2nd Highland Field Ambulance had reported it was now open. No cases were to be left behind at Grevillers, and all blankets, stretchers and medical stores that the unit could possibly carry were, in addition, to be removed.

At 1 p.m. the 3rd Highland Field Ambulance reported all its cases cleared. Shortly after it left the site

THE GERMAN OFFENSIVE, 1918.

all the huts and tentage remaining there were in flames; while it, along with the 2/1st Highland Field Ambulance, moved back to Beaucourt to join the 2nd Highland Field Ambulance; the Forward Evacuation Officer, with a medical officer and party with cars, being left at Grevillers to send back to Beaucourt any Divisional cases that came in. Divisional Headquarters at 2 p.m. moved back to Achiet-le-Petit, and at 7 p.m. again moved to Puisieux; the Field Ambulances at Beaucourt being ordered to retire to Auchonvillers and establish a Main Dressing Station there.

In the evening the Forward Evacuation Officer tried personally to get in touch with Brigade Headquarters at Bancourt with a car and dressings, but could not do so owing to the shelling of the route. He filled his car with wounded, roadside cases, which he evacuated to Albert, returning later to Grevillers; but, finding this place heavily shelled, he proceeded to Main Dressing Station at Auchonvillers.

25th March: Fifth Day of Enemy Offensive.—As the medical officer of the 6th Seaforth Highlanders was now reported a casualty, the Division had up to date lost 12 medical officers. An M.O. was sent up to the Brigade Headquarters, Irles, to join the 6th Seaforth Highlanders; and the Forward Evacuation Officer proceeded to Achiet-le-Petit with a party, cars, and dressings, to endeavour to run a mobile Collecting Post, keeping in touch with Brigade Headquarters through a liaison medical officer sent there with motor cyclist, this officer in turn trying to keep in touch with the R.A.P.s—a very difficult task but the only practical proposition. The Forward Evacuation Officer remained at Achiet-le-Petit until he was shelled out of it, when he moved to Bucquoy and worked with a medical officer and party of a 19th Divisional Ambulance until Bucquoy also had to be vacated owing to enemy fire.

As a Brigade Headquarters was reported in the afternoon at Puisieux, a car with a supply of shell dressings was sent up there at 10 a.m. The M.O. of the 4th Gordon Highlanders reported later at D.H.Q., along with the M.O. of the 7th Argyll and Sutherland Highlanders, both having lost touch with their units through their joint R.A.P. being set on fire and destroyed by enemy shells. These two officers were in a state of complete exhaustion, having worked without sleep since the offensive began.

In the afternoon Divisional Headquarters moved to Colincamps and later to Foncquevillers. A medical officer with three cars was sent to try and reach Puisieux and Brigade Headquarters, taking all available dressings with him. Orders were now sent to the Field Ambulances to move the Main Dressing Station back to Bertrancourt, and to send their cars to scout all routes of retiral and pick up straggling casualties. The Ambulances moved back later to Henu, carrying out the same programme; and cars were also sent to search Mailly-Maillet, where it was reported there was a large number of walking cases from our own and other Divisions.

In the evening the Forward Evacuation Officer, after having conducted his work throughout in the most gallant and efficient manner, was injured through the ambulance car on which he was travelling being upset at Boquemaison, and was evacuated to the Casualty Clearing Station at Frevent.

26th March: Sixth Day of Enemy Offensive.—At 8 a.m. Divisional Headquarters moved to Souastre, the Field Ambulances being busily engaged working with cars on all possible roads where straggling casualties might be found. At 6 p.m. D.H.Q. moved again to Laherliere, the Field Ambulances moving back to Saulty. The Division was withdrawn from the line in the evening. . . .

THE GERMAN OFFENSIVE, 1918.

Owing to the length of time the Division was in the line, the initial heavy losses of R.A.M.C. officers, personnel and motor transport, the nature of the fighting, the difficulty of locating and getting in touch with the constantly moving R.A.P.s, especially at night, the heavy shelling of the routes and the extraordinary traffic congestion on the roads, any collection and evacuation of the wounded throughout the engagement was a most difficult task. Further, the M.A.C., on which the bulk of the evacuation to C.C.S.s always falls, had the additional duty of assisting in the evacuation and removal of the retiring C.C.S.s. At the front the constantly changing line with the R.A.P.s rapidly moving to conform thereto, the loss of M.O.s of battalions (which was usually not known until hours after it had occurred), and the numbers of messages sent back for bearers and stores which never reached their destination, all tended to increase the difficulty. For the first four days the R.A.M.C. in the forward area worked, like the rest of the Division in the line, practically without sleep. A very large number of the more seriously wounded stretcher cases inevitably fell into the enemy's hands, although the most strenuous efforts were made to get them back; but in no case did a Main Dressing Station or other Field Ambulance post, on vacating its position, leave before clearing all its casualties either to the Clearing Station or to the new M.D.S. formed on the route of retiral.

During the enemy offensive 911 lying cases and 60 sick were passed through the books of the Main Dressing Station exclusive of the many hundreds of walking cases dealt with by the Walking Wounded Collecting Station; and, in addition, over 500 stretcher cases were dealt with at Grevillers which had passed through the books of other divisional ambulances and been sent to Grevillers under the belief that the C.C.S.s there were still open. . . .

The foregoing, mainly taken from the official medical

narrative sent in after the Division was withdrawn, gives an idea of the actual moves of the medical units. The main object throughout was to keep them intact as units and near enough to the retreating line to be able to carry out their job; while at the same time to ensure that they were neither captured nor knocked out *en bloc*. Handicapped as the R.A.M.C. was from the outset by the initial loss of 150 all ranks (chiefly from the bearer divisions of the ambulances) and by the constant increase, as the days went on, of M.O. casualties, it was somewhat surprising that so large a number of wounded were actually evacuated.

And not only evacuated, but efficiently dealt with; for the Consultant Surgeon, III Army,[1] wrote:—"What struck me all the time was the extraordinarily good condition in which the wounded arrived at the C.C.S.s. The D.M.S.'s complimentary remarks are thoroughly well deserved." The D.M.S.[2] said:—"Will you please convey to the medical units my congratulations on the good work that has been done"; while the G.O.C., 51st Division, wrote:—"I consider that the R.A.M.C. did everything that could possibly be done under the most difficult circumstances that could occur." The D.D.M.S., IV Corps,[3] also issued his thanks to the 51st Divisional R.A.M.C. "for their excellent work while serving under him."

The further back we got during the retreat the worse the congestion of the roads became; and by the fourth day of the offensive, when we were forced back into the non-devastated, or only partly devastated areas, the retreating troops became increasingly mixed up with civilian refugees. The routes were one steady, slowly moving mass of heterogeneous traffic, two, and some-

[1] Colonel H. M. W. Gray, C.B., C.M.G.
[2] Major-General J. Murray Irwin, C.B., C.M.G.
[3] Colonel C. E. Pollock, C.M.G., D.S.O.

times three, deep; but, while there was inevitable confusion, there was no panic, no loss of discipline. Guns, tractors, g.s. wagons, motor lorries, ambulance wagons and cars—these last often fighting their way against the stream to make for the line—walking wounded, motor ploughs, Labour Companies, Indian coolies shuffling apathetically along, with stick on shoulder and a bundle at each end of it, officers at the roadside, some diverting selections from the traffic stream into the fields in an attempt to reconstruct units, others in charge of stragglers' posts making new combinations of fighting material—all contributed to form an unforgettable picture. Here, perhaps wedged in between a caterpillar and a gun, was a little hooded country cart, loaded to excess with household goods and children—one infant I saw, wrapped in a shawl, was three days old—and the adults, many of them aged men and women, toiling along in the dust beside it. Other such carts, overloaded, lay with a broken or lost wheel in the ditch—abandoned by the owners who had perforce to go on.

One old man I met sat on the front of his loaded *chariot*, where a small crossroad intersected the larger one, gazing dispassionately at the never-ceasing stream of traffic which prevented his crossing to the other side.

> Rusticus expectat dum defluat amnis at ille
> Labitur et labetur. . . .

How long had he been there? "Four hours, Monsieur; but perhaps the opportunity might come soon: one must have patience!" Warning him to be ready to cut in, I went back a few yards and told a g.s. wagon driver to pull up for a second or two when he came opposite the old boy. So he got over; and his venerable cart with its pathetic mixed cargo of domestic relics and human misery went creaking and swaying up the ruts of the sunken road on the other side.

Another peasant, an old woman with long wisps of

grey hair blowing about a hard-featured, black-eyed, aquiline type of face, stood upright in an empty cart on the lip of a deep *chemin creux* into which she could not descend. She had been going against the traffic on the main road, making for a village that must have been long ago in the enemy's hands, and it had been necessary to side-track her for her own safety. It was useless to tell her that her errand was in vain: trembling with rage at having been turned aside, she only replied, with voluble abuse, that she had grandchildren there! And they had sent a message that she must come for them! Had she not sent a reply that she *would* come? These accursed soldiers had led her here, and she could not get further! .. Poor old soul! One could not but admire her steadfast determination, barren as it was bound to be of any practical result.

At Colincamps, where Divisional Headquarters remained for a few hours, the inhabitants were packing up and clearing out—for the second time in this war. Troops were coming and going; the Hun was known to be advancing rapidly; and everywhere was bustle. Standing in the dusk beside an ambulance car, which we had just filled with cases picked up in the village, I was outside the arched entrance to a farmyard, when a two-wheeled handcart, laden with the packs, dixies and other miscellanea of a Labour Company, shot suddenly out into the road, narrowly missing a devastating collision with our car. Between the shafts, but with his big flat feet paddling wildly in the air as he was pressed on high by two excited comrades shoving in the rear of the vehicle, was a very stout little mottle-faced man of middle age, whose appearance suggested (for the moment) an eighteenth century tombstone cherub, and also that it would have been cheaper to have papered his nose than painted it. As he cleared us by a hair's breadth he gave a yell of—

"Hout o' the way, you —— old Irish man-o'-war! Don't you see the Flyin' Corps's a-comin'?"

Then as I came into his line of vision and he landed on his feet with a flop, he added:—

"Beg pardon, sir! But I've 'auled this 'ere little moo-seum hall the way from Bapumey and it ain't gettin' no lighter neither!"

"Bapumey" was Tommy's invariable pronunciation of Bapaume; and when I wished the friendly cherub the best of luck, he replied:—

"Thanky, sir! Same to you!"

And then, with a heave at the trams and a "Come on, you —— couple o' cross-eyed fairies!" to his pals, he went off up the road, cheerfully chaffing his way through the traffic. Bless his affable, Cockney, pothouse soul! I trust that he returned safely in due time to a kindlier environment.

CHAPTER X.

The Battle of the Lys, 1918.

There's water a' owre Flanders where'er ye chance to turn,
But ne'er a hill to set in tune the wimple o' the burn.
O, flat grund's weary, weary, and muckle wad I gie
To hae a glint o' sunset glow on buirdly Benachie!

"9th April, 1918. Shortly after the opening of the bombardment orders had been given to the 51st Division and 55th Division to move up behind Richebourg St. Vaast and Laventie and take up their positions in accordance with the pre-arranged defence scheme. Both these Divisions had been heavily engaged in the Somme battle and had but recently arrived in the neighbourhood. . . .

"11th April. The 51st Division had beaten off incessant attacks with great loss to the enemy, and by vigorous and successful counter-attacks had recaptured positions into which he had forced his way.

"12th April. By a sudden attack just before dawn on 12th April the enemy broke through the left centre of the 51st Division about Pacaut and Riez-du-Vinage, but with the arrival of reinforcements the enemy's progress in this sector of the front was definitely checked."—*(Sir Douglas Haig's Despatches.)*

WHEN the Division had been taken out of the line at Souastre, Divisional Headquarters were successively at Lehurliere, Neuvillette, Foucquieres and Labeuvrieres, while reinforcement and refitting were going on.

On 8th April it entered the XIth Corps, and D.H.Q. moved to Robecq, the little country town near Lillers where our 2nd Field Ambulance had been first billeted on coming to France in May, 1915. Once more I slept in my old room at the kindly (and hereditary) tailor's, who still had his old rheumatic sister, his niece and his gamecocks, his welcome to us being as warm as before. Here there were old acquaintanceships to renew: coffee to be taken with the doctor's widow and her devoted domestic in their little house across the street where,

"Hout o' the way, you —— old Irish man-o'-war! Don't you see the Flyin' Corps's a-comin'?"

Then as I came into his line of vision and he landed on his feet with a flop, he added:—

"Beg pardon, sir! But I've 'auled this 'ere little moo-seum hall the way from Bapumey and it ain't gettin' no lighter neither!"

"Bapumey" was Tommy's invariable pronunciation of Bapaume; and when I wished the friendly cherub the best of luck, he replied:—

"Thanky, sir! Same to you!"

And then, with a heave at the trams and a "Come on, you —— couple o' cross-eyed fairies!" to his pals, he went off up the road, cheerfully chaffing his way through the traffic. Bless his affable, Cockney, pothouse soul! I trust that he returned safely in due time to a kindlier environment.

CHAPTER X.

The Battle of the Lys, 1918.

There's water a' owre Flanders where'er ye chance to turn,
But ne'er a hill to set in tune the wimple o' the burn.
O, flat grund's weary, weary, and muckle wad I gie
To hae a glint o' sunset glow on buirdly Benachie!

"9th April, 1918. Shortly after the opening of the bombardment orders had been given to the 51st Division and 55th Division to move up behind Richebourg St. Vaast and Laventie and take up their positions in accordance with the pre-arranged defence scheme. Both these Divisions had been heavily engaged in the Somme battle and had but recently arrived in the neighbourhood. . . .

"11th April. The 51st Division had beaten off incessant attacks with great loss to the enemy, and by vigorous and successful counter-attacks had recaptured positions into which he had forced his way.

"12th April. By a sudden attack just before dawn on 12th April the enemy broke through the left centre of the 51st Division about Pacaut and Riez-du-Vinage, but with the arrival of reinforcements the enemy's progress in this sector of the front was definitely checked."—(*Sir Douglas Haig's Despatches.*)

WHEN the Division had been taken out of the line at Souastre, Divisional Headquarters were successively at Lehurliere, Neuvillette, Foucquieres and Labeuvrieres, while reinforcement and refitting were going on.

On 8th April it entered the XIth Corps, and D.H.Q. moved to Robecq, the little country town near Lillers where our 2nd Field Ambulance had been first billeted on coming to France in May, 1915. Once more I slept in my old room at the kindly (and hereditary) tailor's, who still had his old rheumatic sister, his niece and his gamecocks, his welcome to us being as warm as before. Here there were old acquaintanceships to renew: coffee to be taken with the doctor's widow and her devoted domestic in their little house across the street where,

MEDICAL POSTS IN THE BATTLE OF LYS, APRIL 1918

Facing page 203.

whatever happened, they expressed their intention of staying, for as the old lady said, "Tous les souvenirs de ma vie sont ici": answers—as soothing as possible—to be given to the groups of anxious-minded people at every doorway.

Here, too, to make good our officer losses in the last battle, we were joined by an excellent and efficient reinforcement of ten Australian medical graduates, who were deservedly popular with all ranks throughout their stay in the 51st Division.

9th April, 1918.

Next morning at 4 a.m. the enemy started a bombardment to have a thrust at the Portuguese troops holding the sector. Shortly afterwards we made the personal acquaintance of a surprising number of our gallant allies; and at 5 a.m. the 152nd Brigade had to hurry into the line. The Field Ambulances were then located at Cantraine, Robecq drawbridge and La Vallée, all at their usual work of collecting and evacuating brigade sick.

An Advanced Dressing Station for the 152nd Brigade was immediately formed near Zelobes by a party of the 3rd F.A., the rest of the unit forming a Main Dressing Station at the drawbridge over La Bassée Canal in front of Robecq. All available bearers were sent up from Cantraine to the M.D.S. to be distributed later as required, with the O.C. 2nd Field Ambulance acting as Forward Evacuation Officer. As the 154th Brigade was going under orders of the 55th Division, the 2/1st F.A. was to be at the disposal of its A.D.M.S.; but telephone communication with him was found to be impossible, and the unit worked throughout under Brigade orders.

By afternoon the Advanced Dressing Station near Zelobes, a Collecting Post at Les Huit Maisons, and the M.D.S. at the drawbridge, La Bassée Canal, were all in full swing and evacuation of wounded going on steadily. An additional M.O., with extra bearers, cars, stretchers, blankets and dressings, was sent up to Zelobes to assist there, as work was rapidly getting heavier. Ford cars were now working right up under fire to the Regimental Aid Posts and in some cases were clearing cases directly back to the Main Dressing Station, as the Advanced Dressing Station accommodation was only farmhouses with no head-cover whatever.

In the evening contradictory and impracticable Corps medical orders came in—one to move the M.D.S. back to Busnes Château (where the Corps Rest Station and a Field Ambulance of the 55th Division were already located); another for it to occupy Robecq Mill (already filled by Marine Artillery); and a third for it to move to Busnes village, where it would be shewn its next location. This last was done — the others being impossible—but the unit found itself side-tracked and useless in Busnes for twelve hours without receiving any further orders. The result was inevitable confusion, as the cases from the Advanced Dressing Stations were evacuated through the 55th Division Field Ambulance at Busnes Château, and our divisional cars made to carry back to the C.C.S.s, thus depleting the supply for the front line and hindering evacuation therefrom.[1]

The 2/1st F.A. had now formed an Advanced Dressing Station for the 154th Brigade at Avelette, with two M.O.s and all available cars and bearers. The 153rd Brigade A.D.S. was at midnight near Pacaut, and fully occupied with numerous casualties.

10th April, 1918.

As the 3rd F.A. was by 9 a.m. still at Busnes without any orders having been received from Corps for its disposal, it was obviously necessary to indulge in the

---

[1]This was the only Corps in our experience which (medically speaking) we were heartily glad to leave.

THE BATTLE OF THE LYS, 1918.

Nelson touch and apply the telescope to the blind eye. The O.C. was therefore instructed to open a Divisional Main Dressing Station on his present site, as our ambulance cars were still running back to the C.C.S. (i.e., doing M.A.C. work instead of their legitimate business), and no record of 51st Division cases was being kept at Busnes Château. The 152nd Brigade Advanced Dressing Station was being kept clear, with two cars evacuating all the wounded from R.A.P.s.

By 11 a.m. the 154th Brigade, less one battalion, was once again in our Division, but by Corps medical operation orders its wounded were still being evacuated through 55th Division medical arrangements.

Numerous wounded French civilians were being taken back from Robecq, which was being badly shelled. One old peasant with an abdominal wound had walked the whole way from Vieille Chapelle. At every street door you met terrified women, children and old men, all seeking a little comfort. A high velocity gun had kept going all night trying for the canal bridges; a Boche aeroplane had flown over in the afternoon and fired a belt of cartridges on the streets; and the inhabitants had not even the spurious safety of cellars, as the ground was too marshy for such things. So here they were, waiting in dread and expectancy for a lead.

My poor old rheumatic landlady, sitting in her armchair, was hoisted on to a motor lorry, *en route* for safer quarters further back. A motley lorry-load it was, embracing as it did an ancient dame of ninety-eight lying on a mattress laid on a long, low barrow—on which movable bed she had spent the last three years of her life— and her daughter of seventy-five. With the latter, I grieve to say, I had "words"; as she, when her mother had been safely loaded, barrow and all, desired to place most of their household gods after her. On being told that the vehicle was only for passengers and that many other of her neighbours needed place therein, she vituperated me as only an excited female can do. This, in a crowded street, was annoying, and led would-be humorous brother officers to ask, "Who's your lady friend?" and indulge in other stereotyped and hoary jests. So I cut it all short by getting two lusty A.S.C. men to hoist her in and pack her out of sight, well to the front of the lorry. Out of sight—Yes! But from the depths, as the lorry rumbled off, came her voice shrilling out, "Féroces! Barbares! Misérables!" with many personal and libellous references to myself, until the conveyance turned the corner and disappeared.

Curious folk they were, and often desperately "sweer" to leave their old homes, even when safety demanded it. At one farm nearer the line—and all this flat fertile country was studded with little farms—the rest of the people had cleared out, leaving only a young woman of twenty-five and her grandfather over seventy. As the fight progressed it became an Advanced Dressing Station, and the vicinity was heavily shelled. At the urgent request of our troops the girl at last went back, but the old man blankly refused. He spent the day sitting at the side of his stove, occasionally going out to feed his pigs and hens. Why not? His alternative was to bundle and go, along shelled roads whither he knew not: the great majority of refugees had no fixed objective: they were simply trying to get away—anywhere—from it all.

By mid-day the A.D.S. of the 153rd Brigade was on the Boheme-Pacaut road and that of the 152nd Brigade behind Zelobes, whence later it moved slightly back to a site more suitable for car loading. In the afternoon both A.D.S.s were near Pacaut and working conjointly to facilitate rapid evacuation. The Forward Evacuation Officer was now sent back to Busnes to superintend and control supply of cars, stretchers, stores, etc., to the A.D.S.s, so as to free the O.C. 3rd F.A. for purely medical work—which was heavy—at the M.D.S. The 2/1st H.F.A., with the 154th Brigade, was doing A.D.S. work, and lending assistance to the 55th Divisional Field Ambulance at Hingette.

By evening motor lorries were taking back walking wounded from Robecq to Busnes, and a better service of M.A.C. cars clearing the Main Dressing Station there.

11th April, 1918.

By morning the 153rd Brigade A.D.S. had again parted company with that of the 152nd Brigade, and was further back on the Pacaut-Merville road, having been shelled out of its previous site; while the 152nd Brigade A.D.S. was near Bacquerolles Farm and liable to be forced back to the drawbridge at La Bassée Canal at any moment. A provisional A.D.S. was, therefore, opened there in view of this eventuality. The 153rd Brigade A.D.S. was later pushed back behind Pacaut, where three extra cars were sent to clear their large list of casualties, and where it again got in touch with the 152nd Brigade A.D.S. for conjoint work, although by afternoon it was once more "on its own" near Riez-du-Vinage. Here it again received extra bearers, while the M.O.s of a Brigade of the 61st Division, which had come up to reinforce, had also to get supplied with our bearers, as their own Field Ambulance had not yet detrained. By evening the Corps Rest Station had at long last evacuated Busnes Château, and this was free to be used by us as a Main Dressing Station. Many civilian and military casualties were cleared from Robecq in the evening; and on two occasions cars had to go to Calonne to clear a R.A.P. there of the 12th Australian Field Artillery Brigade, as the 61st Division's Field Ambulances were still not detrained. At midnight Robecq and the Robecq-Busnes road were being heavily shelled, with many resulting casualties.

12th April, 1918.

In the early morning a message came in from the joint A.D.S. of the 152nd and 153rd Brigades to the drawbridge, La Bassée Canal, to the effect that it was moving back there at once, as the enemy was advancing rapidly and the post was under machine gun fire. The 152nd Brigade H.Q., in their near neighbourhood, had been captured by the enemy, including the liaison M.O.[1] there. A Ford car of the 2nd H.F.A., along with the M.O. 6th Gordon Highlanders and its driver, had also fallen into enemy hands. Although the car was lost, the M.O. and the driver[2] both subsequently escaped in the mist which prevailed. At 9 a.m. Divisional Headquarters moved from Robecq to Busnes, and the Drawbridge A.D.S. in front of Robecq was withdrawn.

Later, the M.D.S. was moved back from Busnes Château to the Red Cross Society's Huts at Ham-en-Artois, and car posts were established at the drawbridge over La Bassée Canal on the Robecq-Busnes road and at Epinette: Busnes Château becoming the A.D.S. in the hands of the 2nd F.A. In the evening an M.O. with motor cyclists was posted to the H.Q. of the Composite Force (now holding the line in front of La Bassèe Canal on the Robecq-Busnes road), with a car in Robecq. 150 other ranks R.A.M.C., reinforcements for losses in March, arrived at Busnes Château, and were distributed to the different Field Ambulances.

13th April, 1918.

Things were quiet, with few casualties passing through, and remained so until D.H.Q. moved back to Lambres, when the Division came out of the line on 16th April. . . .

As the Advanced Dressing Stations were, in every case throughout this engagement, located in farmhouses

---

[1] Captain S. S. Meighan, who was also wounded.
[2] Captain D. McKelvey, M.C., and Private A. E. Highmore, D.C.M.

exposed to shell and machine gun fire and with no overhead cover, rapid evacuation of casualties was the primary necessity. Our only transport losses, fortunately, were one Ford car—the famous "Turra Coo"—captured by the enemy, and one horse ambulance wagon, ditched and abandoned under fire as the horses were killed. Cars throughout ran cases from the R.A.P.s to the A.D.S.s, one Ford car—the lost "Coo"—acting for a considerable time as a mobile R.A.P. while a new site was being searched for further back.

When the Advanced Dressing Stations fell back they had previously cleared all wounded and medical stores, and in several cases this was done with the enemy in sight and the stations under machine gun fire. In spite of this, R.A.M.C. casualties were low—2 M.O.s and one other ranks missing (prisoners), and 7 other ranks wounded. As reinforcements to replace the losses of other ranks sustained in the last battle did not arrive until 12th April, the Field Ambulances were, up to that time, working 150 (mostly bearers) under strength, and had in addition to supply bearers to the units of the Division coming up in support. It was exceedingly fortunate that 10 officers of the Australian A.M.C. had reported on the 8th.

The old difficulty, inevitable under such circumstances, of getting returning cars rapidly back to the Advanced Dressing Stations from the Main Dressing Stations (owing to the congestion of the narrow roads with transport, and at night owing to the darkness), was experienced. Cars also had frequently to pick up a load of stretcher cases *en route* and clear them first to the M.D.S. Only 16 M.A.C. cars were available to clear the M.D.S. from its first unsuitable site in Busnes, and this frequently resulted in our F.A. cars having to do the whole journey to the C.C.S.s until the M.D.S. got entry to Busnes Château, where there was sufficient accommodation for temporarily holding casualties up.

The Corps medical arrangements were, throughout the engagement, confused, imperfect and unworkable. During the 9th, 10th and 11th all the R.A.M.C. in the front line worked, short-handed as they were, without rest and in the most indefatigable manner.

In the course of this battle an officer, dodging his way across country amidst heavy enemy fire, thought he noticed some movement in a shell hole. Going up to it he found an old civilian and his wife, dressed—as these people often were when fleeing from their homes—in their Sunday best, and crouching at the foot of the hole. The old lady, a ruddy-faced agriculturist, had a bonnet fringed with beads and cherries which dangled and bobbed as she ducked at each explosion. Recognising her visitor as a British officer and wishing to express herself in a way he could understand, the poor old dame tersely but comprehensively remarked, "No bon! Ah! No bon!" Later she and her spouse were successfully rescued.

One party of King Edward's Horse gallantly held the enemy in check for several hours in the vicinity of a farmhouse and under very heavy shell and machine gun fire. The men were exhausted and there were many casualties. All the civilians had cleared back except one old woman. During the action she milked her cows, herself taking the milk under fire to the men, and also making hot coffee for them; while, throughout, she tended the wounded as best she could. She was repeatedly pressed to leave, but her reply was always, "Why? I am of use here!" And she only left when the troops retired. No limelight for her: no hysterical female journalism. Just a big-hearted, courageous woman of the old-fashioned type, of which history has given us so many examples, regardless of her own safety while there was the work of the ministering angel to do.

From Lambres D.H.Q. moved to Norrent-Fontes,

CHAPTER XI.

The Second Battle of the Marne, 1918.

Eight she-voos a wagon we had shoved 'em up the ramp
Till our legs was nearly buckled an' our arms a-twist with cramp,
While a bomber hummin' overhead had dowsed each blinkin' lamp—
   Ho! Forty Homs or eight she-voos![1]

Forty homs a wagon on the truck's hard floor,
The cold night wind a-blowin' like a knife below the door.
It warn't no ruddy Pullman they gave us in the war—
   Ho! Forty homs or eight she-voos!

"On the 20th July the 51st and 62nd Divisions of the XXII Corps, attacked in conjunction with the French on the eastern side of the salient, south-west of Rheims. The sector assigned to the British troops covered a front of 8,000 yards astride the Ardre river, and consisted of an open valley bottom, with steep wooded slopes on either side. Both valley and slopes were studded with villages and hamlets, which were for the most part intact and afforded excellent cover for the enemy. On this front our troops were engaged for a period of ten days in continuous fighting of a most difficult and trying nature. Throughout this period steady progress was made in the face of vigorous and determined resistance."—*(Sir Douglas Haig's Despatches.)*

"You, one and all, have added a glorious page to your history. Marfaux, Chaumuzy and the Montagne Bligny, these splendid words will be written in letters of gold in the annals of your regiments. Your French friends will remember your marvellous bravery and your perfect comradeship in arms."—*(General Berthelot, commanding the Fifth French Army, in his order of the day, 1st August, 1918.)*

THE Norrent-Fontes area now gave us for a time a well-earned rest; and our stay here was rendered historic by

---
[1] Hommes, 40; Chevaux, 8.

a visit from that outstanding personality of the day, M. Clemenceau. Divisional Headquarters were in a large and seemly dwelling up a quiet side street of the little country town. Warned of the hour of his arrival, a guard of honour was duly posted; and the General and his staff were lined up in front of the building to receive the great man, as a great man should be received. The hour struck: a loud rumbling on the *pavé* as of approaching cars was heard: the guard presented arms: we came to attention—and into our surprised vision came the Thresh Disinfector on its motor lorry, driven by our old friend the nonchalant civilian in khaki, gazing at the proceedings with his usual air of dispassionate interest. Those not within range of the G.O.C.'s eye grinned happily: the others affected a stern yet sublime calm. Before the General had quite finished a few remarks he evidently thought appropriate to the occasion, the "Tiger" and his entourage, in three limousines, swung into view; and the proceedings, unwittingly rehearsed in honour of the Thresh warrior, were more appropriately repeated. As the cars rolled up the doors opened; and a selection of be-medalled, gloved, spick-and-span French generals and other officers of high rank sprang nimbly out, to be ready for the advent of the man of the moment. In such surroundings he struck a markedly different note. Small, stout, square-built, keen-eyed and with a fierce grey moustache, his dress was as careless as theirs was correct. An old overcoat had its greasy velvet collar one half up and the other half down: black boots were surmounted by a pair of very yellow leather leggings. One baggy trouser leg he had hauled well up before applying its covering, while the other had been equally severely pulled down, with the object, apparently, of shewing two inches of trousering between legging and boot. On top of all was an ancient cloth billy-cock hat. Mumbling what we took to be complimentary remarks,

SECOND BATTLE OF THE MARNE, 1918.

he shook hands with those assembled to do him honour; and then, surrounded by his respectful attendants, made once more for his limousine and was whirled away to repeat the proceedings elsewhere. The whole business was over in three minutes, leaving the G.O.C. free to resume his interrupted remarks on the untimely intrusion of the Thresh Disinfector. And that evening a cloud darkened the usual sparkle of No. 1 H.Q. mess; while, well blanketed and in his steam chamber, untroubled and dreamless was the hard-earned sleep of the civilian in khaki.

The Division, at the beginning of May, took over a sector north of Arras, from Bailleul on the right to Willerval on the left. Here it remained until the early part of July, when it moved to the Dieval-Monchy-Breton-Chelers area for a few days preparatory to moving into Champagne to take part in the French attack there.

The first of the thirty-four troop trains left Brias on the 14th July, and the last left Pernes on the 16th, for their thirty hours journey south via the outskirts of Paris; and on the 15th the first arrivals were detraining in the Nogent-sur-Seine area.

D.H.Q. left Brias by an early train on the 14th, while local sports in honour of the national fête day—celebration of the fall of the Bastille—were going on in the vicinity of the station. The weather was fine and the country interesting; many beautiful woods with plentiful silver birches; grain ripe or ripening; while—when next day we approached, passed through, and left behind the environs of Paris (hearing, incidentally, the arrival of part of "Big Bertha's" output)—there was great cheering with handkerchief waving at all the stations. At one stop an enthusiastic young female started at the head of the train and impartially kissed any man who was willing—and most of them were Barkises—right down the carriages until we started again. The pull-out happily occurred while she was busy dealing with the compartment just ahead of ours, and while we were feverishly and unavailingly engaged in persuading the A.P.M. that as he was young and handsome he was, therefore, our obvious representative in this affair. So we were saved from having cast any slur on the general gallantry of the Division.

Detraining at 1.30 a.m. at Nogent, the D.A.D.M.S. and I left there at 3 in a Ford; and after a run in the darkness of about thirteen kilometres, mostly through woods, we reached Villenauxe, knocked up (after an hour's search for him) the sleep-ridden Camp Commandant to get the location of our billet, and turned in. Daylight shewed the little town to be a most picturesque and charming one, with a XIV century church (in which were some fine old pictures and carved choir stalls) and with booths built in here and there between its buttresses. The inhabitants, numbering about 2,500, were chiefly engaged—in peace time—in manufacturing underclothing and socks, or porcelain plaques for wall decoration. The rest were agriculturists. But now the place was full of French troops of all branches, including *canonniers marins* and *fusilliers marins,* and everyone agog with excitement.

Next morning, after breakfast at "The Horse in Armour" *(Le Cheval Bardé),* "Daddums"[1] and I entered our trusty Ford again and set off in thunder-threatening heat and choking dust for Moussy, on the outskirts of Epernay. The route lay amidst lovely scenery, passing, amongst other places *pittoresques,* through the extensive Forest of Traconne, and Montmort with its fine old château and moat. The roads were crowded with refugees, French troops, guns (chiefly 75's) and motor lorries packed with cheery Jocks. The trees were chiefly poplars (with mistletoe growing on many of them), oaks,

---

[1] For so the D.A.D.M.S.'s title was abbreviated.

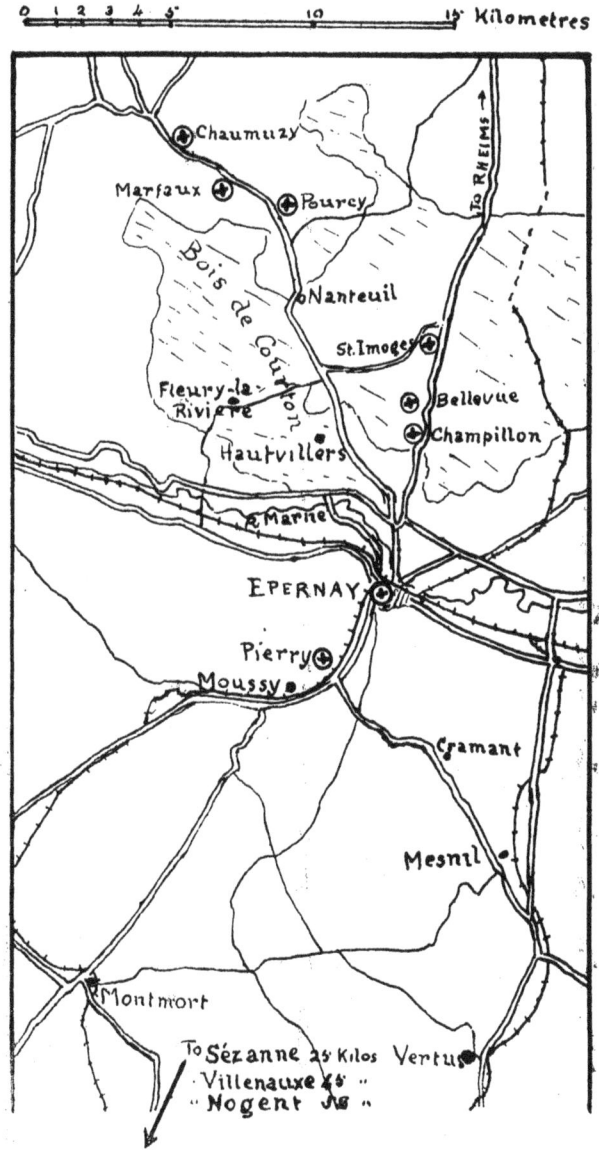

Medical Posts in the Valley of the Ardre.

Facing page 214.

silver birches and acacias; the crops maize, wheat, oats
and rye; picturesque villages with old châteaux and
churches were rife; while a serene blue sky completed
the picture. A visit to Vertus in the evening, to interview
the D.D.M.S. Corps[1] (who turned out to be an old friend
of Armentières days, when he was A.D.M.S. of the New
Zealand Division), finished our day. Vertus, full of
quaint and ancient nooks and corners, made one deeply
regret not being there merely for leisurely exploration.
Running home, the long-expected thunderstorm broke,
with magnificent orange-coloured lightning flashes
illuminating the woods on either side and the straight
white ribbon of dusty road lying ahead.

And now, after a night's rest, to locate the present
position of the three Field Ambulances, which were all
still *en route* from the detraining point. The A.D.M.S.'s
office was in the Moussy village school, where, on the
master's rostrum and behind his desk, I elicited from
a continuous and curious procession of visitors the
natural respect due to such a position. All approached
with the properly deprecating air of an unforgotten
youth. Our earliest arrivals were various sick *poilus*—
one with a sprained knee; another with an acute general
nettle-rash following a wasp sting on the neck. (The
latter was intensely relieved to find that his number was
not up, as he had definitely concluded, and became somewhat emotional at the good news.) A third, rejoining
his unit from leave, was apologetic to a degree at causing
the trouble of having his destination pointed out to him
on the map. Callers in search of *M. l' Instituteur,* on
civilian business, were desolated at their own want of
tact in not having guessed that he was temporarily dis-
placed; and retired with voluble apologies. So it went on
all the hot forenoon; and then the 2/1st H.F.A. was
reported as having reached Mesnil, where we visited it,

[1] Colonel C. Begg, C.B., grandson of the famous Free Church divine.

bivouacked on the edge of a wood above the village, with a widespread view of a beautiful, fertile plain.

Moussy, in the evening, was full of stir. The inhabitants had been warned out by the civil authority, and most of them had trekked—or were trekking—back. The A.P.M.'s Divisional gendarmerie were kept busy till a late hour in streets thronged with Jocks, English, Senegalese, "horizon-blues" and Italians. And here comes in the story of the business enterprise of two hardy Caledonians, who, taking advantage of the place going like a fair, donned the costumes of peasants and sold (to the cosmopolitan crowd of thirsty troops) the contents of a large and varied wine cellar which they had been fortunate enough to discover. Regardless of brand or vintage, and to secure a ready sale with quick returns, each bottle was disposed of at the modest sum of two francs a head! Nay more! To regularise the affair and promote confidence amongst their customers, an obliging confederate did sentry-go with fixed bayonet in front of the establishment, until it was thought safer—owing, alas! to the threats of some of their own countrymen who objected to the high prices!—to bring their operations to a close. Rumour had it that the gallant and provident financiers cleared a well-earned profit of 2,000 francs.

Next day D.H.Q. moved to Hautvillers on the other side of the Marne, a pretty little village well up on the vine-clad slopes of the hill above Epernay, and looking down on it and the river—a view comparable to that obtained of Perth from Kinnoull Hill. The 3rd H.F.A. was still on trek from Nogent to Pierry, while the 2nd had not yet been joined by their transport. The 2/1st, who were to take over the forward evacuation work, had moved forward from Mesnil to Champillon. D.H.Q. were in a large building, the property of the champagne-manufacturing Comte Chandon de Briailles, and recently

SECOND BATTLE OF THE MARNE, 1918.

the residence—since he left Rheims—of the Cardinal Archbishop. Near by were the old church and the remains of an ancient abbey.

In the evening a visit from the D.D.M.S. Corps brought the disturbing news (as the Division was to go into action next morning) that, as it was impossible for any C.C.S. to take over a site and link up in time at Sezanne, it would be necessary for us to form an improvised C.C.S. at Epernay. Four medical officers with surgical experience were to be detailed from the ambulances, along with two tent sub-divisions, to take over from the Italians a pavilion of 140 beds at the Auban-Moet hospital at Epernay.

Farewell, therefore, to a hoped-for night's rest, and off in the Ford to Champillon where the first batch of M.O.s was detailed, and then through Epernay to Pierry for the personnel required from the ambulance there. And next, with a letter from the French general as authorisation, to the Auban-Moet hospital to interview the Italian M.O. at Epernay. My visit most unfortunately coincided with one from an enemy bombing squadron, and the experience was unpleasant. By avoiding the main streets we imagined we lessened our risks; but by the time we got to the hospital and found—with difficulty, owing to the very proper absence of any lights—the pavilion we wanted, my driver and I had had enough experience of bombs at close quarters to make us anxious to waste no unnecessary time.

Entering the ward in pitch darkness I flashed on an electric torch, and found the M.O. in charge (as Sam Weller found the philosophic shoemaker in the Fleet Prison, who had in better days been accustomed to a four-poster) sitting cross-legged under a table so as to enjoy the further security of the increased head cover thus attainable. Joining him there (for he refused to budge), I showed him the French general's letter, and during the next ten minutes sat on the floor and had an acrimonious argument with him over its contents. "It was all very well! Go! *Where* was he to go? Tell him that! *How* could he go? Did I know the town was being bombed?" But with all that I told him I had nothing to do: *I* was not bombing the town: *there* was the general's letter: on that I took my stand (or seat!): that only: go, he had to. And then again the lament:—"But *where* was he to go?" At this, alas! I lost my temper and told him where I personally thought he should go: but that, in any case, if he did not clear out of here to somewhere else in an hour, we should—with great regret, of course—have to push him out. And as our two tent sub-divisions now put in an appearance along with the 4 M.O.s, I left him to their well-known tender mercies. But it had proved quite an interesting debate, as we suffered the equal handicap of having to conduct it in the French language, he knowing no English and I no Italian; while both of us might with the greatest advantage have had more skill of the tongue which we used as ammunition.

Once in the Ford again we made by back streets for the Marne, and just before we hit the street running parallel to the river towards the bridge, a bomb dropped on a house round the corner; leaving us, as we charily crawled into view of it, faced with a street apparently impassable with debris. But, by getting on to the opposite pavement, we bumped Fordishly and miraculously through the ruins, and soon joined the steady stream of traffic on the bridge. When twenty yards over it a jam occurred, and we only got across after several unpleasant stoppages of the same kind, the bombers being still hard at it and the bridge one of their main objectives. The last house at the bridge-end behind us came down by the run, and they also landed on both banks of the river in close proximity. A thick purple pall of smoke hung over everything—it was a beautiful, windless, warm summer's night—and the Marne could be seen on either side luridly lit up by the flames of the fires the bombers had effected in the town, while the flashes from the bursts on the river banks threw great orange-coloured circles against the overhead curtain. As a spectacle, good enough. Yes! But once across we made off at our best pace on the long, winding, uphill road for Champillon, with infinite relief and no desire to see more of it, getting back ultimately to Hautvillers in time for a couple of hours sleep before the battle commenced.

Shortly after daybreak D.H.Q. moved forward to St. Imoges, in the little valley of the Ardre, and once again we were up to the neck in work.

Owing to the necessary haste with which the Division entered the line, there was a lack of the usual time available for linking up Corps with Divisional medical arrangements, and a certain amount of the work usually falling on the Corps was added to that of the Division.

The dismounted personnel of the 2/1st Highland Field Ambulance, the unit detailed for front line evacuation work, had arrived at Mesnil on 17th by buses, the transport joining it subsequently on the 19th. The 2nd Highland Field Ambulance, detailed for working the Main Dressing Station, trekked from the detraining point by forced marches to Soizy, whence the dismounted personnel were taken by bus to Champillon, the transport following; while the 3rd Highland Field Ambulance, the unit in reserve, trekked complete the whole way from train to Pierry, arriving there at midnight of 19th. Both the last two units did over 31 kilometres in one day, and 25 in another, in very trying weather, but arrived in time and in wonderfully good condition to take up their posts.

On the evening of the 19th, when information arrived from Corps that no Casualty Clearing Station would be available until next evening at Sezanne, we were faced with the fact that, apart from the want of this necessary link in the chain of evacuation, the ambulances would be dependent until then upon their War Establishment of stretchers and blankets, as any surplus required in action is drawn from the Casualty Clearing Station by returning empty cars. Further, the Advanced Depot of Medical Stores, from which the units drew their requirements of splints, dressings, drugs, etc., beyond War Establishment, could not possibly arrive at Sezanne until the same time; while only fifteen M.A.C. cars would be available for evacuating from the Main Dressing Station until another M.A.C. got up.

The situation, an unavoidable one under the circumstances, was met, as aforesaid, by sending four medical officers with surgical experience from the ambulances, along with two tent sub-divisions from the unit in reserve at Pierry, to the Auban-Moet Hospital at Epernay, to take over there from the Italians a pavilion accommodating 140 patients, and to act as a temporary Casualty Clearing Station. This accommodation was reserved for serious cases unable to stand the journey to Sezanne, where another temporary Casualty Clearing Station was being run by ambulance personnel of the 62nd Division; while slight cases were sent to Vertus, a portion of the French Hospital there being reserved for their use.

The equally urgent question of supplies of splints and dressings required above War Establishment had to be settled as well as possible by drawing on the French Hospital at Vertus and the *Poste de Secours* of the 120th French Division at St. Imoges. During the last three of the first twelve hours of the action, the available supply of stretchers, blankets, splints and dressings was practically exhausted, as the supplies obtained from the French were, while willingly given, limited, owing to their own requirements. The carpenters of the Advanced Dressing

Station, St. Imoges, were, therefore, turned on to make improvised splints from the material available, while the medical officers and bearers in the line showed great initiative in the making of improvised stretchers, whereby cases were got to the Collecting Posts. A plentiful supply of stout saplings, to serve as stretcher poles, was, fortunately, available in the woods.

By the time, however, that the action commenced on the 20th, the Divisional R.A.M.C. were distributed and working as follows:—

(a) 8 R.A.M.C. bearers with each medical officer of a battalion.

(b) One liaison Field Ambulance medical officer to keep touch with brigades and regimental medical officers. (One had been detailed for each Brigade, as this arrangement had been found to work well in the actions of March and April, but could not be supplied owing to the unexpected demand for four medical officers for temporary Casualty Clearing Station work at Epernay. Thanks to the energy and initiative of the liaison medical officer[1] appointed, very thorough touch was nevertheless kept throughout.)

(c) Advanced Dressing Station and A.D.M.S. office in farm buildings at St. Imoges.

(d) Walking Wounded Collecting Post at Bellevue, run conjointly with the 62nd Division.

(e) Main Dressing Station at Champillon in the village hall and two Adrian Huts in its vicinity. (This was an excellent and elastic site, the only drawback being the narrowness and bad surface of the roads through the village.)

(f) Temporary Casualty Clearing Station at Auban-Moet Hospital, Epernay.

[1] Captain D. McKelvey, M.C.

A MEDICO'S LUCK IN THE WAR.

After the action commenced the position at 10 a.m. of medical posts in the forward area was as in Plan A.

153rd Infantry Brigade.   **154th Infantry Brigade.**
    R A. P. s.   R . A . P . s.

```
  o    o    o              o    o    o
   \   |   /                \   |   /
    BOIS DE COURTON          BOIS DE COURTON
       \|/                      \|/
        o Collecting Post.       o Collecting Post.
          COURTON RUINE.           Hill outside
                                   NANTEUIL.
                \               /
                 \             /
                  \           /
                   \         /
          Advanced o Dressing Station.
                     ST. IMOGES.
                         |
                                        Plan A.
                         |
                         o
                Main Dressing Station.
                    CHAMPILLON.
```

In the course of the forenoon, steps were taken for establishing Collecting Posts farther forward, and by 5 p.m. positions on the right were held as in Plan B, those on the left remaining as before.

By evening of 20th, all initial difficulties had been overcome; a Casualty Clearing Station and Advanced Depot of Medical Stores had reached Sezanne; stretchers, blankets, splints and dressings were got up to the Main Dressing Station and Advanced Dressing Station, and a satisfactory M.A.C. service was established.

On the forenoon of the 21st an Advanced Walking Wounded Collecting Station was established at road bifurcation in Bois de Talma to prevent these cases straggling across country away from Divisional arrangements. Here, after being fed, they were taken by horse

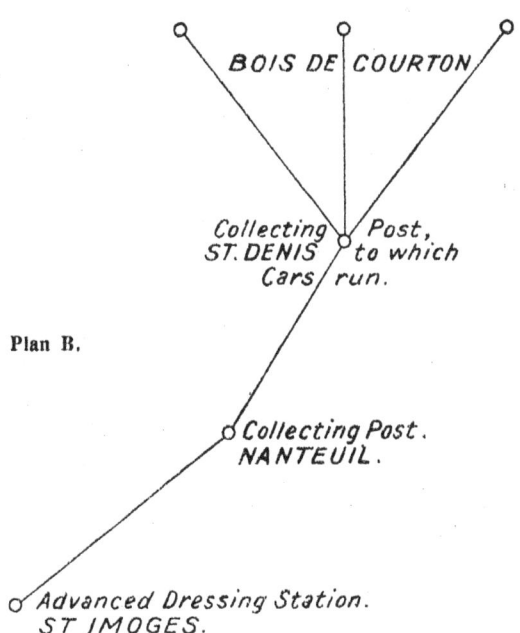

ambulance wagons to Bellevue and evacuated to Sezanne by French motor lorries. The difficulty experienced at Bellevue was that, owing to the length of the journey to Sezanne and the slow progress possible owing to the traffic on the roads, only one trip in twelve hours could be carried out. Further, after dark, owing to the persistent bombing of Epernay, both cars and lorries had to avoid it and go round by Vertus. This, however, was unavoidable; and as the men at Bellevue were under cover in a big barn, receiving medical attendance and being well fed, no unnecessary hardship was entailed by the wait.

As the action proceeded the main route of evacuation became the Nanteuil-Marfaux-Chaumuzy road up the Ardre valley.

On the 25th a new Bearer Relay Post was established in the Bois de Courton, through which the 152nd Infantry Brigade and 7th Gordon Highlanders evacuated to St. Denis Collecting and Car Post.

On the 26th the Courton Ruine Collecting Post was withdrawn, as the Brigade on the left had been relieved on the previous night by the French. On the 27th three new Bearer Relay Posts were established:—

(a) In Bois de Courton,
(b) To right of Bois de Courton,
(c) In Marfaux;

(a) and (b) evacuated through Relay Post in Bois de Courton formed on the 25th.

On 28th the Advanced Dressing Station moved forward to Nanteuil from St. Imoges, its site at the latter place being taken by Main Dressing Station, while the reserve unit moved from Bellevue to Nanteuil.

The various Posts were then distributed as in Plan C.

On the 29th stretcher trollies were being used on the Chaumuzy-Sarcy road to Regimental Aid Posts one mile further forward, as the road, owing to shell holes and debris, was impassable for cars.

Arrangements were working thus until the Division was withdrawn from the line. . . .

In the course of the battle various difficulties arose owing to the nature of the ground fought over.

Except when it was possible to use stretcher trollies on the Chaumuzy-Sarcy road, all carriage from the

In the Bois de Courton.

German Prisoners bringing in French Wounded.
(Imperial War Museum Photograph—Copyright Reserved.)

Facing page 224.

SECOND BATTLE OF THE MARNE, 1918.

Regimental Aid Posts was done by hand to Relay Posts and thence to Collecting Posts. Sense of direction, especially at night, in the dense Bois de Courton was easily lost; and, owing to this and the plentiful shelling by H.E. and gas, such carriage was arduous work. The

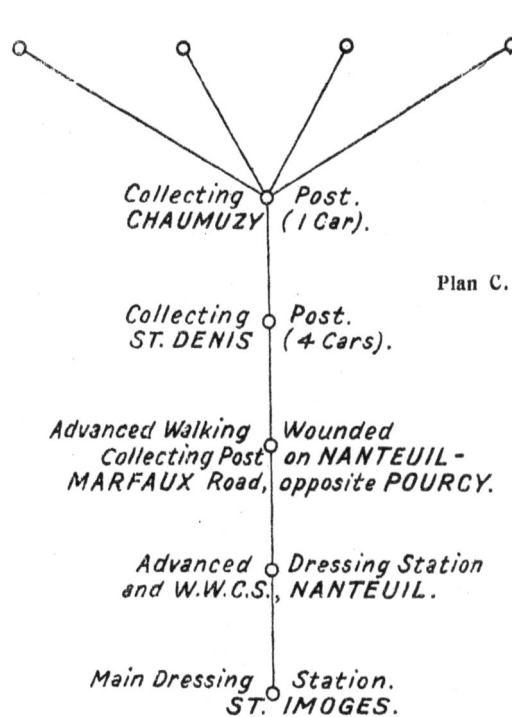

list of R.A.M.C. casualties was, under the circumstances, remarkably small, viz., 1 other rank killed and 25 wounded.

The roads, especially at first, were under enemy observation and fire, and had been previously cut up by shell fire. These were gradually mended as time went on; but up to the relief of the Division, Marfaux,

P

Chaumuzy and the road between was constantly exposed to fire. The only car put out of action, however, was one sent on the 22nd to Fleury-La-Riviere to remove some Divisional cases which had strayed through the Bois de Courton to the French *Poste de Secours* there.

The previous experience of open warfare gained in November, March and April had taught all concerned to make the most of what cover was available in the selection of Regimental Aid Posts, Relay Posts and Collecting Posts. Sunken roads, the shelter of high banks, small quarry holes, cellars in ruined buildings at Marfaux and Chaumuzy, were all duly and promptly taken advantage of. Amongst the N.C.O.s of the bearer divisions of the three ambulances there were by now a large number of excellent men who could be trusted to lead and to show initiative, and it was proved during the action that they had benefited by and acted on the knowledge gained from their previous experience.

At Advanced Dressing Stations and Main Dressing Stations the circumstances were well met, and the units concerned showed that they possessed the power of making the very most of the accommodation available, and of opening out rapidly after a move.

The great necessity for a Field Ambulance is never to lose its sense of mobility. Hence there must be no unnecessary unloading of transport, and transport must be so packed that stores are got at automatically in the order in which they are required. After the long spell of trench warfare, with due warning of any move, it was satisfactory to find that the old pre-war training for mobile warfare plus the experience gained in the field since last November, had had their due effect.

At the improvised Casualty Clearing Station in Epernay a large amount of graver surgical work was done under very difficult circumstances: and in view of the possibility of similar contingencies, a surgical team was definitely detailed from suitable medical officers in the ambulances, who would be able to proceed on such detached work if required. The necessity for this, however, never again happened during the campaign. . . .

Now, of this battle I have several outstanding memories. One was of constantly pleasant relations with my colleague the *médecin chef* of the French Division, the genial Colonel Martin-Deschamps. We used to meet, to discuss matters of mutual interest, in a room of the hunting lodge in St. Imoges, the walls of which were ornamented with the heads of several magnificent wild boars and other *gibier;* for the forest was famous for its game and the sport supplied thereby. Two of his nursing orderlies were interesting men: one possessed a long black beard, another an equally long yellow one: both in peace times were monks—an exchange, therefore, on their part, of the cloister for the clyster.

The trip to the French *Poste de Secours* at Fleury-La-Riviere, to recover divisional casualties who had sideslipped there, resulted in our Ford car straying in the dusk up a side road which ended in a *cul-de-sac* in the forest. With much pulling and pushing and many kangaroo jumps—of which a Ford alone is capable—we got the car turned, and then saw several khaki-breeched bodies, with their tunics off and covering their faces, lying amongst the trees. To identify them we lifted the tunic off one and got an unexpected start. For they were French Senegalese, at no time objects of beauty; but now several days dead, their black faces swollen with decomposition and swarming with flies! Pouf! We were glad to leave the place and find the main road again—my driver sick as a dog.

Fleury lay in a cup-shaped depression fringed with the forest trees of the Bois de Courton: in better times a peaceful and romantic setting. Now—dead horses and men, stench, shell holes, smashed houses and the sound of perpetual gun-fire rumbling over it! The finest sight for us was the *Poste de Secours* itself, several large, roomy, deep caves that ran into a high ivy-clad cliff by the roadside: old places cut years and years ago for storing wine and now delightfully cool and safe.

When, on the 23rd, D.H.Q. moved back again to Hautvillers, we once more commanded the fine view of Epernay and the Marne. Two nights later, as several of us sat smoking on the terraced garden in front of our château, we had a birds-eye and front seat view of the town being fiercely bombed. One of the earliest arrivals hit a French ammunition train at the station, which went west in one long, blinding flash; followed later, for an hour, by a series of explosions as various dumps went up in the succeeding conflagration—two of them being especially terrific even at that distance, and smashing many of our window panes. All the time more bombers were passing overhead and making for the town, where they set various places on fire; one being the large Moet and Chandon works. Epernay was covered with a huge umbrella of black smoke, holed at intervals by the bombs bursting on the town, and lined with the crimson glow of the numerous fires. Over a hundred bombs fell on the town in the course of two hours, and the sight was a weird and unforgettable one.

This Champagne country was a new type of countryside for us, as it was the Division's first irruption into the vineyard regions. And the pleasant sounding place-names were even more marked than elsewhere. Champillon, Fleury-La-Riviere, Nanteuil, St. Imoges, Chaumuzy—all pleased the ear, and suggested, not war, but peace and rural quietude. Near Pierry, as the constant stream of war traffic—horse, foot, guns, caterpillars, whippets, lorries—rattled along, the eye caught the names of three little side streets that made one think of pleasant things—*Ruelle des Vignes, Ruelle des Fées* and the *Rue des Petits Prés*. Think of it! The vines, the fairies and the little meadows! True, the vines and the little meadows were still there, but I am sure the fairies had gone; for up their special lane a French driver was testing the engine of his *camion*, to the tune of horrible noises in a foul cloud of smoke. And in their own Champagne *patois* "the good folk" must, when they left, have expressed much the same opinions as their Scots cousins did on another occasion:—

> Dule, dule to Blelack,
> And dule to Blelack's heir
> Wha banished us frae Seelie Howe
> To the cauld Hill o' Fare.

Amongst the genial folk of Champagne there is a proverb which runs:—"Ninety-nine sheep and a Champenois make a hundred beasts." But *ce vieux dicton*, say they, does not vex the true inhabitants: it is, rather, "a testimony to their good and peaceful character, always inimical to injustice and violence, but excluding neither talent, nor an united defence of their interests and their rights." It arose from a regulation laid down by the authorities of a Champagne town that no flock of less than a hundred sheep had any right of entry to the town, the lowest charge being fixed for that number. A shepherd with a flock of ninety-nine tried to get in free; but the porter at the gate callously gave forth the dictum: "Quatre-vingt-dix-neuf moutons et un Champenois font cent bêtes." And the *berger* was only granted entry at the fee fixed upon, the minimum hundred scale.

One of the French Senegalese blacks got run over by a *camion* and killed on the main road near Bellevue. To ascertain which padre should bury him one of our R.C. chaplains sent a Senegalese N.C.O. to find out his religion. He came back with the report:—"No religion, *monsieur*—Heathen." Asked how the deceased would be buried in his own country, his comrade replied briefly:—

"Killed in battle—not buried—eaten!" And the padre passed the job on to a C. of E. *confrère*—so he told me, anyhow: it was the kind of thing he *did* tell me, for years.

Going along the road through the Forest of Rheims one day I met a procession of French whippet tanks making smartly for the line, with their horizon-blue crews on top, cheery and gallant. On the third car an unexpected touch was given to the show by one merry *poilu* who had resurrected a very ancient "lum" hat, of the species used by their peasantry, as by ours, to attend funerals. Its appearance suggested that it had been a family heirloom since the days of the Little Corporal. But its present owner wore it cocked roguishly over one eye, what time he was not, in response to the chaff of passers by, lifting his tile with an exaggerated *politesse,* and bowing profoundly from his perch to his grinning comrades at the roadside. Me he favoured with a full military salute, regardless of the incongruity of his outfit; an act of correct demeanour which set all of us who saw him off our centres of gravity. Good lad! He was doing a hornpipe on top of the tank as he turned the corner and was lost to view!

At Cramant, when D.H.Q. had moved there from Nanteuil, previous to entraining once again for the north, I came across an old man while strolling up a steep side road amongst the vines, and with him I got into conversation. It was not altogether easy, as he was practically edentulous, spoke very rapidly, and had a Clemenceau type of moustache covering all his mouth and half his chin. But in spite of these preliminary difficulties we discussed for half an hour—to our mutual edification—the best manures for vines, the main differences between Catholic and Protestant worship, the connection (or want of it) between Church and State in France, and what was best for his chronic indigestion. At this stage I got rather a shock, for he said suddenly, "Pardon, monsieur! Mais vous, vous êtes Italien, n'est-ce-pas?" And when I had explained to him, that in spite of all temptation to belong to that estimable allied nation, I still remained a Scotsman, he started off at once on Marie Stuart and her history. Then he stopped and shook his head:—"For the Scots, yes—you are our ancient allies! But the English! Ah, the English!" I asked him what the trouble was, and he said sadly:—"Of course, they too are our allies and we must love them; but for me it is difficult!" And the difficulty on further enquiry turned out to be—*Jeanne D'Arc!* He gave me a learned and emotional *résumé* of her treatment, receiving my respectful sympathy; and I left him in the middle of the dusty cart-track, bowing, with his battered straw hat in hand, a farewell; while he tearfully murmured, "Oui! C'est difficile! La pauvre Pucelle!" For out of the ancient dust, watered with tears, of such memories and prejudices, national sentiment is, century by century, moulded and remoulded.

In Cramant, and the other surrounding villages, were numerous small champagne - manufacturing establishments, bearing no famous brand—the great houses were in Epernay and Rheims—but doing a large local trade. The first two "pressings" of the grape were made into "bubbly"; the third was used as a still wine; the fourth pressing, done under hydraulic pressure, produced a cheap, sour wine, that was used by the peasants who tended and gathered the grapes—truly a muzzling of the ox that trod out the corn! Down below, in the cool, roomy cellars cut out of the rock, the bottles, tilted at various angles according to the stage of manufacture the wine had reached, were stored. But also down below at that time were the family, the bedding, the furniture and the various more valuable household goods: for, owing to the constant bombing of the area, the people of the village had at night been for some time living a subterranean existence.

And there, on 2nd August, we entrained once more for the north, passing again through the outskirts of Paris; reading, smoking, talking; trying to sleep in the very dirty compartment with soiled and torn cushions; getting out at intervals, if a halt occurred, to make for the adjoining cattle truck which was our mess, or precariously finding our way along the footboards when the halt was overdue. Here, perhaps, from the windows one saw great fields of golden grain specked with red poppies and blue cornflowers, spreading back to thick wood with its always copious undergrowth: there, a canal with barges and the water dimpled with a heavy shower, through whose haze might be made out a figure, regardless of wet, phlegmatically fishing from the bank. And again, forest: silver birch, fir, acacia, beech and oak, with the long "rides," cut like canals of green grass, often ending in a glimpse of some lordly château, at whose ancient history one could only guess.

In the morning, at the first stop that promised to be of some duration, all ranks tumbled half-clad out of the train; and with basins, mirrors and shaving tackle set out on the footboards, commenced a hasty toilet. In the middle of the performance—and always without warning —the train would start with a jerk that upset everything; and amidst incendiary language and a wild grabbing— where the difference between *meum* and *tuum* was frequently forgotten—and collecting of paraphernalia, half-washed and shaved officers and men reboarded the train, to wait for another, and similar, opportunity.

And so, detraining at Brias, the Division made for the Villers-Chatel area, where the Field Ambulances found sites at Cambligneul, Jouy-Servins and Aubigny.

CHAPTER XII.

The Battle of the Scarpe, 26th Aug. to 3rd Sept., 1918.

Transport rattles behind us,
  On the Route Nationale,
Dust in our eyes to blind us,
  On the Route Nationale.
Sturdy children at play there,
Lorries lining the way there,
With "What have you salved to-day?" there,
  On the Route Nationale.

"The 51st Division on 26th August attacked north of the Scarpe, and in five days of successful fighting captured Rœux, Greenland Hill and Plouvain."—(*Sir Douglas Haig's Despatch.*)

ON the 19th August the 2nd H.F.A. took over the M.D.S. at St. Catherine, a suburb of Arras, where they had good (and old-standing) accommodation in a little-damaged brewery. The unit was not sorry to see the last of Cambligneul, where they had been freely bombed during their stay: one driver being seriously, and another slightly wounded, with thirteen horses killed and the same number wounded the night before they left. The 2/1st H.F.A. moved the same day to Agnez-les-Duisans to act as Divisional Rest Station, and the 3rd H.F.A. took over the Marœuil Field Ambulance site.

D.H.Q. had now moved to the hutments above Marœuil, and on the night of the 21st we had the highly unpleasant experience of having fifteen bombs dropped amongst us. One landed in front of "Q" office, and an orderly there saved himself only by promptly diving head first into a chalk trench seven feet deep. When brought in for treatment of the many bruises and excoriations that naturally followed this athletic effort, he groused out, "It's a d——d shame they dinna mak steps doon into thae trenches!" On its being pointed out to him that the delay caused by the use of the steps would certainly have led to his demise, he grudgingly allowed, "Aweel, I widna wonder but there's maybe something in that!" It was a curious fact that in the whole camp, where much material destruction was done, he and another man were the only two who sustained any damage from the raid.

On the 25th, D.H.Q. moved to Victory Camp on the Lille road, two kilometres north-east of Arras, and not far from our old Collecting Post at the Vimy Ridge battle in April, 1917. The Collecting Post (over which the R.A.M.C. fatigue parties had expended months of labour) was by now gutted and in use as a billet.

Once more we were working up the Scarpe valley, with Collecting Posts at L'Abbayette and Fampoux: the same villainous old shelled area. Going through Blangy one day a large Hun "dud" landed on a ruined house at the roadside while our car was passing, and battered us with a vigorous shower of broken bricks and dust. There were three passengers inside, and it was with strained and artificial smiles that we simultaneously remarked "Dud!" Next day while working round the various medical posts (at Fampoux; the Sandpit Collecting Post in front of it; and Single Arch Collecting Post on the railway embankment) we got back to the road and ran the car up to the quarry at the *chemin creux* near Rœux, to explore it with the view of its becoming a Relay Bearer Post. Jerry's observation balloon had evidently spotted the car, for (just as we had come out of the place and started on our return journey) the enemy put thirty shells and some shrapnel slick into the quarry. That was the worst of "visibility good." And then, as further harassment, on the road home a couple of horses in a limber bolted out of a farm entrance, drove the pole into our ambulance car, and tore the side covering off in ribbons, luckily without damage to the "insides."

At this time propaganda work of ours amongst the Boches was increasing, and fleets of white balloons used occasionally to sail overhead making for their lines, dropping at intervals showers of leaflets. These, quivering and wavering in the breeze, drifted down like silver lace as the sun shone on them from a serene blue sky.

Behind us in a dip near Anzin was a Japanese battleship gun, made by Armstrongs, mounted on a bogey and pulled about by its own engine. With a shell of nearly a ton weight it fired hourly on Douai, and the whole outfit was said to be worth quarter of a million sterling. It made a devilish noise when it fired; and, on one occasion as we passed, the concussion split the canvas roof and smashed the windows of our ambulance car.

When the Division came out of the line D.H.Q. moved again to the Marœuil hutments on 14th September. How familiar thousands of troops must have become with that blessed village and all its landmarks! Coming up the road from Ecoivres one passed the cemetery on the left, then turned right and downhill a bit before again turning left at right angles along the battered *pavé* that ran between the church and the château. The end of the church that abutted on the street had got, early in the war, a bite taken out of it by a shell, and the gap was propped with a wooden beam. The main ecclesiastical treasure had been long ago removed elsewhere for safety. This was a casket of gilded bronze—XIII century work—containing the relics of Saint Berthilde, who had died a widow at Marœuil about the year 685. Down in the lower part of the village stood her fountain, covered in by a little brick chapel, famous for the cure of diseases of the eye, to which shrine in peace time pilgrimages were regularly made. The water looked clean and clear, but there were, unfortunately, no cases of *maux d'yeux* at the time amongst us whereby to test its efficacy.

On the other side of the little valley was the neighbouring village of Etrun, once the site of a fine country house for the pleasuring of the ancient bishops of Arras. Formerly, also, it had contained a celebrated abbey of Benedictines. But these glories of Etrun had long departed, and its chief interest was now due to the fact that near it were the remains of the old Roman camp of Mont-César. One always lacked, however, the necessary literature—and leisure—to assimilate local archæology; but one sighed for a day there with some French Monkbarns, when all the racket was past and gone.

One of the ever pleasant duties of No. 2 H.Q. mess was to offer on behalf of the Division the most wholehearted hospitality to all visitors who laid claim to it. Entirely free from the inevitable and sometimes oppressive dignity of No. 1, it was in most divisions (certainly in ours) the cheeriest H.Q. mess. With ever memorable representatives of "A" and "Q," we had the A.P.M., "Dados," "Daddums" and other worthies, and as mess president the Claims Officer (better known in his other capacity of O.C. "Balmorals," our famous concert troupe); while the backbone of the whole show was perhaps the O.C. Employment (*alias* "Enjoyment") Company, that genial "Cotswold Highlander" and worshipper of Jorrocks, with his never-failing cheerfulness and caustic wit. Free criticism of each other, as occasion demanded, never interfered with our camaraderie; and if any one of the bunch can look back on those days without many pleasant memories of them, I fear that he has fallen away from the high standard of No. 2 in war time.

On one occasion at Marœuil we received with the usual open arms a very well-known London literary man, who came to us in the guise of a lieutenant from G.H.Q. and as cicerone to several foreign journalists. Of these one was a Spaniard, representative of two newspapers: another a Norwegian from Christiania. The Londoner, like many true intellectuals, successfully concealed the fact (in an environment he evidently considered unsuitable) that he was troubled this way. But the Spaniard, a cheery, cosmopolitan soul with a passable knowledge of English, blossomed forth later and spontaneously as an after-dinner speaker in an eloquent oration which No. 2 received with due and prolonged applause. Then ensued a painful hiatus while we *sotto voce* endeavoured to stimulate our "Q" member—who had resided many years in the Argentine—to reply in the fluent Spanish we had so often heard him speak about. After a blank and ornamentally terse refusal on his part, I was earnestly requested by the mess president to endeavour to save the situation. Alas! what—on the spur of the moment—does the average man know about Spain, save that the Moors had been in it, and that Miguel Cervantes had written *Don Quixote?* And of Norway, what again, save that the Maid of Norway must of necessity have come from there? So, with the aid of these scanty topical touches, a reply was effected; the gallant señor assisting with many valuable interpolations, and the burly descendant of the Vikings (who knew no English) being affected to tears when the only appropriate—and that a doubtfully authentic—verse from *Sir Patrick Spens,*

> To Noroway, to Noroway
> To Noroway o'er the faem,
> The King's daughter o' Noroway
> 'Tis thou maun bring her hame!

was recited. And when, an hour later (and unexpectedly), the G.O.C. sent a message from No. 1 mess that he desired to interview the foreign visitors, we all saw the point of the joke much better than the professional humorist who grimly conducted his voluble charges thither over some open ground which seemed to be even more uneven than his party imagined. Rumour had it next day that the General's manner had been frigid to all concerned.

It was while inspecting the sanitation of the surrounding area that I came one fine day to the village of Gauchin le Gal, some kilometres to the west of that historic landmark, the well-known twin towers of Mont St. Eloi. Standing in the little village market-place, amongst a collection of parked motor lorries and g.s. wagons, were two stones, evidently very old and of a nature that excited the regard of the folk-lorist. One, upright and of the shape and size of a small milestone, had an iron staple let into the top of it; while the other, resembling a large Dutch cheese, had a slice taken off one end. Into the flat surface of the sliced end another iron staple was fixed, and a small incised cross was roughly carved beside it. "This," said I to myself, quoting the exclamation of Mr. Pickwick on the occasion of his great antiquarian discovery, "is very strange!"

Well, when in doubt or when seeking information in France, go to the Maire; and to the Maire I went, to find that he was from home and the schoolmaster acting as his deputy. The latter received me courteously. "The stones? Ah, yes! There *was* a story—a foolish old story—about these stones!" "Would he tell it to me?" "But yes, if monsieur cared for these things. He had written it down some years ago in a little notebook." So with his permission, I copied it, sitting somewhat crampedly at one of the small school desks. And this is how the tale ran:—

"On our village square there is to be seen a large round stone chained to another upright one of red sandstone. Various explanations have been given of these stones. The first is that in an ancient fight between two noblemen one made a prisoner of the other, and to perpetuate the memory of his victory the upright stone was erected to represent the victor, and the round stone chained to it to represent the vanquished. Another version is that the conquered nobleman was made prisoner and tied to a post in the market-place, where he remained exposed to the public gaze till he died, and hence the small cross that can be seen near the fastening of the round stone.

"Yet another story exists, which does not redound to the credit of the ladies of the commune who lived in those far-off days. For it says explicitly that this accursed round stone, then unchained, used to go at night and knock at the doors of husbands whose wives were unfaithful to them. As a large number of households were disturbed in this way, the authorities decided to stop the wandering habits of the stone by chaining it up. Since then the inhabitants of the village sleep in peace. Nowadays one would not be afraid to unchain it, for unfaithful wives are now rare in this countryside, and the stone would have little opportunity of resuming its old occupation."

Eh bien! A good enough story? And at the end a pretty little compliment to the virtue of the commune! *Hélas!* The worthy schoolmaster's little manuscript book had been written before the war and while "the accursed round stone" was still chained. When I saw it, it was once again unchained and had been since 1914, probably at the hands of some mischief maker. Left alone and free to resume its old habits, what had happened? *Ecoutez!* Various French troops had been billeted in the village at the outbreak of war, and one lady had proved—*comment dirais-je?*—more popular than virtuous. Whereupon some of the inhabitants, probably of her own sex, had taken the old round stone and laid it by night on her door-step as a delicate and many-centuries-old hint to her to mend her ways. She, and some of her *bons amis*, naturally annoyed by this advertisement, took the nocturnal visitor and buried it in the back garden. But the other villagers found this out, and, indignant at such an insult to their ancient guardian of morals, went to the Maire, who immediately ordered the offenders to dig it up again and reinstate it on the market-place. One can imagine the scene and the jeers and joy of the local Pharisees! In the market-place, anyhow, it stood once again, unchained and free to look out for fresh work, a tabloid kirk-session to pillory lights o' love. And, also once again, I trust the schoolmaster of Gauchin le Gal can now with a clear conscience proclaim the unassailable virtue of the ladies of his commune. Or has he thought it safer to wait for the rechaining of the *mauvais galet?*

CHAPTER XIII.

The Battle of Cambrai, 1918.

> *Labour cohorts navvy*
>   *On the Route Nationale,*
> *Filling shell-holed pavé*
>   *On the Route Nationale.*
> *Horizon gun-fire glistens,*
> *Abed, the peasant listens*
> *To the tired foot's persistence*
>   *On the Route Nationale.*

"About the end of August and beginning of September the XXII Corps took over on the north and south sides of the Scarpe, and the 51st Division became part of that Corps. In the beginning of October the Corps moved to the south of the Canadian Corps and took part in what is now 'The Battle of Cambrai, 1918,' 8th-9th October, with pursuit to the Selle, 9th-12th October, and on 11th October an advance towards the Selle river was commenced. On the 12th and 13th the 51st Division had hard fighting. The attack was renewed on the 19th, when there were signs of the enemy retiring, and he was closely pressed. The 51st took a prominent part, until the 29th October, in various actions which involved bitter fighting. For a most gallant charge against a counter attack by the enemy the 6th Argyll and Sutherland Highlanders ... were complimented by the Corps Commander. ...

"At the Battle of the Selle river the 51st, as part of the XXII corps, First Army, were on the left of the attack on 24th October. The telegraphic despatches stated that the Division had sharp fighting on the 24th and again on the 27th, when they repulsed a determined counter attack near Maing with the bayonet. Their losses during October were 2,835. At the end of October the Division went out of the line to rest, and its very distinguished fighting career was closed."—*(The Territorial Divisions.)*

ON 8th October Divisional Headquarters moved from the roomy Château D'Acq, near Mont St. Eloi, into a large sandpit—such were the ups and downs of military life—

our correct address then being V 28 d o o (Sheet 51 B). Here we remained for three days in huts tucked into the ever sliding sides of the pit, and—as bombers were rife—covered with green camouflage netting, until on the 10th we moved to Bourlon Château, where "A," "Q," and A.D.M.S. offices conjointly shared the large kitchen. It luckily possessed a huge, old-fashioned open fire-place of the Scots farmhouse type, but had no other merits of any kind whatsoever, except that it was the most habitable part of a building which had been very conscientiously knocked to bits. My bedroom was a little cylindrical vault half way up the kitchen stairs, roomy enough to permit of a bed of sorts being rigged up in it. In peace times it more appropriately functioned as an oven for supplying the family bread.

The 3rd Highland Field Ambulance took over the Chocolate Factory at Ste. Olle—a suburb of Cambrai—as M.D.S. for the 2nd Canadian and 49th Divisions, then in action. This factory, a modern and up-to-date affair with much overhead (and now smashed) glass, was situated on the side of the main road, and had several narrow squeaks during their occupancy of it from the free shelling of the area that was going on.

After a day of rumours and counter-rumours—e.g., that the Kaiser had resigned in favour of his second son—but always with the definite news that we were advancing well, our office got orders in the evening to move out and *rendezvous* at Morenchies on the outskirts of Cambrai. Arriving there in the dusk we waited two hours for orders that never came; so in the dark we pushed on *au pied* to Escaudœuvres, the suburb beyond Cambrai. The greasy *pavé* was stiff with traffic, the place was being shelled by a high velocity gun, and the footpaths were full of shell holes. Advance thereon was further complicated by fallen telegraph poles, so that, scrambling out of the holes into which you fell, you then became hopelessly tied up in a

PLAN OF DRESSING STATIONS. CAMBRAI AREA.

THE BATTLE OF CAMBRAI, 1918. 243

tangle of wire. From several of the houses in which they were billeted, our troops were also engaged in heaving out dead Boches. Progress, therefore, was slow; but after an hour, tired, bruised, wet and muddy, we found D.H.Q., and then managed to get the A.D.M.S. of the 2nd Canadian Division and arrange the various takings-over required before our Division went once again into action.

(a) *First Phase*—11th-12th to 19th October.—*First Day's Advance.*

On the Division entering the line on night of 11th-12th October, the Field Ambulances were located as follows:—

2nd Highland Field Ambulance at Morenchies.

2/1st Highland Field Ambulance at Convent, Escaudœuvres.

3rd Highland Field Ambulance at Chocolate Factory, Ste. Olle.

This last unit was, as already said, temporarily functioning as Main Dressing Station for the 2nd Canadian Division and the 49th Division, until required to act in a similar capacity for the 51st (Highland) Division.

On the evening of the 11th the 2/1st Highland Field Ambulance took over from a Canadian Field Ambulance the Advanced Dressing Station at the Convent, Escaudœuvres; the Canadians also remaining there till the 13th, when their last Brigade came out of the line. Forward Posts were also taken over at Thun St. Martin and Naves.

On the afternoon of the 12th this Advanced Dressing Station was moved forward to St. Hubert, Thun St. Martin, with, for the left sector, a car Collecting Post in the yard and cellars of a *brasserie* near the cemetery at Iwuy, and for the right sector a post on the road N.E. of Naves. As the railway bridges over the roads from the right sector to the Advanced Dressing Station were destroyed, this latter post evacuated cases direct to the Main Dressing Station, Escaudœuvres, now established by the 2nd Highland Field Ambulance which had moved on the morning of 12th October to the Convent. By dint of much hard work in clearing away debris and patching windows and roofs, satisfactory accommodation for over 400 cases was soon provided. In the afternoon the 3rd Highland Field Ambulance arrived at the Convent, Escaudœuvres, from its temporary work with the Canadians at Ste. Olle, and doubled up with the 2nd, joining in the medical work of the Main Dressing Station and in repairing the premises.

In the course of the next day the Regimental Aid Posts moved forward to the neighbourhood of Avesnes-le-Sec, and on the 14th an Advanced Car Collecting Post for Ford cars was established at a site on the Iwuy-Avesnes-le-Sec road, in charge of an N.C.O. and a squad of men. On the 14th, also, the post N.E. of Naves was discontinued and all the cases for evacuation were passed through Iwuy.

On the 15th the Car Collecting Post was moved farther forward along the Iwuy-Avesnes-le-Sec road, and one Ford car stationed there, another from Iwuy replacing it when it came down from the post with cases.

(b) *Second Phase*—19th to 23rd October.—*Across the Selle. At the Ecaillon.*

On the 19th when, under pressure, the enemy began to retire, especially on the left, a Car Collecting Post was established in some buildings beside the level crossing over the railway at Pavé de Valenciennes.

On the forenoon of the 20th an Advanced Car Collecting Post was placed at Frête Au Poirier, on the Iwuy side of the crossroads there, short of where the road had been blown up by the enemy on his retiral. Ford cars brought cases from the Noyelles area to this point, whence they were transferred to large cars and evacuated to the M.D.S., Escaudœuvres.

The post at Iwuy was now moved forward to the cellarage of a house near the church at Avesnes-le-Sec, and at the same time two Walking Wounded Collecting Posts were placed, one at Pavé de Valenciennes and the other at the former Brigade Headquarters on the outskirts of Avesnes-le-Sec. At these Posts horse ambulance wagons picked up walking cases and took them back to the Corps Walking Wounded Collecting Station at Escaudœuvres.

Next day the post at Avesnes-Le-Sec was vacated and an Advanced Car Collecting Post established at Croix Sainte Marie on the Douchy-Valenciennes road. As the main-road bridge at Douchy had been blown up and a temporary one was still in process of erection, Ford cars were man-handled by squads of men across the badly cut-up fields beside the road and over the small R.E. trestle bridge crossing the Selle two hundred yards north of Douchy. These Fords then ran forward and brought cases down from Croix Sainte Marie to a post in Douchy, whence they were carried by hand across the bridge and loaded again on large cars waiting on the west side of the river.

The same day the Main Dressing Station in charge of the 2nd Highland Field Ambulance moved from Convent, Escaudœuvres, to the Château at Iwuy, the Convent being taken over by the 3rd Highland Field Ambulance as a Divisional Rest Station, while the Advanced Dressing Station moved forward to Pavé de Valenciennes.

On the 22nd the Advanced Walking Wounded Collecting Posts were moved forward to Frête au Poirier and Noyelles, and cases evacuated by horse ambulance wagon to the Corps Walking Wounded Collecting Post, now at Iwuy, relay wagons being got at a post at Pavé de Valenciennes.

An Advanced Ford Car Post was next established on the west side of the demolished railway bridge at Thiant, it being at the time impossible to get cars farther forward until the debris of the fallen-in stonework had been cleared from the road.

The same day a dispensary for civilian sick of the district was established at Douchy, and a soup kitchen was also started there to feed the starving population of Douchy, Neuville and Noyelles. These were very necessary and much appreciated.

(c) *Third Phase*—23rd to 25th October.—*The Crossing of the Ecaillon.*

The main-road bridge at Douchy having now been reconstructed and allowing of the passage of large cars, an Advanced Dressing Station was established in the Salle du Patronage, Douchy, and the Main Dressing Station moved forward from Iwuy Château to the Bakery, an extensive factory building at Pavé de Valenciennes. Iwuy Château was then taken over by the 3rd Highland Field Ambulance as a Divisional Rest Station.

During the night of the 22nd-23rd the Croix Sainte Marie post was badly gassed, and in the course of the day 25 shells came into Douchy; one, which caused 21 casualties, landing thirty feet from the Advanced Dressing Station in the village hall. A large number of local wounded, military and civilian, had to be dealt with.

A dispensary for civilian sick and a soup kitchen were installed at Haulchin on the 23rd.

On the 24th, many gassed cases, including several civilians, were evacuated from the village of Thiant by hand carriage over the ruins of the collapsed railway bridge, and thence by cars. Douchy was again shelled, causing several local casualties.

THE BATTLE OF CAMBRAI, 1918.

Relay Bearer Posts were established on the 25th at the Bolt Factory, Thiant, and in front of the village. In the evening a further post was pushed forward on the Thiant-Maing road. The bridge across the Ecaillon river, which had been blown up by the enemy when retreating, was now reconstructed, and the road had been cleared during the day.

(d) *Fourth Phase*—25th to 28th October.—*The Advance beyond Maing. The Fighting in Famars. The Struggle for Mont Houy.*

On the 25th the Advanced Dressing Station moved forward to La Pyramide de Denain, where there was excellent cellarage in a farmhouse, while the Main Dressing Station moved forward from Pavé de Valenciennes to the School, Douchy.

The Relay Post for horse wagons collecting walking wounded closed at Pavé de Valenciennes on the 26th, all walking wounded now going direct from Croix Sainte Marie to the new Corps Walking Wounded Collecting Post at Haspres.

The main car post at Bolt Factory, Thiant, with Ford cars stationed on the Thiant-Maing road, was now collecting direct from Regimental Aid Posts on S.W. side of Maing, until on the 28th, the Advanced Dressing Station and forward posts were relieved by a W. Riding Field Ambulance of the 49th Division, when the Highland Division came out of the line after its last battle. . . .

As occurred in the retreat of March and April, the Battle of the Lys, and the action in Champagne, new types of difficulty arose in this action, the overcoming of which lent fresh interest to the work.

The demolition of crossroads by mines, and the blocking of evacuation routes by the blowing up of railway arches and bridges, rendered the getting away of the casualties no easy matter. The value of the Ford type of ambulance car was prominently brought out; as, owing to its lightness, it could cross fields, dodge through roads cut up by shell holes, climb banks, and be manhandled through soft, cut-up ground quite impassable for the larger type of car.

Owing to the fact that in most cases during the advance Fords could be run up practically to the Regimental Aid Posts, a large amount of the motor transport Field Ambulance work was done under heavy shell fire. In the village of Iwuy one Ford twice received a hit; the second time, an orderly being killed and a medical officer slightly wounded. In both cases the driver[1] managed temporarily to repair his car under fire and get his cases away safely.

As the Division advanced, the shelling of the evacuation routes, the greasy condition of the pavé, cut-up, too, with shell holes and mine craters, made night work doubly difficult. The blowing up of the bridge over the Selle on the main road through Douchy, and the repeated blocking of the road into Thiant by the debris of the constantly shelled railway bridge were serious obstacles; but before the action finished Ford cars were running into Maing and large cars into Thiant. The work of the bearers and the motor transport was, as always, carried out with great gallantry and efficiency.

The Advanced Dressing Station and the Main Dressing Station, while at Douchy, both came under shell fire. Under the circumstances the R.A.M.C. casualties were fortunately few.

During the advance we were faced for the first time with an entirely new problem. The civilian population were either being evacuated from the danger zone or

---

[1] Private A. E. Highmore, D.C.M. A wheel of his car was wrecked, which he replaced by one "taken on loan" from a Canadian Ford parked in a yard nearby, its driver being, very sensibly, down below in a cellar. Highmore courteously left his own damaged wheel as a souvenir.

THE BATTLE OF CAMBRAI, 1918.

returning from the back area to their now freed homes. About half of these people were ill, largely owing to exhaustion, exposure and the long continued under-feeding while in enemy hands. A very large proportion was found to be tubercular; e.g., in the village of Haulchin, with a population of 1,500, over 90 cases (by no means the total) of tubercular disease of the lung received medical treatment, many of them in an advanced stage of the disease. Venereal disease was also common.

In co-operation with the French Mission (and the civil authorities when they were functioning) medical attendance on the sick was organised through the Field Ambulances and medical officers of units. In one village alone (Neuville sur L'Escaut) over 200 cases were visited at their homes. The graver cases were evacuated through our medical channels to the French *Hôpital St. Jean,* Arras.

Soup kitchens and centres for distribution of cook-house bones were quickly installed and handed over to the French authorities to provide food for the villages of Douchy, Neuville sur L'Escaut, Noyelles, Haulchin, Bouchain, Iwuy, Thun St. Martin, Thun L'Evêque, Paillencourt, Estrun and Hordain. It is estimated that nearly 4,000 civilians were thus daily supplied with good nourishing food, in addition to the rations and medical comforts issued, and the greatest appreciation was shown by the French authorities and by the people themselves of the efforts of the Division on their behalf.

34 civilian wounded (gun-shot wounds and gassed) and seriously sick (advanced phthisis, pneumonia, etc.) were evacuated, most of the gassed being from Famars.

In all the re-occupied area sanitation was very bad. Considering the vaunted efficiency of the enemy in this respect, it is more than possible that the conditions found were largely intentional. This state of affairs was increased by the amount of debris which had to be cleared out of the houses before our troops occupied them as billets, and by the insanitary habits of the returning civilians, many of them merely birds of passage. The large amount of dead horses all over the area contributed to make matters worse; while owing to the multiplicity of breeding grounds and the abnormally mild weather there was a plague of flies. Incineration, the usual safeguard in such cases, was severely handicapped by the fact that it had to be carried out with great caution owing to the large amount of loose bombs and hand grenades lying about. "Booby-traps" were frequently met with. At Iwuy a bomb had been placed inside a soiled mattress, and, on this being burnt, an explosion resulted in one man being mortally and another slightly wounded. At Douchy a refuse pit, full of dry refuse inviting the application of a match was, on examination, found to have the bottom lined with hand grenades laid in a regular layer.

Officers commanding Field Ambulances were instructed to co-operate, as far as their other duties permitted, with Town Majors and medical officers of units, in the remedying of existing conditions, and a very large amount of sanitary work was carried out before the Division was relieved.

During the battle D.H.Q. moved first from Escaudœuvres to Naves, some three kilometres distant, a much battered and (then) very dirty village. Here I shared, with Daddums and Dados,[1] the coal cellar beneath the A.D.M.S. office as a bedroom, having taken it over from the Huns as a going concern with all plenishings, including three beds and a clock affixed to the wall. The clock was going too, and we sincerely wished it wasn't, owing to our knowledge of the numerous booby-trap efforts the enemy had left in his wake. The

[1] D.A.D.M.S. and D.A.D.O.S.

THE BATTLE OF CAMBRAI, 1918.

puzzle was whether to stop the evil time-piece and thereby possibly set off some infernal contraption inside, or to let it run down with results probably similar. Pleading the possession of an absolutely unmechanical mind, I tried to persuade Dados to take a look over it some afternoon when he was out of a job, but he "wasn't having any." An R.E. sergeant, called in as a consultant, had no doubt (and stated his opinion in a most convinced manner) that it was much the best course to let it run down! So for two nights we all fell off to sleep with the horrible clock stolidly tick-ticking, while we affected a composure we did not feel. In one corner of our cellar—a fuggy vaulted hole twenty feet by ten—was a heap made up in equal parts of coals and potatoes; and our strained nerves were further shattered one midnight by the Ordnance merchant suddenly asserting that he heard a steady ticking noise proceeding from it! Daddums lit a candle, while Dados, on hands and knees, crawled about in the neighbourhood of the heap and applied his ear to various likely parts. I offered him the loan of a stethoscope, as I had reason to be really interested in the proceedings; but Dados was quite rude about it, and huffily got into bed with his hands, knees and temper in a most unseemly condition.

The next move was to the château at Avesnes-le-Sec —why *sec* was the conundrum there. It had been badly knocked about, and rain got in only too readily.

The Basseville of Bouchain was our next location, where Nos. 1 and 2 H.Q. Mess were in a large house in the narrow and dirty main street. Soon after our arrival the owner, a quiet, cultured old man with white side-whiskers, turned up along with his daughter, son-in-law and three maids and politely asked to be allotted accommodation in his own house! He had been a mill-owner there before the war, and gave a bad account of the Boche. One of their generals had been billeted in his house, and, after departing, sent back two motor lorries to lift all the furniture he had specially favoured. This was done; but the house in the town to which it had been removed was set on fire during a drunken orgy and everything was destroyed.

The A.D.M.S. office was in a neighbouring private house which had been very thoroughly looted from the basement to the attics. The well-filled library was one of the saddest sights of the war; bookcases smashed; all the French classics—finely tooled leather-bound books —torn, burst or half burnt, lying about in heaps that had been trodden and re-trodden by muddy boots. Many old legal documents were also scattered around in disorder. Even the children's nursery on the top flat had not been missed: bedding cut open, furniture smashed, and the rocking-horse, dolls and other children's toys broken to bits with an axe. Fritz was a dirty devil when he got going on the lines of malicious destruction.

But we had more to do than gaze at the devastation which *Kultur* had effected, for, besides the ordinary Field Ambulance work of a Division in the line, we had now the extra work—most willingly undertaken by one and all— of feeding and medically treating the unfortunate French population of the area, plus the added refugees passing through, who for four years had steadily suffered the vilest ill-usage at the hands of a brutal and unscrupulous foe. And, in the present atmosphere of international criticism, one may perhaps, even at some length, fitly recall how our help was then appreciated by the French.

On 30th December, 1918, M. Clemenceau wrote a letter from Paris to Sir Douglas Haig, in which he said: "Field-Marshal Foch has just communicated to me a complete report concerning the aid rendered the population of liberated territories by the British troops at the time of their victorious advance from Oct. 1 to Nov. 25, 1918. You generously undertook for four days to feed the French population of over 700,000 souls, who had been restored to their country. You did not, however, consider this enough. Wherever our civil authorities were unable to succour our compatriots, worn out by long privations, and systematically deprived of the means of subsistence, your effective assistance was continued for as long as was necessary. Thus, in the course of one month, over five million rations were distributed by the British troops. Your different Service branches, your officers and men, vied with each other in ingenuity and efforts to procure fresh meat, white bread, and hot food for our women and aged people, and with wise and touching forethought, took special pains to guarantee a supply of milk for the children and invalids. Thousands of our refugees, sick and repatriated prisoners of war, were transported by you; your heroic drivers exposing themselves to the enemy's fire in order to save the victims of his bombardment. Further to assist our wounded compatriots, you improvised complete hospitals within a few kilometres of the firing line. Innumerable lives were thus saved by your devoted doctors and nurses, who have moreover been unremitting in their efforts to overcome the terrible epidemic of influenza which has lately visited our unfortunate population.

"I wish it were possible to quote the many individual acts of devotion and proofs of the comradeship in the report that lies before me. Words cannot express all that the British Army, whilst unceasingly engaged in heavy fighting, endured in order to render practical assistance to our unfortunate compatriots. France owes you the salvation of a whole region. I am proud, M. le Marechal, to acknowledge the debt. The Government and People of France will never forget it." And again, in the report forwarded to the Quartermaster-General of the British Armies in France by the Chief of Staff of the French Military Mission attached to the British Army, the covering letter says:—"I avail myself of this opportunity to tell you how all those who have seen your officers and men at work in these circumstances have admitted the ingenious and untiring efforts displayed in order to relieve our suffering populations, and beg to express to you my personal and deep gratitude for the same."

The report itself contains the following passages:—
"On Oct. 1, 1918, the British Army began to enter a district from which the population had only been partly evacuated by the Germans. The British Army was going to find, up to the Belgian border, 700,000 inhabitants. The order strictly forbidding the placing of British batteries near inhabited villages, in order to diminish for them the risks of being shelled, throughout the 1st British Army area, illustrates the attitude which our Allies were adopting towards our fellow countrymen. The main question was going to be the provision of food. The British Army had promised to supply the liberated inhabitants, as it advanced, with four days' preserved rations, calculated at the scale of one Army ration to four civilians. At the end of this period the care of feeding the population was to fall upon the French authorities. The object of the present report is to show what the British troops have in reality done for a population consisting mostly of old people, women and children, who had been insufficiently fed for several years, who were suffering from a violent epidemic of influenza, and who were also, except in the Lille area, entirely short of foodstuffs.

"Throughout their areas and as they advanced, the British have fed the civilian population for four days as promised. But at no place, on the fifth day, were the French authorities in a position to ensure, even partly, the feeding of the civilian population. The first provisions sent by the French authorities only arrived in

THE BATTLE OF CAMBRAI, 1918.

the First Army area (Denain, Valenciennes) eighteen days, in the Third Army area (Le Cateau, Avesnes) twenty-nine days, and in the Fourth Army area (Le Quesnoy, Maubeuge) thirty-eight days after the first civilians had been liberated. During all that period and in spite of difficulties of transportation which, on several occasions, compelled the British troops to reduce their own rations, the British have assumed the enormous task of carrying out this prolonged supply, distributing officially a minimum quantity of 5,084,000 civilian rations, the transportation of which represents, for instance, for the area of a single corps, viz., the Eighth, from Oct. 19 to Nov. 15, 284 days of motor lorry and 602 days of two-horsed wagon transportation. The British have, therefore, saved in this way from starvation at least 400,000 French people whom the retreating Germans had systematically deprived of all means of subsistence.

"When at last, after waiting for weeks, the first provisions sent by the civil authorities arrived at railheads, at all places the number of lorries placed at the disposal of the prefects was utterly out of proportion to the requirements. For instance, on Nov. 11, in the First British Army area (Denain, Valenciennes), the Prefect of the Nord only had eighteen motor lorries in working order for supplying 177,000 inhabitants. Provisions were accumulating at railways stations, fresh arrivals had been stopped for two days, and complete starvation would have prevailed throughout the district had it not been for the forty motor lorries, and afterwards sixty, which were placed by the First British Army at the disposal of the French authorities for all the time required. This state of affairs occurred everywhere; and everywhere, in response to the applications made by the French Military Mission, the various British armies have employed every day, regardless of numbers, hundreds of motor lorries and wagons for conveying the provisions to the *centres de ravitaillement* and distributing them afterwards between the respective localities. This constitutes an enormous effort which was made all along the British front, and which resulted in saving the liberated populations from an unprecedented disaster.

"In addition to the transportation of provisions, the British have constantly placed the whole of their empty motor lorries at the disposal of refugees, evacuated people, and released prisoners of war. Everywhere proper routes of circulation were established, by which tens of thousands of people have benefited. The untiring obligingness of the British drivers, their courage in removing under fire civilians to be evacuated, the help which they have spontaneously given everywhere to women and children, form one of the most striking features of the assistance rendered by the British during the war. It is even impossible to calculate the thousands of journeys made by motor lorries loaded with civilians since the beginning of the advance. To give an idea—from Oct. 19 to Nov. 15, the First British Army officially employed for the conveyance either of provisions or of French refugees, 2,279 days of motor lorry transportation. This figure does not include, however, the innumerable transportations of civilians, with their baggage, spontaneously carried by the drivers on roads, and which reach an amount at least double the above figure.

"Owing to delay in the arrival of the provisions to be provided by the French authorities, the scale foreseen of one army ration to four inhabitants proved to be distinctly insufficient for a diet of any duration. The British have at all places done their utmost in order to remedy this disquieting state of affairs. In many cases the British troops supplied, free of charge, thousands of rations in addition, which are not included in statistics. Moreover, the directors of the Medical Services of corps

THE BATTLE OF CAMBRAI, 1918.

and divisions have been instructed to specify what should be given to the civilian population.

"On the other hand, a physically weakened population requires other things than preserves and biscuits. Wherever possible considerable quantities of fresh meat have been substituted for corned beef. In addition to the rations furnished, the Veterinary Services arranged for some of the sound horses to be slaughtered, and the flesh to be distributed between the various localities. At the recommendation of medical officers fresh bread was substituted for biscuits nearly everywhere, and an enormous quantity of tins of condensed milk was distributed to children and sick people.

"At all places in face of the piteous condition of the civilian population, cases of personal initiative took place. The 51st Division alone thus provided food, free of charge, for 3,500 persons a day. An admirable ingenuity was displayed in the supply of ingredients for the making of these free soups: flesh from wounded horses destroyed, rations in excess, and bones from neighbouring units, vegetables fetched from a distance by fatigue parties, were added to the Bovril, Oxo, and tea given by the British Army. The Ambulance in the neighbourhood furnished the cooks."

The report says later:—"This was a marvellous impetus of systematic and ingenious charity which turned the British Army, even at the periods of the heaviest fighting, into a sort of huge society for the relief of the liberated French people. It is impossible to estimate the number of human lives saved in this way."

Reference is also made to the fine work of the British hospitals in caring for this exhausted population, amongst whom influenza, bronchitis and pneumonia were making terrible ravages, and whose villages the departing Germans were, moreover, bombarding with gas shells.

Summing up the services rendered, the report adds: "It is impossible to do justice to the admirable efforts displayed by all the British Armies, which, amidst heavy and victorious fighting, unceasingly thought about saving human lives and giving help to the French civilian population, regardless of cost. For this fine achievement both officers and men deserve the deepest gratitude of the French nation at large."

Of Divisions, the 51st and the 66th—both Territorial—were the only two referred to by name in the report for their work in this connection. At Mons, after the armistice, Captain St. André of the G.H.Q. French Mission, specially sent by Marshal Foch to enquire into the medical work done by the R.A.M.C., expressed to me his cordial thanks, on behalf of his country, for the efforts put forth by the 51st Division in their area to assist the unfortunate inhabitants.

Looking back on it all, I do not suppose that many housewives would have whole-heartedly admired our first efforts at soup-making. We had not enough trained cooks to go round, and these genial amateurs who ran the first *soupes populaires* went solely—guided by taste and fancy—on the lines of making the liquid refreshment "grateful and comforting." We were up against the fact that the usual local authorities—the *Maire,* his deputy, etc.—had had all their initiative knocked out of them by four years of German repression and brutality, and it was absolutely essential to act at once. So, on entering a half-smashed village, the first hunt was for a "boiler" or "copper"—the kind of thing found in a washing-house for boiling clothes or in a farmyard for making hens' meat and cattle food—of sufficient capacity for the job. This when found was thoroughly cleaned out, filled with water, and a fire lit beneath. Into the water went the contents of several tins of "bully," a bag of biscuits, some Bovril, or a piece of meat cut from some convenient and recently shell-killed horse. The neighbouring remains of gardens were searched for possible turnips, carrots, cabbages, or any green things of the vegetable order; and (after due washing and chopping) in they went too. A wooden "spurtle" had been now manufactured, and "the whole hypothec" was vigorously stirred.

The news—and the fragrant odour—of what we were manufacturing soon got abroad, and the starving inhabitants commenced to gather around the scene of operations, their numbers swelled further by the refugees passing through with their little handcarts. An announcement was made to the crowd of the hours (twice daily) when the distribution would be carried out, and they were warned to bring jugs and a statement of the number for whom they claimed food.

At this stage, if wisdom abode in you, the attendance of some village authority was demanded—the *Maire,* a "notable" or at least the *garde champêtre*—to check the demands of the applicants: a hungry man may be an angry man, but he certainly is apt to handle the truth very carelessly. At one of our earliest distributions a long, gaunt, middle-aged man turned up with a Gargantuan jug and claimed supplies for himself, a wife, and five children. An aged inhabitant, physically weak in all but tongue power, whom we had secured as umpire, broke forth at once:—

"Ah, villain! Five children? Who knows! But a wife—*jamais, jamais! Va t'en, misérable!*

But as we thought hunger might have damaged the exactness of his memory, we gave the "misérable" a sufficiency for his personal requirements, to the high disapproval of "Father William," who immediately tendered his resignation!

As things developed, the bones from all the units' cookhouses were systematically collected in sandbags and distributed to the soup centres according to the estimated population requiring aliment. In some cases the request was made by the people that these should be divided up and handed over so that each family should make its own soup. In the very small villages this was possible and was done; but in the larger ones it was not, and in some of the latter the authorities required persuasion to adopt the communal method.

I entered one such place just as Jerry commenced to shell it—for shell all these villages he did, although he knew they were still full of inhabitants. The street was empty, save for one phlegmatic old dame who was drawing water from a pump in the middle of it. "The house of M. le Maire? The fourth on the left, *Monsieur.*" Knocking at the door, I was hastily ushered in by a perturbed lady to a room where a "council of notables" was in session over local affairs, and, after introductions all round, was voted into the chair. From there, and in what I knew of the French language (practically sentence about with the chief of the Divisional French Mission, who kindly drove my points home), I explained our scheme. Solemnly these old worthies discussed it, and then divided into "Wets" and "Drys"; the former in favour of the central soup kitchen, the latter plumping for distributing the bones. The discussion promised to be both of interest and some length, but was prematurely brought to a close by a shell landing too near the *Mairie* for comfort; so the meeting broke up without the usual votes of thanks. But we had a soup kitchen going there in the afternoon all the same: I was always a consistent "Wet" on such occasions, because the food went further.

The conditions generally were pitiful in the extreme: a history of four long years of semi-starvation and brutal treatment by the enemy.

"You find the soup good?" I anxiously asked one woman, because, somehow, it did not look to me like "what mother used to make."

"*Mais oui, monsieur!* It is the first good food we have had for years," she replied.

A widow with five children, this woman had on one occasion left the village to go to a neighbouring one in search of food for them. Having done this without permission, she was kept there for nine months without news of her family, working in the fields with a gang of other women under the orders of a German soldier.

At Famars, several days after the cessation of hostilities, we found the *Maire*—a working stone-mason—in great distress. He had just got the news that his son, a prisoner in Belgium, had been—along with several others—shot by the enemy for cheering when the news of the armistice had been given out.

At Croix Sainte Marie I saw the first meeting after four years—and it was a touching scene—between a father and mother and their only child, a cripple daughter of eighteen lying in an invalid chair. All the time of the war she had been in Valenciennes, where she had gone on a visit to relatives a few days before it broke out. Only seven kilometres away, the parents had been steadily refused a *laissez-passer* to go and visit her.

At Iwuy we had for several days charge of an infant six weeks old. Its sole food during that time had been two tins of condensed milk, and, for the four days immediately previous to our getting it, nothing but water. The mother—far gone in phthisis and with three other children—had, four days after the birth, been ordered to move from Douchy to Denain, and for the privilege of lying on the bare boards of a German wagon that was going there in any case, had paid the driver her all—a sum of twenty-five francs. Rigging up an emergency feeding-bottle with the aid of a piece of sterilised stethoscope-tubing, we had the child in a fair way to recovery before we handed it over to the French hospital at Cambrai. But the mother was dying.

Dying, too, was an old woman with cardiac dropsy who had managed to make her way back to Iwuy, whence she and her husband had been forced to go by the Huns, as they retreated, to the other side of Valenciennes. Her husband, a frail old man, had dropped dead on the road, and two sons had previously been killed in the war. When we were arranging for her removal to a French refugee hospital in Cambrai, she pleaded earnestly to be allowed to die "at home"—"home" being the one half-habitable room in her destroyed cottage. Getting another old woman to look after her, we granted her request, and she died two days afterwards—at home.

One refugee, who had been doing forced labour for three years at a jam factory for German troops in Belgium, told me that many children were also compelled to work there, and that he had seen them knocked down by blows from a stick on the back of the head for tasting the stuff. Two of them had died as a result. He had seen other children struck on the mouth and their teeth knocked out for the same "offence."

But why go on ? Any one of the continual procession of refugees, pulling along their pitiable little collections of personal belongings in home-made handcarts, with whom one chanced to converse, had similar stories to tell. To get back to their homes, and meantime to get food and a night's lodging, was all they asked. Anything sadder than that perpetual stream of old folk and children, to be met by night and by day stumbling along in the wet, over greasy pavé or muddy road, it would be hard to conceive.

Paying a call one evening on the Chief of the Divisional French Mission,[1] I knocked at the door of his billet to be met with a cry of "Who's there ? I am busy ! Go away !" Giving my name I was allowed to enter,

[1] The gallant M. Pic.

and found him on his knees in front of a tub of steaming water, busily engaged in washing a pretty little boy of some five years of age. He modestly apologised for his occupation, which certainly recalled the famous old statuary advertisement of Pears' soap, so to make him feel more at ease I lent him a hand. The little chap was literally "nobody's bairn." He had neither local habitation, name nor relations. My friend had got him handed over that afternoon by some refugees in whose charge he had been for a year; they, in turn, having got him from strangers to whom he had been entrusted by previous unknown compatriots. So his tragic little history—he must have been about a year old when war broke out—ran back into sheer obscurity. His clothing was only fit for the incinerator, where it went; and we rigged him out in a white sweater and a pair of old Tommy slacks cut down to requirements. And to see the small chap when we had finished with him, strutting proudly about—a bundle of white wool with a Dutch stern of khaki—was a sight for the gods. I wonder if he was ever by any chance claimed by his own folk, or whether his own folk were alive to claim him. There were long, long odds against it.

Grateful to a degree the people were for what was being done: but after the *soupe populaire* became a fixed public institution, it was, like all public institutions, liable to criticism. Tinned milk—issued only to children, old folk and invalids—had ultimately to be diluted with sterilized water and served out by the pint; as the temptation of supping it undiluted was too much for some sybarites. And besides food, in some districts, an attempt had to be made to supply firewood and coal. Many of the villages were colliery villages, and a central depot for such things, to make the limited supply go fairly round, was a necessity. And, of course, with such a population, accusations of favouritism would arise.

Antoine would declare Anatole was "too far ben" with the M.O. in charge: Pauline, aged and voluble, would assert that her many infirmities were not assessed at their proper food value. Coming across a fire of such statements one day, I intimated that any further complaints would be met by removing the doctor, the soup kitchen and the fuel depot to another village. Next day I called for the M.O. to take him over with me to inspect another place where we meant to instal a branch soup kitchen; and, when we entered the car, many of the inhabitants, believing the threatened removal was in progress, mobbed us with promises of better behaviour and loud praises of the M.O.[1]—who, incidentally, thoroughly deserved them. One of his proudest possessions may well be the illiterate address of appreciation—all they could give him—with which he was presented by these poor folk when we finally left the area.

And then after the Armistice we moved into Belgium to the Lalouvière area—again a coal-mining district—on the other side of Mons, where we stayed until demobilisation in April, 1919. Our war work abroad was done....

So there you have the tale, such as it is. Not much in it, perhaps—you can read it in your arm-chair, of an evening, with your toes at the fire—but it took us the best part of four strenuous years to do what it tells of. As I said at the beginning, it is, changing the dates and the names, the tale of any British Field Ambulance in France: we were not "the only pebbles on the beach." To those who were there it may recall many memories: to those who were not it may give a general idea of our life and work. And if I have told the tale badly—well, *mea culpa;* but, let me add, *sit meritum voluisse.* For in the years to come a rough and ready record may be better than none.

---

[1] Captain J. M. Morgan, M.C.

www.ingramcontent.com/pod-product-compliance
Lightning Source LLC
Chambersburg PA
CBHW020808100426
42814CB00014B/376/J